LIVE FROM CAPITOL HILL!

Newswork 4

LIVE FROM CAPITOL HILL!

Studies of Congress and the Media

STEPHEN HESS

The Brookings Institution
Washington, D.C.

Library of Congress Cataloging-in-publication Data:

Hess, Stephen.
    Live from Capitol Hill! : studies of Congress and the media /
Stephen Hess.
        p.   cm.
    Includes bibliographical references and index.
    ISBN 0-8157-3628-2 (cloth)
    ISBN 0-8157-3627-4 (pbk.)
    1. Press and politics—United States.   2. United States.
Congress—Reporters and reporting.   3. Journalists—Washington
(D.C.)   4. Government and the press—United States.   I. Title.
PN4888.P6H48   1991
071'.3—dc20   91-15538
                                                                              CIP

9 8 7 6 5 4 3 2 1

The paper used in this publication meets the minimum
requirements of the American National Standard for Information Sciences—Permanence of paper for Printed Library
Materials, ANSI Z39.48-1984

Set in Linotron Electra
Composition by NK Graphics
    Baltimore, MD
Printed by R.R. Donnelley and Sons Co.
    Harrisonburg, VA

THE BROOKINGS INSTITUTION

The Brookings Institution is an independent organization devoted to nonpartisan research, education, and publication in economics, government, foreign policy, and the social sciences generally. Its principal purposes are to aid in the development of sound public policies and to promote public understanding of issues of national importance.

The Institution was founded on December 8, 1927, to merge the activities of the Institute for Government Research, founded in 1916, the Institute of Economics, founded in 1922, and the Robert Brookings Graduate School of Economics and Government, founded in 1924.

The Board of Trustees is responsible for the general administration of the Institution, while the immediate direction of the policies, program, and staff is vested in the President, assisted by an advisory committee of the officers and staff. The by-laws of the Institution state: "It is the function of the Trustees to make possible the conduct of scientific research, and publication, under the most favorable conditions, and to safeguard the independence of the research staff in the pursuit of their studies and in the publication of the results of such studies. It is not a part of their function to determine, control, or influence the conduct of particular investigations or the conclusions reached."

The President bears final responsibility for the decision to publish a manuscript as a Brookings book. In reaching his judgment on the competence, accuracy, and objectivity of each study, the President is advised by the director of the appropriate research program and weighs the views of a panel of expert outside readers who report to him in confidence on the quality of the work. Publication of a work signifies that it is deemed a competent treatment worthy of public consideration but does not imply endorsement of conclusions or recommendations.

The Institution maintains its position of neutrality on issues of public policy in order to safeguard the intellectual freedom of the staff. Hence interpretations or conclusions in Brookings publications should be understood to be solely those of the authors and should not be attributed to the Institution, to its trustees, officers, or other staff members, or to the organizations that support its research.

foreword

TEN YEARS ago, Brookings published the first volume of the Newswork series by Stephen Hess, a senior fellow in our Governmental Studies program. "In the vast literature about how Americans govern themselves," I wrote in that book's foreword, "the role of the press is often neglected. Yet the press—no less than the presidency, the judiciary, and the legislature—is a public policy institution and deserves a place in the explanations of the governmental process." Today the press is no longer a neglected subject of inquiry. One scholar preparing a bibliographic essay on trends in political communication has said she read more than 600 works published during the 1980s. And clearly, Stephen Hess has contributed to this investigation.

In Newswork 1, *The Washington Reporters* (1981), the author began his discussion of the interactions between government officials and journalists by surveying the personnel and organization of the press corps. In the next volume, *The Government/Press Connection* (1984), he investigated the interactions from the other side of the briefer's podium, reporting on how five executive agencies, including the White House, State Department, and Pentagon, conducted their press relations. Newswork 3, *The Ultimate Insiders*, explored the reasons the national media deemed certain senators newsworthy and others not.

Now in Newswork 4, *Live from Capitol Hill!*, Hess not only expands his canvas to include the U.S. House of Representatives and regional reporting from Washington, but examines a number of the myths that have grown up around the role of journalists and the power of the media. And as is often true of careful research, things are not always as they appear. Although the book is a series of discrete studies, each of which is designed to stand on its own, the totality presents a picture that is sometimes at odds with standard accounts of how legislators try to use the media and how the media report on legislators. It questions the received wisdom of the media's pervasive power to influence electoral outcomes and lawmakers' power to manipulate the media to influence legislative and electoral outcomes. The ubiquity of television on Capitol Hill, he argues in a postscript, has more to do with legislators' egos than with public policy.

Brookings received grants for this research from the Cissy Patterson Trust Fund, the Dirksen Congressional Center, the Earhart Foundation, and the National Press Foundation.

The manuscript benefited from the critiques of Ross Baker, Thomas E. Mann, and Steven S. Smith. Various chapters also received thoughtful comments from Senator Daniel Patrick Moynihan, former U.S. Congressman Bill Frenzel, and journalists Frank Aukofer, Helen Dewar, Jacqueline Frank, Steve Gerstel, and Julia Malone. The goodwill of Superintendent Robert E. Peterson of the Senate Press Gallery and Lawrence J. Janezich of the Senate Radio and Television Gallery was especially helpful.

Interns who assisted the author were Athena E. Andrew (Occidental), Sarai Brachman (Harvard), Jon Buffington (Northwestern), Julie S. Darnell (St. Mary's), Jennifer Dowling (Haverford), Francis L. Dymond II (Ripon), Jung M. Lee (Georgetown), Ilene G. Lovesky (Middlebury), John H. Sharon III (Connecticut College), Mark Sheft (Princeton), Paul Schoeman (Princeton), Lori Silva (Richmond), James Smith (Hobart), Jeffrey S. VanderLinden (Wesleyan), Karen L. Yashar (Yale), and Richard A. Wilde (Williams).

Computer work for the project was conducted by Dorothy Poole, Carole H. Newman, and Christine C. de Fontenay. Library services were provided by Laura Walker and her colleagues; duplicating services by Louis A. Holliday and his colleagues.

The author's research assistant was Deborah Kalb; personal assistants, Vida R. Megahed and Antoinette T. Williams; administrative and logistical support supervisors, Sandra Z. Riegler, Eloise C. Stinger, Susan A. Stewart, and Renuka D. Deonarain.

The verification assistant was Todd L. Quinn; proofreader, Donna Verdier; indexer, Margaret Lynch; and production assistant, Susan L. Woollen.

The author is pleased to note that the team of Hess and editor James R. Schneider have now worked together on five Brookings books.

The views expressed in this book are those of the author and should not be ascribed to the trustees, officers, or other staff members of the Brookings Institution.

BRUCE K. MACLAURY
President

May 1991
Washington, D.C.

To the Memory of

Malcolm Moos
(1916–1982)

Contents

In the Gallery

"THIS IS the last old-fashioned newsroom," comments Joan McKinney of the *Morning Advocate* as she looks around the Senate Press Gallery.[1] "It's still cluttered and funky, and I like it. It doesn't look like an insurance office, as mine does in Baton Rouge where there are partitions so you can't shout across the room." The press gallery consists of four rooms carved out of a vaulted corridor on the north side, third floor, of the Capitol. In S-315, the large room in the middle, a rack of press releases runs almost floor to ceiling along one wall, with handouts and documents spilling over onto the windowsills. The other walls are lined with telephone booths—ten of them—and bulletin boards, filing cabinets, a rack for daily newspapers, a photocopier, a watercooler, and a television set. Brown leather couches and stuffed armchairs, deep and worn, crowd the center of the room. Swinging doors lead to seats (really fixed stools) from which the reporters look down on the Senate chamber from behind the presiding officer's chair. (From here the reporters once threw spitballs on the head of Blair Moody, a former colleague from the *Detroit News*, who had been appointed to fill a Senate seat.) "There is something incongruous about the Minton tiles [on the floor], marble walls, and decorated ceilings in this newsroom," Senator Robert Byrd of West Virginia once said, "but, from the signs of clutter, I gather that the reporters have made themselves comfortable nevertheless."[2]

The reporters' desks are accommodated in rooms on either side of S-315. In S-316 the Associated Press and United Press International face each other across a center aisle, as if the two wire services were opposing sides in a perpetual game; the *Wall Street Journal* is wedged into a corner. Reuters, the British news agency, is in S-314, as is the Coke machine and the coffee-maker. Next to S-314, in a part of the original corridor, the *New York Times*

---

1. All people are identified by their position or affiliation in 1984, the year of the site observations for this chapter.
2. Robert C. Byrd, "The Senate Press Galleries," *Congressional Record*, vol. 126 (November 24, 1980), p. S14906.

and the *Washington Post* burrow into window niches slightly separating them from the likes of the *Milwaukee Journal, Chicago Tribune,* and *Sacramento Bee.* Another room, S-313, contains telecopiers and an office for the gallery's staff.

Other facilities for the reporters are available in the House of Representatives. Those with assigned desks on the Senate side are not there because they are covering the Senate exclusively but because of squatters' rights, longevity, or bureaucratic politics. AP's allotted space is better in the Senate Press Gallery, so its senior correspondents want to be housed there. Some law of hydraulics seems to govern: news organizations flow into space as it becomes available. (The cramped quarters add a territorial imperative to the politics of the galleries, which was a factor in deposing the Senate Press Gallery superintendent in 1983.)[3]

On the west side of the Senate's gallery level, two small additional rooms are reserved for the periodical press and photographers; on the east side, until they moved in 1986, the radio and television reporters were jammed into a space so tiny that it had to be tiered to make room for the desks. It was here in 1984 that senators were interviewed in a studio lined with faded blue curtains and old bound copies of the *Congressional Record,* which lent a formal and judicious air to contrast with the burlap stapled on the walls. There were also closet-sized offices for ABC, CBS, and NBC television and recording booths for the major radio outlets.[4]

Congress supplies the reporters with the space (for some it is their only office), telephones, writing paper, typewriters, special elevators, a pressroom in the Russell Senate Office Building, separate tables in two Capitol dining rooms, and a few parking spaces. A combined staff of seventeen answers the phones and provides other services in the four Senate galleries. From time to time a member of Congress will make an issue of these perks. Minnesota's Representative Bill Frenzel told me, "Once I moved to cut one or two press gallery employees from the federal payroll and you would have sworn that I had shredded the First Amendment."[5]

3. The superintendent, Sandy Hays, was accused of not defending properly the reporters' interests when the Senate Armed Services Committee staked a claim on space in the Dirksen Office Building that was being used as a pressroom.

4. There is a good physical description of the old Senate broadcast gallery in William L. Rivers, *The Other Government: Power and the Washington Media* (Universe Books, 1982), pp. 73–75. The new Senate Radio and Television Gallery is now located off the south corridor of the third floor in what used to be the document room.

5. Representative David R. Obey of Wisconsin became particularly agitated in 1977, noting that he did not object to spending an estimated million dollars a year to maintain the press galleries, but that he did mind "the misplaced sanctimony of some of the reporters." The Standing Committee of Correspondents, the reporters' elected representatives, then debated whether news organizations should be billed but concluded

The press gallery generally echoes with a mix of familiar sounds. A public address system pages reporters to the telephones or announces that a roll call is about to begin or that a senator has arrived for a press conference. The television set is on. There is the more or less constant clack of personal computers, interrupted by the bell of an occasional typewriter. There is laughter, especially just before lunch. Pye Chamberlayne of UPI radio has noted that today's newsrooms have the noise level of a library or a hospital. Not so the Senate Press Gallery.

The disorder, the cramped quarters, and the noise reflect the singular atmosphere of Capitol Hill, a workplace for elected politicians. Reporters here absorb the karma of Congress. It is different from the feel and look of the State Department and Pentagon, where they take their cues from diplomats and generals. There is a herding instinct in politicians and journalists, and it is especially keen among congressional reporters, who seem to like each other. "It's lonely back in the office," says Frank Aukofer of the *Milwaukee Journal*, explaining why he prefers to file his stories from the press gallery. A reason for this congeniality—so different from the attitude of White House press corps—is that most Hill reporters are not in direct competition. When Lee Bandy of the Columbia, South Carolina, *State* talks about the press gallery as one big newsroom, the analogy is to a bunch of reporters having different beats: "If Helen Dewar [*Washington Post*] runs across some tidbit about South Carolina, she'll pass it along to me." Even when competition is direct, as it is for the television networks, the stakes are not as high as they are for reporters covering the president. Indeed, there is a certain comradeship among Capitol Hill's network television reporters because of the struggle they have in common to get anything at all on the evening news.[6] And unlike the daily White House story, there can be more than one "right" story, which tends to divert eyeball-to-eyeball rivalry.

As the reporters fan out to cover Congress, there are several ways that they can arrange to divide Capitol Hill into manageable portions. Recalling the 1950s, when Jack Bell was chief of the Senate correspondents for the Associated Press and Bill Arbogast was his counterpart in the House of Represen-

---

that supporting a desk in the gallery could be a hardship for the smaller operations. Instead it suggested that the organizations make voluntary contributions to the U.S. Treasury. (Several, notably the *Wall Street Journal* and Knight-Ridder Newspapers, sent checks for the estimated value of what they received.) See James M. Perry, "You're Right, Congressman Obey, the Press IS Riding Too High," *Quill*, vol. 65 (July–August 1977), p. 31. Also see Norman C. Miller, "The 'Free' Press Makes Out Okay at Public Expense," *Wall Street Journal*, June 17, 1977, p. 8; and Laura Foreman, "Capitol Hill's Press Challenged on Costs," *New York Times*, July 6, 1977, p. 38.

6. See Norman Ornstein and Michael Robinson, "Where's All the Coverage? The Case of Our Disappearing Congress," *TV Guide*, January 11, 1986, pp. 4–10.

tatives, Carl Leubsdorf said, "They were like Clarence Cannon and Carl Hayden [the powerful committee chairmen who ruled the administration of the House and Senate, respectively], with a line drawn through the Capitol distinguishing turf. A tax bill would be handled on the House side by one reporter and on the Senate side by another." By the late 1970s, however, major news organizations began to abandon this segregated system, combining Senate and House beats into one congressional bureau. Dennis Farney of the *Wall Street Journal*, which made the change in 1984, explained, "It provides better coverage in that you might previously have been immersing yourself in a subject in the House that wasn't going to go anywhere in the Senate." The wire services now divide workloads along substantive lines—budget, taxes, foreign relations, defense, and so forth.

Most bureaus with two or three national reporters, such as the *New York Times*, assign work largely according to which stories deserve the most attention each day. "We're short-order cooks," Martin Tolchin of the *Times* says. If the *Washington Post* still retains Senate and House reporters, "It's because Helen [Dewar] got there first and loves the Senate," explained Tom Reid, who used to cover the House. Still, the *Post* and other major papers send specialists to Capitol Hill for the more technical issues. Reporters from the *Post*'s business and finance section regularly cover tax legislation, for example, although its congressional reporters retain control over budget stories.

Regional reporters, usually one to a newspaper, who are stationed in Washington primarily to follow a state's congressional delegation, tend to divide their time equally between House and Senate. From the beginning of March to the end of September 1984, for instance, 37 percent of Lee Bandy's articles focused on senators and 33 percent on House members. (South Carolina has two senators and six representatives, so that while each senator received 18.5 percent of Bandy's total attention, no House member got more than 7 percent and several got less than 1 percent.) There are also special circumstances that determine how reporters spend their time. Bandy emphasized the Senate in 1984 because South Carolina's Ernest F. Hollings was trying to become the Democratic nominee for president. David Lynch used to focus on House members when he worked for a Buffalo newspaper because New York senators generally get enough attention from the wire services and the national news outlets. Now that he reports for Nebraska and Iowa papers, he finds that his editors are more interested in the states' senators.

The national news reporters lean toward Senate stories. For the television networks the leading senators are attractive because they are instantly recognizable and there is always the possibility that they may run for president. But even the major newspapers are Senate oriented. When President Reagan removed the Marines from Beirut in February 1984 after a terrorist attack against them, the "reaction from Congress" story in the *New York Times* quoted six senators and four House members, the *Washington Post* eight senators and three House members.[7] (The personal preferences of reporters may also make some difference. The story in the *Times*, for instance, was written by Steven Roberts, whose wife's father and mother were Democratic members of the House—Roberts jokes that his in-laws had only two biases, against Republicans and senators.) Whether House or Senate is the more interesting body is, by the way, a matter of modest dispute in the press galleries. Commenting on the former House members in the Senate, for example, NBC's Roberta Hornig Draper believes something about the Senate can turn "a perfectly nice young congressman into a very pompous senator."

Freelance reporters cover House or Senate on the basis of marketability. Carol Bennett of the Alabama Information Network, whose client is a collaboration of ninety-one Alabama radio stations, considers the Senate the better hunting ground because all her stations can use the same story. For most radio freelancers, however, there are more stories in the House, so they tend to hang out in the pressroom of the Rayburn House Office Building, where they have been given some workspace. The larger House offers a gaggle of one-minute speeches at the beginning of each session (with press secretaries alerting the reporters in advance) as well as more possibilities of selling one story over and over again by simply substituting a name, as in this piece sent to local stations by Hanna Gutmann on March 1, 1985: "A group of 10 governors, 14 senators, and 17 representatives, including _____, have formed an independent council to help shape Democratic Party policy and rules. . . ."

7. Steven V. Roberts in "Redeployment of Marines Is Praised," *New York Times*, February 8, 1984, p. A11, quotes Senators Howard Baker, John Glenn, Charles Mathias, Jr., Barry Goldwater, Alan Cranston, and Gary Hart and House members Thomas P. O'Neill, Samuel Stratton, Robert Matsui, and Tony Coelho. Helen Dewar and Margaret Shapiro in "Lawmakers Relieved at Announcement of Troop Pullback," *Washington Post*, February 8, 1984, p. A21, quote Senators Barry Goldwater, Howard Baker, Claiborne Pell, Joseph Biden, Alan Cranston, John Glenn, Ernest Hollings, and Gary Hart and House members Thomas P. O'Neill, Robert H. Michel, and Tony Coelho. The listing illustrates one of the reasons why senators get more attention—all but Mathias and Pell have run for president. Of the House members, O'Neill was the Speaker and Coelho was majority leader.

Specialists have various priorities. Gretchen Chell (*The Daily Bond Buyer*) and Jean Christensen (Commodity News Services) spend more time on the House side because the Constitution decrees that tax actions begin there. *Congressional Quarterly* reporter Dale Tate's specialization is the Senate: as it debates civil rights legislation on October 2, 1984, she says, "Most [daily] stories say, 'The Senate is tied up in procedural knots,' and move on, while I will have to write a story about the procedural knots."

MORNINGS BEFORE 11:00 the Senate Press Gallery is quiet. Congressional committees are meeting. The gallery's staff members post a schedule the afternoon before to help reporters find potential stories: Foreign Relations Committee, 10:00 A.M., on arms control overview; Joint Economic Committee, 9:30 A.M., on the June employment situation; Select Committee on Intelligence, 10:30 A.M., closed.

Each committee meeting produces its own configuration of senators, reporters, and spectators. For the Finance Committee meeting on January 25, 1984, a long line of spectators waits to get in as the reporters show their passes and sit at three press tables. The room is bathed in light for the television cameras. There is to be a confrontation between the senators and the Social Security Administration over disability insurance procedures. A crowd of handicapped persons will be seen leaving the hearing (apparently as a protest) on "CBS Evening News." On February 2 the committee hears Treasury Secretary Donald Regan review the budget. The audience is mostly tourists and students, and the press tables are filled with economics reporters. Senators make short statements, copies of which are distributed at the press table, and leave. On February 3 the committee takes up a technical subject, Foreign Sales Corporation legislation. There is a small audience of lawyers, lobbyists, and trade publication reporters. There are no bright lights, no television cameras. Only two senators are present. Reporters, as usual, are choosing in the daily bazaar of issues and personalities. During seven days in May 1984, for example, the AP chose to cover 65 percent of Senate committee meetings, but it ignored hearings of the Committee on Energy and Natural Resources on revising the boundaries of the Chattahoochee River National Recreation Area in Georgia and designating Mono Lake, California, as a national monument, subjects that interested regional reporters from Georgia and California, respectively. It also ignored a hearing of the Committee on Small Business that was considering technical changes in loans by the Small Business Administration, a topic worthy of note in specialized business journals.[8] "Hearings are staged and mostly boring," Representative Barney Frank of Massachusetts has commented, but reporters know hearings provide stories without demanding legwork.

The Senate convenes in late morning. Fifteen minutes before the chaplain gives the opening prayer, reporters gather around the majority leader's desk. As many as thirty are present on a busy day, a dozen on an ordinary day, mostly from the national media. If the majority leader is absent, the briefing is conducted by the majority whip. The minority leader may also choose to see the reporters at this time. If so, he goes first, then drifts away when the majority leader appears. Questioning is on the record, but the reporters are not allowed to use tape recorders. They ask questions until the bell sounds to signal that the session is about to begin. The majority leader adjusts the amount of questioning by his time of arrival. He may show up on the Senate floor three minutes before the reporters must leave it. (In 1984 Majority Leader Howard Baker's press secretary, Tom Griscom, followed up each session with a backgrounder, held in an alcove immediately outside the Senate chamber, which usually lasted for ten minutes. The press secretary's sessions were dropped when Bob Dole succeeded Baker in 1985.) The majority leader's responsibility is to explain scheduling and legislative tactics to the reporters. His press secretary fills in the gaps.[9] The minority leader is the point man for the opposition.

These mini–press conferences are called "dugout chatter," named, it is thought, after an interview show that preceded radio broadcasts of the Washington Senators baseball games in the 1950s.[10] A staff member from the press gallery and another from the radio and television gallery take notes, which are then posted.

[Excerpts from dugout chatter, September 5, 1984]
[*Minority Leader*] *Byrd*: Hopes president can be "smoked out" on his plan to balance the budget. Congress has right to know and needs to know what programs will be affected. . . . Democrats in the House

8. See Stephen Hess, *The Ultimate Insiders: U.S. Senators in the National Media* (Brookings, 1986), p. 33.

9. See Martin Tolchin, "A Press Secretary Can Say Things a Senator Can't," *New York Times*, April 20, 1983, p. B6.

10. See Warren Weaver, Jr., "Dugout Chatter, a Senate Tradition," *New York Times*, January 27, 1982, p. A20. For comparable leadership and press procedures in the House of Representatives, see Cokie Roberts, "Leadership and the Media in the 101st Congress," in John J. Kornacki, ed., *Leading Congress: New Styles, New Strategies* (Washington: CQ Press, 1990), p. 86.

will introduce legislation to require the president to submit a balanced budget to the Congress. . . .

[*Majority Leader*] *Baker:* Sen. Baker will meet with the Speaker today at 2:30 to discuss the next 30 days legislative schedule. [He] laid down a list of legislation that he will attempt to have passed before adjourning sine die on October 5th. The Banking bill will be laid down today but not finished until next week. Military Construction will follow. . . .

The session begins. But reporters are seldom drawn into the gallery. Senators discuss procedural matters or make for-the-record presentations. Real debates—over a constitutional amendment on school prayer or a controversial Supreme Court nominee—are rare. Press gallery staff members, rotating at forty-five-minute intervals, take notes on the floor action. These, too, are posted on the bulletin board.

[*Excerpts from Senate floor summary, April 5, 1984*]
10 to 10:45 A.M. The Senate resumed consideration of the supplemental appropriations bill shortly after 10:30 A.M. today with Sen. Levin offering an amendment that prohibits giving funds to groups that want to overthrow a government that has full diplomatic relations with the United States (i.e., Nicaragua). Sens. Levin and Inouye spoke in favor of the amendment and Sen. Stevens was speaking against it at the close of period. . . .

The press gallery's staff—in addition to paging reporters to the phones (and keeping a log of the calls), compiling a list of the next day's committee meetings, making arrangements for press seating at hearings, and taking notes on the dugout chatter and the floor activities—maintains research files and prepares background papers. Files fill two cabinet drawers in room S-315—some 180 subjects ranging from *Abortion* through *Women in the Senate*, and including *Flags flown over Capitol*, *Lying in State*, and *Snuff Boxes of Senate*. The radio and television gallery's background papers, prepared by Larry Janezich on domestic affairs and Jason Cooke on foreign policy, are especially elaborate. "The White House press office was good," said Ann Compton of ABC, pointing to these briefs, "but this is marvelous." Reporters also have access to a wide array of research materials that Congress prepares for its own use: the legislative bulletins and weekly legislative updates of the Democratic Senators' Policy Committee, notices from the Democratic whip, committee digests from the Republican Senators' Conference Committee, and news summaries distributed by the Republican Policy Committee. A small Senate library offers a comfortable reading room to members of the press and access to various data bases that can provide summaries of the contents and status of legislative proposals. Yet this is all quite incidental to how reporters gather most of their information, which is by asking questions.

They send messages down to the floor of the Senate chamber requesting interviews. Then senator and reporter meet in the "President's Room," adjacent to the chamber, under a ceiling of frescoes by Constantino Brumidi, where three walls are dominated by gilt-framed mirrors reflecting a Victorian chandelier, and busts of two assassinated presidents, James Garfield and William McKinley, stand guard. On most days at least one senator schedules a news conference in the press gallery, usually to promote some piece of legislation, as announced in the following press releases:

DANFORTH SEEKS TO EXPAND TELECOM EXPORTS:
WOULD USE AT&T AS NEGOTIATING LEVER
Senator Jack Danforth (R-Mo) said today [May 1, 1984] that the United States should call on other nations to open their markets to American telecommunications exports as the price of expanded access to the U.S. market. Danforth, Chairman of the Senate International Trade Subcommittee, introduced legislation that would set a three-year timetable for negotiations to liberalize world telecommunications trade.

NEWS FROM SEN. JOHN MELCHER
Sen. John Melcher, D-Mont, today [July 25, 1984] introduced a bill to tighten the U.S. Department of Agriculture's authority to close down meat packers who continually violate the law by butchering dead or diseased animals under poor sanitation conditions that endanger consumers.

Because each news medium maintains its own gallery, Senators Danforth and Melcher then troop next door to the radio and television gallery and repeat their performances. Meetings with print reporters may run for thirty minutes and are apt to become technical (during the press conference the senator may refer questions to staff aides). Radio and television reporters need sound bites—short, concise statements—and sessions rarely last more than ten minutes. Of the many brands of Capitol Hill news conferences, these can be the most intimate: three radio reporters questioned Danforth, Melcher spoke to four print reporters. But not always. Eight television camera crews and dozens of print reporters recorded the September 11 news conference on civil rights legislation called by Senators Edward Kennedy of Massachusetts and Bob Packwood of Oregon, for which members of the press had received simulated engraved invitations promising a breakfast danish and a chance to meet such U.S. Olympic athletes as Mary Decker, Flo Hyman, and Cheryl Miller.

Press conferences and hearings, morning activities, are followed by a quick lunch. The White House press office may provide a "luncheon lid," guaranteeing it will release no news for an hour or two so that reporters will have time to eat undisturbed (or do their banking). But congressional reporters usually eat a fast meal at tables reserved for them in dining rooms on the Senate and House sides of the Capitol. They thus seem grateful for the respite provided by Senator Ted Stevens of Alaska, who hosts a semiannual Alaska seafood lunch, even if they are expected to listen to him discuss "current issues before the Senate" in exchange for a spread of sable fish and berry jams.[11] Otherwise, lunch is a utilitarian affair for congressional reporters—not work-related and not a deductible business expense. When I surveyed twenty-four Senate committee staff aides, for instance—the sort of sources who would be wooed if they worked for the president—eighteen said they never had lunch with a reporter and six said they did so only rarely or occasionally. None claimed that lunching was a common part of their interaction with the press.

At lunchtime on Tuesdays, Republican and Democratic senators hold their party caucuses. As they leave the meetings, reporters drift from one to another, what Helen Dewar calls "trolling the waters." Much of this activity takes place as the legislators wait for an elevator, just time enough for reporters to get in a question or two on a day when senators' schedules may be otherwise hopelessly crowded. It may not be the best way of gathering news, but it has a certain casual efficiency familiar to both sides. In January 1984, when the Senate sergeant-at-arms ruled that the reporters would no longer be allowed to stand in front of the elevators (presumably a measure taken to tighten access to various parts of the Capitol following the detonation of a bomb outside the Senate chamber on the night of November 7,

11. "Stevens to Host Media Luncheon July 26," press release, July 20, 1984.

1983), New York's Daniel P. Moynihan took the floor: "To cut off access—free, spontaneous, adventitious, and often calamitous—between Senators and the accredited members of the Press Gallery would be to change our institution. It would begin to cut us off from the people who send us here. . . ."[12] Senator Moynihan was apparently not alone in his sentiments. Senate rules were quickly returned to the status quo ante.[13]

WITHOUT EXACTLY being second-class citizens (largely because too many other reporters in their organizations want their jobs), those who cover Congress nevertheless do not receive the deference accorded some of their colleagues. They are rarely the ones invited to ask questions on the networks' Sunday morning television programs, nor are they recognized by name at presidential press conferences or given seats on the secretary of state's plane. What hurts more, however, are comments that they do not do a very good job. Two Duke University professors, for instance, accuse them of a dangerous lassitude or ineptitude: "By failing independently to investigate legislators' activities and decisions in Washington, by failing to probe into the 435 individual stories in the House, or the 100 in the Senate, the mass media let more than one sleeping dog lie. The result: the press contributes to the public's deepening despair about Congress while helping to insure the reelection—the power—of the kind of people who make that body what it is."[14]

Worse is criticism from fellow journalists. "In this wasteland," Lou Cannon has commented, "a symbiotic relationship flourishes between congressman and correspondent, a relationship based on mutual need and sometimes on mutual laziness."[15] Ben H. Bagdikian leveled a similar complaint: "The majority of them practice herd journalism."[16] And, with perhaps the unkindest cut, Peter Gruenstein stated flatly that "many Congressional reporters now survive quite nicely by doing little more than rewriting press releases."[17]

How accurate are these charges?

12. Daniel P. Moynihan, "The Press," *Congressional Record*, vol. 130 (January 26, 1984), p. S230.
13. Rich Burkhardt, "Capitol Access Expanded for Hill Aides and Press," *Roll Call*, February 2, 1984, p. 1.
14. David L. Paletz and Robert M. Entman, *Media.Power.Politics* (Free Press, 1981), pp. 97–98.
15. Lou Cannon, *Reporting: An Inside View* (Sacramento: California Journal Press, 1977), p. 182.
16. Ben H. Bagdikian, "Congress and the Media: Partners in Propaganda," *Columbia Journalism Review*, vol. 12 (January–February 1974), p. 5.
17. Peter Gruenstein, "Press Release Politics: How Congressmen Manage the News," *Progressive*, vol. 38 (January 1974), p. 40. For a positive assessment, see Bill Hogan, "The Congressional Correspondent," *Washington Journalism Review*, vol. 3 (June 1981), pp. 34–35.

A problem with assessing congressional reporting is that most of the arti-cles appear in newspapers we never read, published in somebody else's city. So to get a sense of what Hill reporters do write, I asked my assistant, Deborah Kalb, to gather a full file of clippings for March 1985, a month in which Congress was in session, from the *Atlanta Journal, Atlanta Consti-tution, Cleveland Plain Dealer, Dallas Morning News, Dallas Times Herald, Dayton Daily News, Detroit News, Milwaukee Journal,* and Donrey Newspapers. She also compiled a partial file from the *Richmond News Leader.* Donrey is a chain of fifty-five small papers, such as the *Examiner-Enterprise* of Bartlesville, Oklahoma, with a circulation of 14,000. The Atlanta and Dayton papers are owned by Cox and the Richmond paper by Media General. The others were independents at the time. The biggest was the *Detroit News,* with a daily circulation of 650,000.[18]

Laziness is the easiest claim to measure, at least quantitatively. At the *Dallas Morning News,* Mark Nelson, the reporter whose beat was the Texas congressional delegation, had a byline on seventeen stories, nearly 11,000 words, among them, "House Democrats Say Party Is Healing" (March 4), "Washington Snaps Up Former Aides to Tower" (March 11), and "Study Shows Gramm Led in PAC Funds" (March 13). The economics reporter, Mike McNamee, went to Capitol Hill for thirteen stories, 6,400 words, on "Strong Dollar Hurting U.S., Bentsen Says" (March 13) and "Congressional Myopia Distorts Tax Reform Issue" (March 28), among others. Another twelve articles, 7,600 words, came from four other *News* reporters, including Richard Whittle on the defense beat ("House Group Cancels Arms Talks Trip" on March 5) and Jim Landers on the energy beat, whose March 22 story, "Energy Agency's Credibility Questioned," begins, "Two Texas Democratic members of Congress on Thursday challenged the credibility of the Energy Department for ranking Deaf Smith County as one of the top three sites for the nation's first high-level nuclear waste burial site." This total of forty-two stories, some 25,000 words relating to Congress, repre-sented 40 percent of the bureau's March output. The two-man bureau of the *Milwaukee Journal,* John Kole and Frank Aukofer, produced thirty-seven stories in March, of which thirty-two were about the Wisconsin congres-sional delegation or votes in Congress or were based on information that came from congressional hearings and reports. Bob Dart and Greg McDonald, the regional reporters for Cox's Atlanta papers, wrote fifty-two

---

18. A systematic coding of contents relating to Congress, including editorials, columns, op-ed pieces, and cartoons from ten major newspapers for one month (July–August 1978), can be found in Charles M. Tidmarch and John J. Pitney, Jr., "Covering Congress," *Polity,* vol. 17 (Spring 1985), pp. 463–83.

stories, thirty-six of them focusing on Congress. In terms of words and number of stories, these congressional reporters were a prolific lot.

But what about quality? How many pieces reflect the inquisitive work implied by the headlines already mentioned? Sometimes they do not. On March 24, for example, a story in the *Dayton Daily News*, "McEwen Making Mark as Ohio's 'Rising Star,' " began, "From Saginaw, Mich., came thanks for 'the superb job you did as speaker at our Lincoln Day dinner' and a comment that 'Your belief in the Republican Party, coupled with your abilities and appearance, portend a great future.' " The praise was for Congressman Bob McEwen, who was said to be "rapidly establishing himself nationally as a rising young star of the conservative movement and in Ohio as a strong contender for statewide office in the not-too-distant future." On March 8 a *Detroit News* profile noted Representative Bill Shuette's "receptive mind," "outgoing personality," and, in the opinion of his mother, capability of becoming president someday "if he would only learn to eat meals at the right time." But flattery was the exception, as was calumny. On a scale from positive to neutral to negative, my researchers found the month's worth of stories about Washington legislators to be almost totally neutral in tone.

The charge of herd or pack journalism, of reporters rushing to the same subject, perhaps using the same sources and taking similar slants, has been more serious. To examine the allegation, we compared the competing coverage of the *Dallas Morning News* and the *Dallas Times Herald* for March 1985. On March 12, for instance, the superintendent of the Dallas schools testified on the Hill, an event that could be expected to be of local interest. Both papers covered the story, and in a similar manner.

WRIGHT URGES LIMIT ON LEGAL-FEE AWARDS
by Mark Nelson [*Morning News* Washington Bureau]
Dallas school Superintendent Linus Wright urged a congressional subcommittee Tuesday to limit the award of legal fees in cases involving the rights of handicapped students.

DISD CHIEF OPPOSES LEGAL FEES BILL
by Susan Brenna [*Times Herald* Washington Bureau]
In testimony Tuesday, before a congressional committee, Linus Wright . . . criticized proposed legislation directing school districts to pay legal fees incurred by parents of handicapped children who sue school districts.

Each also covered that month a report from the Joint Economic Committee charging that "the overvalued dollar" had cost 69,000 jobs in Texas, a Defense Department admission that AWACS reconnaissance aircraft were being used to patrol the Texas-Mexican border to help check drug smuggling, and a report criticizing the federal government for wanting to build another nuclear waste dump, possibly in Texas. These were subjects that both papers should have cared about and did. Yet of twenty-six stories from the *Times Herald*'s Washington bureau, only nine were also reported in the *News*. The papers were almost complementary in approach, the *Times Herald* choosing to focus more tightly on how Washington affects Texas, the larger *News* putting its stories in a wider, more international context. For example, only 43 percent of the members of Congress mentioned in the *News* stories were Texans; in *Times Herald* stories, 75 percent were from the state.

Even if reporters sometimes work on the same stories, they do not necessarily produce interchangeable copy. The major congressional actions of March 1985 were close votes in the Senate and House on whether to go ahead with the production of MX missiles. Regional reporters saw the events through the lens of their state's delegation. The *Atlanta Constitution* reported, "Sam Nunn on Thursday endorsed continued production of the MX missile. . . . Because Nunn is the ranking Democrat on the Senate Armed Services Committee and an authority on defense matters, his support will substantially boost President Reagan's efforts." The *Cleveland Plain Dealer* reported, "Much as he did on the SALT II treaty vote during President Jimmy Carter's administration, [Senator John] Glenn used his credentials as a former Marine and astronaut to try to persuade colleagues that voting for the MX was pouring money down the drain." In Milwaukee the *Journal*'s story said that Congressman Les Aspin's backing for the MX "brought him criticism from some constituents and from liberal colleagues in the House. There have been published reports that he made a deal with the liberals in which he promised to withdraw his support for the MX in exchange for votes in the caucus of House Democrats that won him the chairmanship of the Armed Services Committee. However, Aspin denied Thursday that he had made such a deal." The *Detroit News* noted that "For 20 minutes on Monday, [Paul] Henry, who has been in Congress less than three months, was closeted in the White House with President Reagan, Vice President Bush and National Security Adviser Robert MacFarlane. He also spoke with [arms negotiator Max] Kempelman and was summoned to a meeting with House Republican Leaders Bob Michel and Trent Lott. President Ford called from California for a 20-minute conversation. Despite the high level arm-twisting, Henry remained resolute in his opposition to MX."[19] Finally, from the *Dallas Morning News*:

> After the 217–210 vote for approval of Reagan's $1.5 billion request for 21 more missiles, Rep. Tom Loeffler walked into the warm sunshine outside the Capitol and accepted the congratulations of the White House lobbying team. "I feel like a football player at the end of a game who suddenly realizes his legs are tired," the Hunt Republican said of his three-week effort to line up support from both parties.[20]

The reporters' stories were, of course, far more diverse when they reflected their regions' economic interests. In Dallas the concern in March 1985 was oil production; in Detroit, auto imports:

> OKLAHOMANS, OIL EXECS TELL REAGAN OF TAX FEARS
> by Jim Landers [*Dallas Morning News*, March 1]
> Oklahoma's two Republican members of Congress, along with four oil company executives from the state, met with President Reagan Thursday and urged him to avoid "devastating" changes in tax laws covering the petroleum industry.

> REAGAN WON'T ASK FOR CAR IMPORT LIDS
> by Gary F. Schuster [*Detroit News*, March 2]
> President Reagan decided against urging Japan to extend its voluntary export restraints on cars shipped to America. . . . Michigan Rep. John Dingell said that "the so-called free-trade mentality of the Reagan administration strikes again."

In Ohio the savings and loan crisis struck that month:

---

19. Greg McDonald, "Nunn Endorses Continued Production of MX," *Atlanta Constitution*, March 8, 1985, p. 5A; Thomas J. Brazaitis, "Reagan Wins Battle of MX in Senate Vote," *Cleveland Plain Dealer*, March 20, 1985, p. 5A; Frank Aukofer, "Aspin Is Expected to Vote for MX," *Milwaukee Journal*, March 7, 1985, p. 4; and "Reagan Fends Off House MX Threat to Win New Vote," *Detroit News*, March 27, 1985, p. 1A.

20. Mark Nelson, "House Hands Reagan 4th Victory on MX," *Dallas Morning News*, March 29, 1985, p. 1A.

U.S. Grants Coverage to One S&L in Ohio
by Tom Diemer [Cleveland Plain Dealer, March 16]
The Federal Home Loan Bank Board, moving to calm depositors' fears in Ohio, granted federal insurance coverage yesterday to the Columbia Savings & Loan Co., of Cincinnati. "I think that should restore a modicum of confidence out there," said Rep. Chalmers P. Wylie, R-15, of Columbus.

As with stories about home-state legislators, the tone of most articles on regional economic issues was neutral, although out of seven auto stories in the *Detroit News*, one dealt with the poor safety record of "two hot-selling new American cars" and another with complaints about defects in General Motors X-body cars.

After reporters have covered the congressional agenda (MX missiles) and the regional agenda (oil, autos), two other agendas can generate stories from Congress: the interests of their local senators and representatives and their own interests. Applying these four classifications to the March output of the *Cleveland Plain Dealer*, which had an energetic four-person bureau in Washington, we found the following mix of stories: congressional agenda, four; regional agenda, twenty-eight; legislators' agendas, thirteen; reporters' agendas, fourteen. The totals do not include twenty-one stories that had no congressional references and sixteen very short fillers. The modest number of articles from the congressional agenda probably meant that the paper was using the Associated Press and one of the supplemental services (such as those of the *New York Times* or *Los Angeles Times–Washington Post*) to concentrate its own resources on stories that could not otherwise easily be covered.[21] The large number of stories from the regional agenda stemmed from the Ohio savings and loan crisis.

Most criticism of congressional reporting, at least from other journalists, is that stories too often uncritically reflect the legislators' agendas. As Andrew Barnes, the managing editor of the *St. Petersburg Times*, said in 1978, "A great deal of what I see as I move around [the country] is puff for the local congressman, ascribing to him a power and influence he does not, in fact, have."[22] But stories from the legislators' agendas are not automatically puff pieces. The one *Plain Dealer* article that could be put in this category

---

21. For a summary list of the full-time national reporters covering Capitol Hill in 1984, see Hess, *Ultimate Insiders*, p. xv, note 1.
22. Quoted in Edmund B. Lambeth and John A. Byrne, "Pipelines from Washington," *Columbia Journalism Review*, vol. 17 (May–June 1978), p. 54.

describes the activities of Representative Mary Rose Oakar, "the plucky former amateur actress," who was trying to save Washington's Folger Theatre. On the other hand, several stories about Representative Edward F. Feighan's efforts on behalf of human rights in South Korea were deserving of national attention. As for stories from congressional hearings, another part of legislators' agendas, *Plain Dealer* reporters filed only three during the month. Yet it should not be assumed that reporters' agendas are necessarily more important than legislators' agendas—only that such stories show journalistic initiative. The consumer health stories devised by Judy Grande were consistently useful, and "Who Sent Feighan to Korea, and Why," Tom Diemer's story of the group that paid for Representative Feighan's trip to Korea, was a good piece of enterprise reporting. In general, however, as Richard E. Cohen of the *National Journal* has pointed out, "Home-state reporters do not usually play an adversary role. . . . Nor do many nationally based congressional reporters spend time investigating the 535 members." Rather, he noted, "Congressional reporters are better suited to report on the legislative record of the members they cover."[23] This press corps could not be categorized as combative. Looking around at his friends in the Senate Press Gallery, Martin Tolchin says, "These are not hardball players."

Press release journalism, the final charge against congressional reporters, very much relates to what press releases are apt to be about, namely legislators claiming credit for good things that happen because of their actions. "Bethel has been approved for federal assistance in constructing a new sewer system, reports Congressman Harold Volkmer." "U.S. Senator John Heinz (R-Pa) today announced the award of a $10 million Navy contract to the Medley Tool and Model Company located in the heart of economically depressed North Philadelphia."[24] "They're worthless," says Tom Raum of the AP, picking up a pile of press releases from his in-box in the Senate Press Gallery to illustrate the point. It is a view that would be shared by all national reporters, the correspondents who are there to cover the "big picture." But there are other reporters for whom press releases are useful. In the Rayburn pressroom, where six UPI regional reporters were working the phones in March 1984, each producing on average nine brief stories a day about such events as the awarding of a grant or contract, the press release was often the place to start getting the story. And just off Capitol Hill, on March 27, 1984, Don Brownlee, bureau chief of a television freelance service,

23. Richard E. Cohen, "Prime Time," *National Journal*, September 3, 1988, p. 2221.
24. "Volkmer Announces Bethel Sewer Grant," press release, September 26, 1989; and "Heinz Announces $10 Million Navy Contract to North Philadelphia Company," press release, February 14, 1984.

Potomac News, dispatches an intern to the press galleries to gather handouts.
It is 6:00 P.M. and he has not yet located enough business to occupy his
crews tomorrow. Perhaps there is a story in a press release that will interest
a local station's news director. Press releases are also a staple of the weeklies,
which do not have reporters in Washington and get their information
directly from the legislators' offices.[25] With the exception of the small papers
in the Donrey group, the news organizations in my informal survey do not
devote much space to constituent services, although 26 percent of all Americans consider them the most important function a legislator can perform.[26]

To WHAT EXTENT, then, did these newspapers bear out the conventional crit-
icisms about congressional reporting? The charges, it seems to me, were not
proven. The reporters were energetic not lazy, the stories more diverse than
alike, and their tone professionally neutral. Press releases play a role, but a
small one. Perhaps in another set of newspapers the results would have
turned out otherwise. Individually, paper by paper, there are always differences—reflecting the size of the bureau, the skill of the reporters, the interests of the editors, the wealth of the owners, the intelligence of the readers.
But taken together, the papers show how much of Congress is reported,
somewhere. It is the coverage of Walter Lippmann's searchlight beam,
moving "restlessly about, bringing one episode and then another out of dark-
ness."[27] Like a three-ring circus, it is hard to watch all the action at the same
time. Instead we may focus, seriatim, on a legislator, a committee, a piece
of legislation. For this is the confusing branch of government, 535 men and
women, increasingly leaderless in an age without strong political parties,
searching for solutions (and reelection). Yet strangely, remarkably, and I
think quite accidentally, an imperfect press, almost because of its imperfec-
tion, captures the confusing essence of today's imperfect Congress. Unfor-
tunately, no one except an occasional researcher will read all these stories
and thus see Congress from this vantage point.

25. A book by the Ralph Nader Congress Project claims, "One 1965 study found that about a third of the
members of the House said that newspapers in their districts printed their news releases verbatim. . . ." See
Mark J. Green, James M. Fallows, and David R. Zwick, *Who Runs Congress?* (Bantam, 1972), p. 239. A
Wisconsin study shows, however, that a House member got only 6.6 percent of his press releases' possible
uses in a sample of fifty weekly newspapers and that the two Wisconsin senators received considerably less
(0.38 percent for Gaylord Nelson and 0.58 percent for William Proxmire). See Leslie D. Polk, John Eddy,
and Ann Andre, "Use of Congressional Publicity in Wisconsin District," *Journalism Quarterly*, vol. 52
(Autumn 1975), pp. 543–46.
26. See Bruce Cain, John Ferejohn, and Morris Fiorina, *The Personal Vote: Constituency Service and
Electoral Independence* (Harvard University Press, 1987), pp. 38–39.
27. Walter Lippmann, *Public Opinion* (Harcourt, Brace, 1922), p. 364.

Watching the
Watchdog

"IT IS HARD to think of another occupation of comparable importance to society that exercises so little formal control over itself," claim the authors of a journalism textbook.[1] Given the perceived power of the press, especially in Washington, the question of who watches the watchdog, and how effectively, is increasingly pertinent. There are various informal avenues of media criticism, of course—ombudsmen or readers' representatives on some papers, a news council in one state that adjudicates complaints, journalism reviews and academic journals, organized monitoring groups of both the political left and the right, popular letters-to-the-editor columns. But on Capitol Hill, Congress has created an institution whose watching carries a different kind of weight.

Reporters who wish to be members of the congressional press galleries are subject to a formal policing mechanism: four committees of the correspondents themselves, one each for those who work for daily newspapers, periodicals, radio and television, and as photographers. It is a unique arrangement. A branch of government (Congress) has given a group of private citizens (journalists elected by their peers) almost absolute control over space and facilities in a government building (the Capitol) and the power to hire and fire government employees (the staffs of the galleries). In return, the committees determine who gets press passes and can censure or withdraw the privileges of those who break their rules. The legislators thus avoid becoming the arbiters of journalists' conduct, a responsibility that would be hazardous politically and dangerous constitutionally, and the journalists achieve a measure of control over their own behavior that defines other professions.

These self-governing and virtually autonomous committees have been the children of necessity and pragmatic administration. Initially Congress itself determined the admission or banishment of reporters from its chambers.

---

1. The authors, Peter M. Sandman, David M. Rubin, and David B. Sachsman, are quoted in Tom Goldstein, *The News At Any Cost: How Journalists Compromise Their Ethics to Shape the News* (Simon and Schuster, 1985), p. 157.

And there was always some tension. The reputations of Washington reporters in the nineteenth century were sometimes shady and occasionally deservedly bad. Addressing his colleagues from the floor of the Senate in 1839, Connecticut Democrat John M. Niles asked who were these persons who styled themselves reporters? "Why miserable slanderers, hirelings hanging on to the skirts of literature, earning a miserable subsistence from their vile and dirty misrepresentations of the proceedings here . . . venal and profligate scribblers, who were sent here to earn a disreputable living by catering to the depraved appetite of the papers they work for."[2] Sometimes the scribblers, guilty perhaps of misrepresentation, or what amounted to the same thing, outrageously partisan bias, were expelled from the Senate or House chambers. Sometimes congressional action was more stern. In 1848 a *New York Herald* reporter was arrested by the Senate for publishing the secret text of the Treaty of Guadalupe Hidalgo, which ended the Mexican-American War, and was confined to a committee room in the Capitol for more than a month. In 1871 the Senate held two *New York Tribune* reporters prisoner in a committee room for a similar offense, although their imprisonment seems to have been less than harsh. According to Senator Robert Byrd, "Accounts indicate that their wives and friends, including several senators, visited them every day; that they received books and fresh flowers; ate meals sent in from the Senate restaurant; and that they were entrusted with the key to their prison door."[3]

In these same years, however, Congress had to grapple with clear breaches of reportorial ethics, violations that endangered the stability of its own code of behavior. "There were never-ending efforts by lobbyists and claim agents to pose as correspondents and secure the newspapermen's privileges. Some department clerks engaged in part-time reporting. Some legitimate reporters used their press gallery privileges and congressional contacts to branch out into such profitable sidelines as lobbying, pressing claims and selling tips to lobbyists and speculators."[4] In 1855 the House of Representatives expelled a reporter who was in the pay of the Colt's Patent Fire Arms Manufacturing Company; two years later it expelled a *New York Times* corre-

2. Quoted in Frederick B. Marbut, "The United States Senate and the Press, 1838–41," *Journalism Quarterly*, vol. 28 (Summer 1951), p. 344.
3. See Robert C. Byrd, "The Senate Press Galleries," *Congressional Record*, vol. 126 (November 24, 1980), p. S14906.
4. Frederick B. Marbut, "Congress and the Standing Committee of Correspondents," *Journalism Quarterly*, vol. 38 (Winter 1961), p. 53. A claim agent was a person who promoted bills in Congress to pay individuals for war services. Many of the claims were specious, and the practice led to the creation of the U.S. Court of Claims in 1854.

spondent who had admitted being offered money to help pass a Wisconsin land bill. In 1875 a House investigation revealed that four reporters had been paid fees ranging from $5,000 to $30,000 to help secure a subsidy for the Pacific Mail Steamship Line. *Many Secrets Revealed; or, Ten Years Behind the Scenes in Washington City*, a book by a Washington journalist of the time, described some of the reporters as "perhaps the most unscrupulous and unprincipled set of men" in the capital. "As a rule these men accept their journalistic trusts because of the fine facilities they present for bleeding corporations and getting money easily from divers lobbying schemes. There are about a dozen of these journalistic sharpers in Washington."[5]

By the last quarter of the nineteenth century, oversight of the press had become too burdensome for Congress. The numbers of Washington reporters had exploded with the rise of the penny newspaper, and case-by-case examination of credentials and complaints was diverting energy that could be applied more appropriately elsewhere. To address the problem, Speaker of the House Sam Randall met with a group of reputable congressional journalists in 1877 to create a self-policing system. The newsmen were to elect a committee from among their number to whom the House would then delegate the power of determining which journalists should be admitted to the press gallery. In 1884 the Senate Rules Committee also accepted the reporters' committee, and since 1888 the rules for governance of the press galleries as adopted by the Standing Committee of Correspondents have been approved by the Speaker of the House and the Senate Rules Committee, and published in the *Congressional Directory*.

Once the reporters were given the authority to determine who would be let in, they set about devising ways to make sure that others would be kept out. Women were initially excluded by a rule requiring accredited correspondents to file their dispatches by telegraph (none of the eleven women reporters in the 1870s qualified).[6] Blacks were excluded by a rule requiring that accredited reporters work for daily newspapers: blacks worked for weeklies. (The Senate Rules Committee forced the correspondents to revise this rule in 1947.)[7] When radio reporters applied for membership in the 1930s, the print reporters refused them. The galleries were already too crowded, they claimed, and letting in the radio reporters would open the door for even

5. I am indebted to Neil MacNeil, of *Time* magazine, for a very useful memorandum, "Origins of the Senate and House Periodical Press Galleries and their Rules," December 3, 1973.
6. See Donald A. Ritchie, *Press Gallery: Congress and the Washington Correspondents* (Harvard University Press, 1991), p. 145.
7. See Byrd, "Senate Press Galleries," p. S14908. Also see Ritchie, *Press Gallery*, p. 215.

less desirable groups.[8] Led by Fulton Lewis, Jr., the radio broadcasters won separate galleries of their own in 1939 (now used by television broadcasters as well). Two years later, correspondents for the periodicals got their own House and Senate galleries; and the photographers' gallery was started in 1955. Membership widened again in 1971 when, after weeks of "anguished debate," the newspaper correspondents' committee, by a vote of three to two, accredited a "radical" journalist, Thomas King Forcade of the Underground Press Service, who had once thrown a pie in the face of a member of the U.S. Commission on Obscenity and Pornography.[9] The galleries also had to decide whether they should admit journalists from government-controlled foreign news outlets. The newspaper journalists agreed to accredit *Pravda*, *Izvestia*, and TASS reporters as voting members, apparently because the State Department had warned that the Soviet Union would retaliate against American correspondents in Moscow if it refused. Reporters for the Voice of America, however, were granted membership in the radio and television galleries without the right to vote in elections.

CAMPAIGNS FOR SEATS on the governing committees provide congressional correspondents with an experience of participatory democracy writ small, a concave mirror image of the matters that make up the rest of their working days. When Helen Dewar, the *Washington Post's* Senate reporter, was a candidate for the Standing Committee of Correspondents in 1981, she went to the top of the National Press Building and worked her way down, floor by floor, office by office (including those of the foreign correspondents), shaking hands, smiling, making promises. She gives a sample of the politician's smile: "Yes, I'll see what can be done about a parking space. . . ." Elections have become hotly contested in recent years. Winning is no longer a by-product "simply of being well-known and an old-timer, as was once the case," according to Larry Jenezich, superintendent of the Senate Radio and Television Gallery. The voters, the journalists accredited to each gallery, now expect to be wooed. Jacqueline Frank of Reuters claims that in 1984 she visited every newspaper office listed in the *Congressional Directory*. It took her three days. She talked about everything from getting a better coffeemaker to the necessity of providing training programs for the galleries' staffs. "It's fun," she said. "It's Byzantine," said Dewar.

    8. Frederick B. Marbut, *News from the Capital: The Story of Washington Reporting* (Southern Illinois University Press, 1971), p. 212.
    9. See James Doyle, "Radical Press Gets Foothold at Capitol," *Washington Evening Star*, September 8, 1971, p. A7.

Fun? Perhaps. Being voted up or down does not suit everyone, but for those willing to risk their egos, the campaign for the standing committee can be as calculated and stimulating as a race for president of the senior class. The personalities of politicians and journalists, as I have written elsewhere, are much alike.[10] Still, the business of politics is active and reporting is passive. For some reporters who spend their working lives covering legislators, a brief fling as a politician in a professionally sanctioned election must have a cathartic effect.

As for the Byzantine quality, the better analogy might be to elections in cities controlled by machine politics. Consider the role of the two American wire services. The Associated Press has 16 or 17 reporters who work out of the congressional press galleries, United Press International about half that number. But the AP's Washington bureau employs more than 90 reporters and editors who are eligible to vote in committee elections, and UPI about 70. These are sizable blocs in contests that usually can be won with 260 votes.[11] Most of these voters have limited personal knowledge of the candidates and are willing to take instruction from those within their organizations who do. According to an AP executive, a notice is posted on the office bulletin board announcing "good" candidates and offering reporters time off to vote and cab fare to the polling place. Each ballot must be marked with as many X's as there are seats available (the standing committee consists of five members; two are elected in even-numbered years, three in odd-numbered years). For the representative of a small newspaper, then, the probability of getting elected may depend largely on the endorsement of the wire services. David Lynch, a reporter for the *Buffalo Courier-Express* when he was elected in 1978, has acknowledged, "I was anointed by Steve Gerstel [the Capitol Hill bureau chief for UPI]. He's the kingmaker."

If the wire services have kingmakers, each large newspaper bureau has a "political boss," a label that a *Los Angeles Times* reporter affectionately pinned on Paul Houston, the paper's Senate correspondent, in 1984.

He comes around the bureau urging us to vote. He'll tell you who the good guys are, apparently the candidates who will be good for us. We get these letters, and they come here and he introduces them to us. I've never figured out what we get out of it. Once someone said it had something to do with the location of a computer, another time it was

---

10. Stephen Hess, *The Washington Reporters* (Brookings, 1981), pp. 124–27. Similarly, there must be personality parallels between journalists and actors—on television, of course—but also to be seen when print reporters exhibit themselves in funny costumes at the annual Gridiron Club show in Washington.

11. In eight standing committee elections (1978–85), total votes cast ranged from 224 to 456.

an extra floor pass at the [presidential] conventions. So every January we troop down to vote. They can't tell who you vote for, of course, but they do check you off on a list.

At the time, the *Los Angeles Times* bureau had nearly 30 voters; the *Washington Times* nearly 40; the *New York Times* and *Wall Street Journal* about 50 each; and the *Washington Post* more than 100. Yet getting out the vote is not necessarily synonymous with winning: a *Post* reporter, an apparently reluctant candidate propelled into the contest by the institutional ego of his organization, was badly defeated in 1979.[12]

While some winners come from small organizations, the losers almost always come from small organizations, and some correspondents claim there is tension between large and small. Susan Stolov, a freelance television reporter, was one of six candidates for three slots on her gallery's executive committee in 1984. Phil Jones of CBS television came in first with 191 votes; Stolov was fifth. "My 87 votes may have represented 75 different organizations," she commented. "I wonder how many votes a network has?"

The arrangement between AP and UPI is that they will not run against each other. They field a candidate only in odd-numbered years. The UPI runs twice, then the AP runs twice. Because winners get two-year terms, and the highest vote-getter becomes chairman in the second year, the wire services are angling to win the chairmanship in the even-numbered years, which happen to include presidential election years. The reason for these machinations is that since 1904 for the Republicans and 1912 for the Democrats, the standing committee has been in charge of press facilities at the parties' nominating conventions.[13] "You've never seen a convention where we were not well positioned [in terms of working space in the auditorium]," an AP executive says. "We take care of ourselves."

I attended the meeting of the Standing Committee of Correspondents when it decided on seating assignments for the 1984 Democratic National Convention. The committee consisted of Tom Raum, Associated Press (chairman), Julia Malone, *Christian Science Monitor* (secretary), Robert

---

12. See Mick Rood, "Politicking in the Press Corps: Just Like the Real Thing," *Washington Monthly*, vol. 11 (April 1979), pp. 55–59, for an account of the 1979 standing committee election in which Robert Kaiser, the *Post's* Senate correspondent, was defeated, as was the article's author, who worked for States News Service. "I felt kind of silly after it was over," Rood quotes Kaiser. "They're not going to screw the *Washington Post* out of convention seats. Sure it's silly. But by running, it would assure us our seats and then Mrs. Graham can send some of her friends to the convention" (p. 59).

13. The congressional galleries are also responsible for press arrangements for the presidential inaugural events that take place at the Capitol. According to Max Barber, former superintendent of the Senate Radio and Television Gallery, "We once handled press tickets for all inaugural events, but the inaugural committee would give us 25 tickets for which there were 400 requests, and we had to play the bad guy. So now we tell the inaugural committee to play its own bad guy."

Merry, *Wall Street Journal*, Jacqueline Frank, Reuters, and Steven Roberts, *New York Times*. Senate Press Gallery Superintendent Bob Petersen explained that the staff had made tentative allocations by comparing requests for seats with the number of reporters the news organizations sent to the conventions in 1980 and 1976, thereby assessing whether requests were padded for bargaining purposes. The committee's job was to pare down 1,500 requests to match 1,000 available slots, but instead the *New York Times* thought the *Washington Post's* allocation should be increased, the *Wall Street Journal* felt the *Baltimore Sun* needed additional space, and the *Christian Science Monitor* wanted extra seats for the *Los Angeles Times*.[14] Later, when I noted the committee's generosity, a member replied that their terms in office were short and next time someone would have to look after their interests. Leo Rennert, Washington bureau chief of the McClatchy Newspapers, laughs about the politics of the press galleries. "But I've never heard of any crass deals. What's to deal? We get all the [convention] space we need without deals." He is right. Yet reporters in their temporary roles as politicians love to act as if there are deals that must be cut.

A study prepared in 1977 for the Commission on the Operation of the Senate concluded that "as a general rule, less than 10 percent of the Senate press corps uses the media galleries frequently during the week."[15] The galleries' membership at that time was about 3,000. It is now more than 4,000, but the percentage of frequent users probably has not changed. A third of the membership turns out for the standing committee elections.[16] The game of standing committee politics is thus played by a small gang of national media reporters and those regional reporters who use the galleries as their office and clubhouse.

MOST OF THE COMMITTEES' time is taken up with housekeeping chores. At the meeting of September 24, 1984, for example, the press galleries' committee received a report recommending that dues should be doubled to $10 annually; passed a resolution of appreciation for the work of the galleries'

14. "Minutes of the Standing Committee," May 25, 1984. Minutes of the most recent standing committee meeting are posted in the main room of the Senate Press Gallery; bound volumes of past minutes are available in the press gallery's office.

15. Charles E. Bosley, "Senate Media Galleries," in Commission on the Operation of the Senate, *Senate Communications with the Public: A Compilation of Papers Prepared for the Commission on the Operation of the Senate* (Government Printing Office, 1977), p. 81. See also Len Allen, "Makeup of the Senate Press," p. 24, in the same volume.

16. A comparison of the membership lists of the media galleries as published in the *Congressional Directory* with the official tallies of Senate Standing Committee elections shows a 38 percent turnout in 1979, 36 percent in 1981, and 32 percent in 1983 and 1985, about the same as the national figures for the United States in midterm elections.

staffs at the presidential conventions; discussed problems that might arise for press facilities at the 1985 presidential inauguration; reviewed various problems of security in the Capitol; agreed to have a party for Tom Griscom, press secretary for retiring Senator Howard Baker; discussed a vacation policy for the staff; adopted a series of staff job descriptions; and approved a design for the 1985 gallery cards. But because membership in a congressional press gallery is increasingly required by federal executive agencies as proof of gainful employment in the news business and therefore presumably of serious and ethical intent on the part of a reporter, the standing committees have been turned into government credentialing bodies. They may not be in a class with the American Medical Association, but they are as close as there is in Washington journalism.

The basic criteria for membership, slightly different for each gallery, are that the applicants must be "bona fide correspondents of repute in their profession"; their principal income must come from a news organization that meets the standing committees' definitions of acceptability; and they must not engage in certain activities, notably "paid publicity or promotion work" or lobbying. Each type of consideration has created controversy at some time and has even led to court cases.

Although it has not happened often, members of the standing committees have been called upon to judge the professional ethics or reputation of a colleague. In 1961, for example, they reprimanded a correspondent for two Missouri papers who had sold "ghost-written college theses, book reviews, and other assignments which should be prepared by students themselves."[17] The next year they took up the matter of an overly aggressive colleague who was accused of drowning his scruples in quest of a scoop.

The Standing Committee of Correspondents at a meeting today [September 18, 1962] considered complaints in connection with a news story published in the September 7, 1962, edition of the *Los Angeles Times* concerning the candidacy for reelection of Rep. D. S. Saund of California. The Committee invited John H. Averill, author of the story and a member of the Congressional Press Galleries, to appear and explain the circumstances under which the news story in question was obtained and published. Mr. Averill appeared before the Committee. He acknowledged that at about 9:30 P.M. on September 6, 1962, he gained entry by subterfuge into the office of Rep. Saund, and took from that office, Room 1223, Longworth House Office

---

17. "Minutes of the Standing Committee," November 14, 1961.

Building, a copy of a press release; that he then wrote and filed a news story containing the text of the press release; and that the story was published September 7, 1962, despite the fact that the release was embargoed until September 10.

The committee concluded that these were "unethical actions prejudicial to the repute and privileges of members of the Congressional Press Galleries."

A reporter's conduct was again questioned in 1979 in a statement presented to the Standing Committee by Chairman Michael Posner of Reuters:

On Friday, May 18, the Standing Committee met in executive session to receive from Sergeant of Arms of the House Ken Harding police documents regarding Mr. Gary Schuster, of the *Detroit News*, an accredited member of the gallery. . . . In sum, the police make a prima facie case that Mr. Schuster postured as a Michigan Congressman on March 26 by riding a "For Congressmen Only" bus to attend the Mideast peace treaty signing that day on the lawn of the White House. . . .

One of [the committee's] responsibilities is to see that only bona fide reporters of repute in the profession are admitted to cover Congress. On this point, reporters seek accreditation. We do not offer it to them. It is not necessary to have a gallery card to cover Congress, although it certainly makes it a lot easier. If we have a responsibility to issue cards, we have a responsibility to see that credentials are not abused. I look at our task now as to answer this question: can we as the Standing Committee of Correspondents, elected by our colleagues to issue credentials and review them, condone an accredited reporter posturing as a Congressman?[18]

The committee unanimously went "on record as strongly disapproving the conduct attributed to Mr. Schuster" and conveyed to him its "reproof." "Reproof," a word more fitting in a Jane Austen novel, seems to have been chosen as constituting less of a rebuke than the traditional "reprimand." The committee, for example, unanimously reprimanded syndicated columnist Jack Anderson in 1989 for carrying a gun and a bullet into the Capitol. He had defended himself on grounds that his purpose was "to save lives by dramatizing that the Capitol security system was vulnerable."[19]

---

18. "Minutes of the Standing Committee," May 25, 1979.
19. Helen Dewar, "Columnist Rebuked for Carrying Gun into Capitol," *Washington Post*, June 27, 1989, p. A21; and George Garneau, "Anderson's Gun Incident Has Journalists up in Arms," *Editor & Publisher*, vol. 122 (June 24, 1989), pp. 22, 42.

Unlike disciplinary actions taken in response to proscribed activities—mostly lobbying and promotion work—about which standing committees have been fairly active in recent years, judgments about professional repute are avoided if possible. Frank Aukofer of the *Milwaukee Journal* probably spoke for most of the galleries' members when he commented, "The Standing Committee should not legislate ethics for reporters. Ethics should be between the reporters and their papers."

Reporters may be of repute and still be denied membership in the congressional press galleries if they do not work for organizations that fit the committees' definitions of acceptability. Such was the case with a correspondent from *Consumer Reports*, whose rejection became a case in the federal courts as *Consumers Union of United States, Inc. v. Periodical Correspondents' Association* (1973–75). Under the rules of the Periodical Press Galleries' Executive Committee, members have to work for publications that "must be owned and operated independently of any government, industry, institution, association, or lobbying organization." *Consumer Reports'* Washington correspondent was denied admission to the periodical galleries because the magazine was owned by Consumers Union, a nonprofit advocacy organization. U.S. District Court Judge Gerhard A. Gesell ruled that the exclusion was an "abridgement of the freedom of the press" and other rights guaranteed by the First and Fourth Amendments to the Constitution.[20] A higher court overruled the decision, however, arguing that the case was "not justiciable" in that the Constitution gives Congress the power to make its own rules (and the rules of the Standing Committee of Correspondents have been incorporated into the rules of the Senate and the House).[21]

Recent definitional problems have had to do with the on-line computer services that are increasingly seeking accreditation. The Standing Committee of Correspondents has been handling applications one by one, but after several years the outline of a general policy is emerging. One criterion has been the general availability of the product. The committee turned down an on-line service that was charging a small number of business corporations about $100,000 a year for its product, then approved another that was available to a home computer user for about $100 a month. A second criterion

---

20. David Pike, "Ban at Hill Press Gallery Ruled Invalid by Gesell," *Washington Star-News*, October 12, 1973, p. A2; and Timothy S. Robinson, "Magazine Wins Suit on Rights," *Washington Post*, October 12, 1973, p. A6.

21. *Consumers Union of United States, Inc. v. Periodical Correspondents' Association*, F. 2d 1262 (D.C. Circ. 1975). The arguments for and against the *Consumer Reports* decision were made in *Harper's*, March 1977, under the title "Whisperings in the Press Gallery," by Peter H. Schuck, pp. 113–15, and Neil MacNeil, pp. 113, 116–17.

has been the standard meaning of "news." The committee has disapproved of financial tip sheets and other on-line operations that would not have qualified for admission as newspapers or periodicals, but has approved on-line operations that were simply delivering "news" through a different technology.

At its March 15, 1985, meeting, for example, the committee considered the application of Market Information, Inc., an on-line service that transmits futures quotes and agriculture prices to clients for a fee of between $300 and $400 a month. The vice president of the company told the committee that "Market Information needs Congressional accreditation to gain access to releases from government agencies such as the Departments of Commerce and Agriculture as well as to gain access to crowded Congressional hearings." The committee members then voiced objections. Lance Gay, Scripps-Howard News Service, believed "the service does not fall within gallery rules because it is not of broad general interest and seems to be geared toward providing information to corporations and financial institutions for trading purposes, and therefore differs little from consultants and lobbyists who monitor hearings for information that will be of value to their clients." Jeff Raimundo, *Sacramento Bee*, was concerned that "there are no newspapers or members of the public among Market Information's clientele." Jacqueline Frank, Reuters, was concerned because "Mr. Reed was primarily interested in credentials in order to gain access to the press lockups at the Department of Treasury, Commerce and Agriculture." Steven Roberts, *New York Times*, thought Market Information was in "the business of providing inside information at a high price and [he] was concerned at the precedent that would be set by accrediting it." The committee then unanimously rejected the application "on grounds that the service is mainly intended as an investor service rather than to disseminate news of interest to a broad section of the public."

SINCE ITS INCEPTION, the primary purpose of the Standing Committee of Correspondents—from the perspective of Congress—has been to protect the legislators from lobbyists acting in the guise of reporters. In 1928 J. Frederick Essary, Washington correspondent of the *Baltimore Sun*, recounted an example of the committee doing its duty:

> The correspondent of a Philadelphia newspaper was found a few months ago to be on the payroll of the Washington headquarters of the so-called Power Trust. This fact was brought out in sworn testimony before the Federal Trade Commission. . . .[The correspondent's]

private employers, when called upon to explain his association with themselves, went to pains to explain that he was not a press agent but a "mere tip-off man." There was no condoning such a relationship, of course, and although the correspondent enjoyed great personal popularity, the standing committee barred him from the press galleries and his newspaper promptly discharged him from its service.[22]

In other cases relating to whether gallery members had engaged in "any lobbying activity" or in "paid publicity or promotion work"—outlawed under rules 4(b) and 4(c) in "Rules Governing Press Galleries"—the committee found against columnist Drew Pearson for endorsing Listerine mouthwash in radio and television commercials (1962); against Earl Voss of the *Washington Star* for having "accepted payment for an article from an agent of the Nicaraguan Government" (1963); against columnist Jack Anderson for failing to report being a director of an airline (1964); and against Lester Kinsolving, then of the McNaught Syndicate, for having received corporate stocks from a lobbyist for South Africa (1977).[23] On the other hand, in 1978 columnist James J. Kilpatrick was declared not to have broken the galleries' rules by writing for *Nation's Business*, a publication of the U.S. Chamber of Commerce, because there was no "promotion in the articles," and, therefore, this was a legitimate freelance activity.[24]

In 1973 the standing committee construed its rule against paid advertising, publicity, or promotion work to include "paid appearances on television interview shows sponsored by members of Congress or the federal government."[25] This was unacceptable to Richard L. Strout, who had been covering Washington since 1923 for the *Christian Science Monitor*, and who appeared from time to time on a Voice of America program (he had received $240 in 1973). The venerable journalist felt that the ban was "worse than nonsense," that it was an "infringement on the rights of journalists."[26] The reaction to Strout's loss of accreditation was so considerable that the committee held a special open meeting at which the correspondent said he

22. J. Frederick Essary, "President, Congress, and the Press Correspondents," *American Political Science Review,* vol. 22 (November 1928), p. 904.

23. For the judgment on Pearson, see "Minutes of the Standing Committee," January 16, 1962. In a similar case in 1957, Marguerite Higgins of the *New York Herald Tribune* resigned from the press galleries rather than give up appearing in television commercials. The "Minutes of the Standing Committee," November 8, 1963, discuss the case of Earl Voss; the "Minutes of the Standing Committee," January 16, 1964, discuss Anderson's case; and the "Minutes of the Standing Committee," March 18, 1977, and February 23, 1978, discuss Kinsolving's case.

24. "Minutes of the Standing Committee," April 13, 1978.

25. "Minutes of the Standing Committee," January 8, 1973.

26. Quoted in Martin Arnold, "50-Year Newsman and Capitol Press Gallery Tempest," *New York Times,* January 29, 1974, p. 35.

"did not feel compromised [by taking the government's money]. He said he did not want to volunteer his services and preferred payment."[27] But the committee refused to back down. It later said, "The salient factor not made clear in publicity of recent weeks surrounding this issue is the fact that Mr. Strout is not barred from performing on Voice of America. If, however, he takes pay for such performance then he would be in violation of the galleries' rule. It is a simple rule, applicable to all members."[28] In 1977 the rule was revoked as "unfair and impossible to enforce."[29] In 1986 it was reinstated. The Periodical Press Galleries voted the ban in 1988, repealed it in 1989. So the policies governing newspaper and magazine journalists, for the moment at least, are at odds.[30]

In connection with testimony before the Senate Committee on Rules and Administration in 1983, reporters John Fogarty and Julia Malone prepared a list of twenty-one enforcement actions taken by the Standing Committee of Correspondents since 1913. All but two had come since 1951, suggesting that reporters are taking their self-policing responsibilities more seriously in recent years. Indeed, the most celebrated brouhaha came in 1989 when the Executive Committee of the periodicals galleries voted 4–3 to require members to file "an itemized list of public appearances, freelance articles or consulting work, giving the precise source—but not the amount—of income."[31] Roll Call editorially asked, "Is it in the public interest to know that a reporter who is writing about oil companies has just taken a $1,000 speaking fee from an association of petroleum producers?" The answer was "You bet it is," but that such revelations should not come from the files of the press galleries.[32] Other critics of the regulation, such as Morton Kondracke of the New Republic, "fumed" (according to a Washington Post story) that this was "a privacy issue" and that the committee was "just a bunch of busybodies."[33] The four committee members who had voted for the stricter disclosure rule were swept from office at the next election, and the offensive proviso was then repealed.[34]

27. "Minutes of the Standing Committee," October 4, 1973.

28. "Minutes of the Standing Committee," February 25, 1974.

29. "Minutes of the Standing Committee," July 25, 1977; also see "Minutes of the Standing Committee," November 7, 1975, and May 20, 1977.

30. John P. Gregg, "Press Bars Fed Fees," Roll Call, November 27, 1988, pp. 1, 17; and George Garneau, "Periodical Press Gallery Reverses Disclosure Rules," Editor & Publisher, vol. 122 (March 11, 1989), p. 18.

31. Rick Maze, "Journalists' Double Standard," New York Times, February 9, 1989, p. A27.

32. "The Press Gallery," Roll Call, February 19, 1989.

33. Eleanor Randolph, "Query Makes Reporters Cringe," Washington Post, January 25, 1989, p. A19.

34. John P. Gregg, "Press Gallery Gives Incumbents the Boot," Roll Call, February 12, 1989, pp. 1, 14; and "Members Keep Closer Eye on Press Gallery as It Repeals Disclosure Rules on Outside Income," Roll Call, February 27–March 5, 1989.

Making rules and regulations, the reporters have found, can be complicated (if one tries to anticipate every possibility) and unfair. There are advantages to a case-by-case approach. There are also disadvantages: it is terribly time-consuming, because adjudicators continually reinvent the wheel, and it presents opportunities for favoritism. The reporters' committees have been attacked for failing to provide proper protections for those who run afoul of their rules.[35] Moreover, like the legislators they write about, they can look very foolish in the act of legislating. Or as one member of the periodical panel "muttered" to another during a 1989 meeting, "Your conduct is outrageous."[36]

Norman Isaacs, a distinguished editor, has written that "the most sacred cow in journalism's holy credo [is] its self-proclaimed right to reject any type of examination of its performance."[37] Yet journalism organizations love to write codes of ethical conduct. They "have a nice ring to them," journalism educator H. Eugene Goodwin has stated. He has also noted that they always lack enforcing machinery.[38] Within this context, then, it is perhaps only a small note, but notable nonetheless, that the reporters who cover Congress have had a self-policing mechanism in place for more than a century, a watchdog of sorts, and, if hardly a junkyard dog, one that does occasionally bark.

35. See Stephen F. Mannenbach, "How Broad Discretion? Congressional Delegation of Authority to the Standing Committee of Correspondents," *Administrative Law Review*, vol. 31 (Summer 1979), pp. 367–84.
36. John P. Gregg, "Canadian Reporter Denied Credentials," *Roll Call*, March 13–19, 1989, p. 12.
37. Norman E. Isaacs, *Untended Gates: The Mismanaged Press* (Columbia University Press, 1986), p. 99.
38. H. Eugene Goodwin, *Groping for Ethics in Journalism*, 2d ed. (Iowa State University Press, 1987), pp. 15, 352.

Live from
Capitol Hill!

IN THE 1980s, Washington, especially Congress and particularly the House of Representatives, discovered the charms of local television news. "Hometown TV Coverage Is Booming," a headline in the *National Journal* pronounced in 1987: "Congress has come to be the target of constant surveillance by reporters hungry for a Washington story with a local angle."[1] If local stations wanted to cover Congress, Congress very much wanted to be covered. "I'm never too busy to talk to local TV, period, exclamation point," said House member Dan Glickman of Kansas.[2] Television coverage of the Senate, Robert Dole believed, would be "an electronic bridge to the American people."[3] Presumably, expanded coverage would benefit both legislators and electorate, increasing the public's awareness of what Congress does, while at the same time increasing constituents' appreciation of their representatives in Washington.

The interest of local television stations in reporting events on Capitol Hill was indeed a relatively new phenomenon. When Washington's first television news bureau to produce material for individual stations was opened in 1957, stories had to be filmed, the film developed, and the canisters delivered to an airport, put on board the next scheduled flight, off-loaded, and rushed to the station, where the film was then edited. This was not a successful formula for covering late-breaking news. The market was further restricted because local newscasts made up only a small part of a station's daily program menu. By 1979 there were still fewer than eighty regional television reporters in the capital.[4]

1. Dan Tuden, "Hometown TV Coverage Is Booming," *National Journal*, vol. 19 (August 29, 1987), p. 2175.
2. Quoted in Peter Osterlund, "Media-Savvy Congress Turns to TV," *Christian Science Monitor*, June 3, 1988, p. 3.
3. Quoted in Jacqueline Calmes, "Senate's Romance with TV Ends in Marriage," *Congressional Quarterly Weekly Report*, vol. 44 (August 2, 1986), p. 1744.
4. See Ed Lambeth, "Reporting Washington for Main Street," *Washington Journalism Review*, vol. 2 (December 1980), pp. 26–28.

At the opening of the 1980s, however, technological innovations and changes in the operating conditions of local stations altered news operations dramatically. Relatively inexpensive lightweight video cameras became available, giving journalists a new mobility and requiring a smaller crew. Tape, which was reusable, did not have to be developed, and was easy to edit, replaced film. Most important, commercial satellites could instantly transmit edited or live pictures to ground stations. Station managers now had more news alternatives, and more vivid ones, than before.

And they had a reason to need them. Local newscasts were becoming huge moneymakers—one securities analyst estimated that 40 percent to 50 percent of the profitability of most stations came from news programs.[5] Stations were very profitable. Pretax profit was 35 percent of gross for a typical network affiliate and could reach 47 percent in the top ten markets.[6] The market value of the stations also soared, partly because the Federal Communications Commission ruled in 1982 that owners no longer had to hold broadcast licenses for at least three years before selling them. In another ruling, the FCC allowed the networks to buy more outlets. To increase sales of commercial time, stations went to longer evening newscasts and added morning segments and daytime newsbreaks. In 1982, also, the stations dropped their voluntary code limiting the number of advertising minutes in each broadcast hour. They needed material to fill the expanded formats, and with the increased profits were able to afford costly Washington bureaus.

The immediate consequences for Washington-based regional reporters were heady. Tim Hillard of Fisher Broadcasting, with stations in the Pacific Northwest, recalls, "We were so enamored with the technology [that] for a year we went live every night."[7] Rapid development of Washington news operations followed. Bruce Finland had come to Washington in 1975 from Spartanburg, South Carolina, with a tape recorder and a plan to originate freelance radio news. When he had earned enough money to buy a camera, he switched to television reporting, called himself Potomac News, and began to customize Washington stories for stations that did not choose to have their own reporters in the capital. By 1984 he owned $300,000 in equipment and three editing benches, fielded four camera crews, and employed ten people.[8]

5. Dennis Liebowitz, quoted in *Broadcasting*, October 5, 1987, p. 61. See also Sig Mickelson, *From Whistle Stop to Sound Bite: Four Decades of Politics and Television* (Praeger, 1989), p. 169.

6. See Leo Bogart, *Press and Public*, 2d ed. (Hillsdale, N.J.: Lawrence Erlbaum Associates), p. 45. Also see Geraldine Fabrikant, "3 TV Stations' High Margins," *New York Times*, July 1, 1985, pp. D1, D2.

7. See Carol Matlack, "Live from Capitol Hill," *National Journal*, vol. 21 (February 18, 1989), p. 392.

8. Finland's company was reported to have had revenues of $7 million in 1989; the next year he sold his interest for "more than $1 million and less than $5 million" and became the operating head of the media

The growth of local news was clearly reflected in the Senate Radio and Television Gallery, which had 750 members in 1979 and 2,300 by 1987, of whom 500 were reporters.[9] The networks had about the same number of correspondents in each year, so the growth was attributable to the influx of regional reporters.

The possibilities held out by the new technology caught the interest of legislators. In 1979, the same year that commercial satellites went into orbit, the House of Representatives voted to televise its floor proceedings. Illinois Representative John Anderson's argument that the coverage would constitute "one more incumbent protection device at taxpayers' expense" had not discouraged his colleagues from installing the cameras.[10] The cameras were controlled by the House itself and the images were carried by C-SPAN, the Cable Satellite Public Affairs Network. The new network reached only 3.5 million subscribing households, but still, the exposure was alluring.[11] As Senator Charles McC. Mathias observed a few years later, "I see those little clips every night on the nightly news. Some House member is orating on something. Maybe it's only for 10 seconds, but it's part of the national dialogue and we're not part of it."[12] This exclusion worried Senator Arlen Specter, who warned, "The U.S. Senate will soon become the subordinate legislative body . . . if the Senate is not televised and the House continues to be televised." He also noted, "It may be that there are some benefits to incumbency and one of them may be the possibility of having television coverage of the U.S. Senate."[13] Finally, in 1986 the Senate agreed that its sessions should be televised, and C-SPAN II was created.[14]

The White House also made an effort to appeal to regional reporters (President Reagan's style meshed well with hometown television coverage).[15] But basically, local newscasts were expected to be the medium of Congress, just as the networks' national brand of news was dominated by the presi-

company of which Potomac was to be a part. See Paul Farhi, "Moon Associate Ties Up D.C. Media Operations," *Washington Post*, February 3, 1990, p. C1.

9. According to Max Barber, then superintendent of the gallery. See Howard Fields, "D.C. Crowded as Stations Elbow in for News Feeds," *Television/Radio Age*, September 14, 1987, p. 51.

10. Ann Cooper, "Curtain Rising on House TV Amid Aid-to-Incumbent Fears," *Congressional Quarterly Weekly Report*, vol. 37 (February 10, 1979), p. 252.

11. John Schachter, "Congress Begins Second Decade under TV's Watchful Glare," *Congressional Quarterly Weekly Report*, vol. 47 (March 11, 1989), p. 508.

12. Steven V. Roberts, "Senators Ponder Value of Letting TV in the Door," *New York Times*, September 16, 1985, p. B6.

13. *Congressional Record*, daily ed., September 17, 1984, p. S11225.

14. Brian Lamb, *C-SPAN: America's Town Hall* (Washington: Acropolis, 1988), pp. 11–16.

15. See Thomas B. Rosenstiel, " 'Local' News Bureaus Polish Reagan Image," *Los Angeles Times*, July 14, 1984, p. 1; and John Anthony Maltese, "Presidential Power and the Media: The Role of the White House Office of Communications," Ph.D. dissertation, Johns Hopkins University, 1988, pp. 353–54.

dent. Most of the regional bureaus were housed on Capitol Hill. At the
same time, some legislators were learning the techniques of producing their
own video releases and of beaming interviews and even whole programs to
stations in their districts.[16] Necessarily, they created an infrastructure of
staff, committees, consultants, and party organs to assist in these publicity
efforts.[17]

All this activity itself fascinated print journalists, who kept their readers
informed of how Congress was playing to a television audience. The articles
usually contained caveats that television was not for all legislators—some
would never be comfortable with the immediacy and brevity of the new
medium, others came from districts that did not fit comfortably into any
station's market. But in general they concluded, as did a *Christian Science
Monitor* account in 1988, that "many members are . . . transforming themselves into virtual television stars back home and, in the process, boosting
their prospects for reelection."[18]

Political scientists began to comment on the effect that changes in the
media were having on Congress as an institution, on the election prospects
of its members, and even on the character of the people who would become
legislators in the television era.[19] The network evening news became the unit
by which scholars most often measured the impact of television on politics,
in part owing to the excellent abstracts of these programs prepared monthly
at Vanderbilt University.[20] Soon there were statistics to show that network
news focused more on the president than on the Congress. Not only were
there more stories on the presidency, but they were longer than congres-

16. See, for example, "Sen. Trible Will Be Host of Monthly TV Program," *Richmond News Leader*,
March 6, 1985; Richard S. Dunham, "Heeeeeere's Phil, Gramm Starring in Own Show for Texas TV,"
Dallas Times Herald, March 28, 1985; and Tom Kenworthy, "House Incumbents Ride the Airwaves,"
Washington Post, October 17, 1990, p. A1.

17. See, for example, Emily Yoffe, "Bargain Basement Broadcasting," *Washington Journalism Review*,
vol. 3 (June 1981), p. 25; Anne Haskell, "Live from Capitol Hill," *Washington Journalism Review*, vol. 4
(November 1982), pp. 48–50; Martin Tolchin, "TV Studio Serves Congress," *New York Times*, March 7,
1984, p. C22; Paul West, "The Video Connection," *Washington Journalism Review*, vol. 7 (June 1985), pp.
48–50; Shannon Bradley, "Democrats Are Falling in Love with Television," *Roll Call*, July 5, 1987,
p. 24; and Mary Collins, "News of the Congress BY the Congress," *Washington Journalism Review*, vol. 12
(June 1990), pp. 30–34.

18. Peter Osterlund, "Media-Savvy Congress Turns to TV," *Christian Science Monitor*, June 3, 1988,
p. 3.

19. See Michael J. Robinson, "Three Faces of Congressional Media," in Thomas E. Mann and Norman
J. Ornstein, eds., *The New Congress* (Washington: American Enterprise Institute for Public Policy Research,
1981), pp. 55–96; Norman J. Ornstein, "The Open Congress Meets the President," in Anthony King, ed.,
Both Ends of the Avenue: The Presidency, the Executive Branch, and Congress in the 1980s (Washington:
American Enterprise Institute for Public Policy Research, 1983), pp. 185–211; and Ornstein, "The Media
and the Open Congress," in Stephen Bates, ed., *The Media and the Congress* (Columbus, Ohio: Publishing
Horizons, 1987), pp. 7–19.

20. Also, starting in 1987 the Center for Media and Public Affairs in Washington began *Media Monitor*,
a content analysis (one topic or theme per issue) of network news. The editors are S. Robert Lichter and Linda
S. Lichter.

sional stories and were given better placement.[21] Michael J. Robinson and Margaret A. Sheehan summarized, "the office of the president has become the *sine qua non* of network journalism"; and Kathleen Hall Jamieson commented, "435 members of the House and 100 members of the Senate compete for the crumbs of network time left after the president has gotten his share."[22] Other scholars proved that network journalism was more interested in the Senate than the House. Joe S. Foote showed that during the Ninety-ninth Congress (1985–86) senators averaged six times more exposure than House members on the three network evening news programs. Other studies showed how network television homed in on legislative leaders and those legislators who were potential presidential candidates; the networks had little time for rank-and-file members of the House and Senate.[23]

Strangely, perhaps, there is no similar body of information about local newscasts, even though they draw bigger audiences than the comparable network programs. (When I examined ratings in 1986 and 1987, the popularity of local news topped that of national news for eighteen of twenty-two stations.)[24] In the absence of careful examination, the fears of Senators Mathias and Specter about the primacy of House members' exposure on local television, the assertion of Representative Anderson that exposure would be an incumbent protection device, and the assumptions of the press that legislators were playing to a television audience have taken on an air of certitude.

If, as assumed, these popular local newscasts are the mirror image of the networks, more focused on the legislature than the executive, would this not constitute a new "check and balance" in our political system? Hardly something designed by the founding fathers, but also hardly unimportant in a period of divided government, when one party often controls the White

21. See Lynda Lee Kaid and Joe Foote, "How Network Television Coverage of the President and Congress Compare," *Journalism Quarterly*, vol. 62 (Spring 1985), pp. 59–65. Also see Robert E. Gilbert, "President versus Congress: The Struggle for Public Attention," *Congress & The Presidency*, vol. 16 (Autumn 1989), pp. 83–102.

22. Michael J. Robinson and Margaret A. Sheehan, *Over the Wire and on TV: CBS and UPI in Campaign '80* (Russell Sage Foundation, 1983), p. 191; and Kathleen Hall Jamieson, *Eloquence in an Electronic Age: The Transformation of Political Speechmaking* (Oxford University Press, 1988), p. 14. When I measured stories about Congress and the president on the three networks' evening news programs for a week in April 1978, I concluded that the split was 59 percent to 41 percent in favor of the president. See Stephen Hess, *The Washington Reporters* (Brookings, 1981), p. 98.

23. Joe S. Foote, "99th Congress Network News Visibility Study," press release, Southern Illinois University, August 17, 1987; Timothy E. Cook, *Making Laws and Making News: Media Strategies in the U.S. House of Representatives* (Brookings, 1989), pp. 32–70; Stephen Hess, *The Ultimate Insiders: U.S. Senators in the National Media* (Brookings, 1986), pp. 9–29; and Feverill Squire, "Who Gets National News Coverage in the U.S. Senate?" *American Politics Quarterly*, vol. 16 (April 1988), pp. 139–56.

24. I used the Arbitron rating system, November 1986 and January 1987, for San Francisco, Detroit, Seattle, Charlotte, Oklahoma City, Salt Lake City, Toledo, and Charleston, S.C. Local news averaged nearly 4 points better than the evening network news. Also see Martin Schram, *The Great American Video Game: Presidential Politics in the Television Age* (Morrow, 1987), pp. 181–82.

House and the other Capitol Hill. If, as assumed, local television also corrects the network imbalance of Senate-House news, this could have political ramifications, encouraging more House members to reach for Senate seats. If rank-and-file members of Congress dominate their local newscasts, as assumed, is this not additional evidence of the role television can play in tilting the electoral balance between incumbents and challengers? This is a worthy topic for consideration before we attempt to reform campaign financing, the use of the franking privilege and other congressional perks, and any practices that prevent elections from being conducted even handedly.

This chapter thus examines local television coverage of Washington officials and institutions. Does local news favor the president or Congress? House or Senate? And does any of it make a difference? There are two parts to the investigation. The first looks at the news produced by local stations' bureaus and by independent news services in Washington. The second looks at what actually appears on local newscasts. They are not the same. Rather, as we will see, our design resembles seeing an event first through one end of a telescope and then through the other.

Washington from the Washington Bureaus

This is an examination of the stories produced by ten Washington bureaus for their television stations or groups of stations and of two independent news services that specialized in freelance stories with a Washington focus. When we contacted the bureaus in 1986, they reported for 33 stations: 12 in the West, 10 in the Middle West, 9 in the South, and 2 in the Northeast (see appendix table B-1 for a list of the stations). The freelancers sold stories to 156 stations in 40 states, although 49 stations bought only one or two during the period under study.

Our vacuum cleaner approach sucked up whatever program logs or scripts my research assistant, Deborah Kalb, could beg from busy reporters, whose records had gaps and whose notations had not been prepared to be part of a scholarly study. The material covers seven years of stories, starting with 12 from 1979 and ending with 6,781 produced in 1985, a total of 18,213. Although the sample is not meant to be scientific, its size and breadth are sufficient to give what we believe is an accurate reflection of regional television news stories produced in Washington during the first half of the 1980s.

We coded the stories to classify the people and institutions identified in them. The people were classified as House members or senators from the station's state; members of Congress from other states; local people, such as governors and mayors, visiting Washington; and executive branch personnel. Executive branch personnel associated with the White House—president, vice president, national security adviser, OMB director, and so forth—were also coded separately. In all cases, we noted whether the person was seen or merely mentioned. The institutions identified in the stories were classified as *Senate, House, House and Senate, executive, executive and legislative,* and *other.* A story about Senator Jake Garn's intentions of accompanying the crew on a space shuttle mission was coded as a *Senate* story unless it had a sound bite from a NASA official, in which case it was coded *executive and legislative.* Comments from House members and senators in a single story made it *House and Senate.* If the president sent a message to Congress or if there was a Senate confirmation hearing on a presidential nominee, the story was coded *executive and legislative.* Stories about the Supreme Court or about local people doing things unrelated to government were *other.*

In a further breakdown, when a story was classified as being about a senator from a station's state, we determined whether the content was local or national: *local* if it involved a matter primarily affecting the state or region, *national* if the senator was acting or commenting on a national issue. Consider the following reports:

> Senator Dan Evans made up his mind today and voted in favor of continued funding for the MX missile . . . joining a surprisingly large majority in the Senate . . . which approved the missile on a vote of 55 to 45. Channel 7's John Hollenhorst has the story from the nation's capital. [*KIRO, Seattle, March 19, 1985*]

> The House is expected to follow the Senate's lead and approve these new missiles next week. . . . And it should keep a few thousand Utahns on the job for at least the next five years. . . . Morton Thiokol is building the first stage of the MX missile [and] Hercules the third. . . . Between them, defense contracts account for millions of dollars and nearly 2,000 jobs. [*Mike Goldfein in Washington for KUTV, Salt Lake City, March 19, 1985*]

The same event, yet we coded Senator Evans's vote *national* and the effect of that vote on Utah *local.*

When we counted the legislators who were seen in these stories, our survey reflected what we had been led to expect from reading newspaper and magazine reports about the relationship between members of Congress and local television news broadcasts: House members get more attention than senators. House members appeared or were mentioned in 53 percent of the bureau stories on Congress run by their states' television stations. Senators were involved in 47 percent (appendix table B-1). House members received more coverage from twenty-seven of thirty-three stations—and two of the exceptions were in very small states where, as Carolyn Gorman, Outlet Broadcasting's bureau chief in 1986, said of Rhode Island, "people know their senators the way people in other states know their congressman." She added, "Rhode Island House members lose out on coverage because of this."

However, in terms of institutions, stories about Congress focused less frequently on the House (46 percent of the time) than on the Senate (54 percent). And it must be remembered that the survey antedated C-SPAN II coverage. As Charles Sherrill, Bonneville Broadcasting's Washington bureau chief, told me one day in 1985, "There's a story today on the Superfund. If it was on the Senate floor, we wouldn't do it. We would have to stay there all day and get an artist. But in the House we can tape the floor." What appeared to have happened was that more House members were seen in House stories than senators were seen in Senate stories. But there were more Senate stories. Thus local news broadcasters in Washington favored House members and the Senate.

Another finding that seemed to conform with expectations is that members of Congress get on local news broadcasts more often than people from the executive branch—nearly three times as often (appendix table B-2). But the imbalance is not so drastic as it might first appear. The president, although not seen as often on the "Live at Five" segments, often provides a motor force for Washington stories:

> Local government leaders from around Utah today complained that their budgets would be devastated by the elimination of federal revenue sharing, proposed by President Reagan. Charles Sherrill reports from Washington. [*KSL, Salt Lake City, March 5, 1985*]

And classifying stories by the institutions covered, a more difficult tabulation than simply counting the positions of the people appearing in them, further erodes the imbalance.

People seen	Percent	Institutions	Percent
Senators from region	21.0	Senate	14.4
House members from region	21.9	House	12.5
Legislators outside region	9.9	House and Senate	7.4
Executive branch	20.6	Executive and legislative	22.3
Locals	24.5	Executive	28.3
		Other	15.1

Our institutions scale showed Congress leading the executive branch 54 percent to 46 percent.

One member of Congress out of every five who appeared in these stories was not from the area to which the story was beamed. Part of the explanation is that Washington bureaus increasingly report for more than one station, and the stations are often located in different regions of the country. Cox Broadcasting, for instance, owns stations in San Francisco, Orlando, Dayton, Detroit, Pittsburgh, Atlanta, and Charlotte. From 1983 to 1985 the company's Washington operation produced more than 6,000 stories and distributed nearly a fourth of them to all stations. A local angle is therefore not always possible, but the bureaus try to compromise. Cox bureau chief Andy Cassells said that if a story was to be about the space shuttle, he would try to interview Ohio Senator John Glenn, the former astronaut. This would make Dayton happy and would do nothing to lessen the value of the story for the Orlando station. An interview with Dayton's congressman, however, would not enhance the story for Florida viewers.

Still, the choice of what is to be aired is made by the individual stations, and even a story featuring a member of Congress from a station's region may not be local enough. King Broadcasting has stations in Seattle, Portland, and Boise: on June 6, 1986, its Washington bureau produced a story with a prominent sound bite from Representative Norman Dicks of Tacoma, which Chris Ramsey, evening news producer for KGW in Portland, decided against using because Dicks was not a household name there; in turn, Linda Gist, assistant news director for the Seattle station, commented that her viewers were not interested in the Washington bureau's coverage of Idaho Congressman George Hansen's trial, although it was "a huge story in Boise." The demands on a multistation Washington bureau may thus work in favor of showing nationally known senators and against the rationale of localized reporting.

Washington bureaus viewed the House and Senate in distinctly different ways. Although WJBK in Detroit asked Representative Donald Albosta to comment on a dioxin study being conducted in the Great Lakes area, it asked Senator Donald Riegle for his reaction to the president's State of the Union message. The House is stereotypically a city council writ large, and 60 percent of all stories about House members covered the local angle. There was considerable variation among bureaus, of course. From 1983 to 1985, for instance, WFAA in Dallas showed House members in a local context 48 percent of the time. Texas senators were given a local angle only 25 percent of the time: it was more typical to show Senator Lloyd Bentsen commenting on the Grenada invasion or other matters of national interest. Washington's regional reporters, however, seemed to let senators designate their own news orientation, depending on whether they wanted to be seen primarily as national or local legislators. Our survey showed senators' appearances evenly divided on local television, with 49 percent coded as local-angle stories. But again, the range was considerable: Wisconsin's William Proxmire was mentioned in a national context 91 percent of the time; Roger Jepsen of Iowa was mentioned in a local context 75 percent of the time. Unlike network news, which is attracted to powerful senior senators, the regional reporters, interested largely in where senators come from rather than whether they chair committees, gave senior and junior senators from their states equal attention, with the edge (51 percent) in favor of the junior senator, who may work harder at press relations.

This should not imply that all senators are equally interesting or make themselves equally available to the broadcast reporters from their states. The disparity was considerable in five states in our sample where one senator received at least twice as much attention as the other.[25] In a 1986 interview, Jan McDaniel, Washington bureau chief of Chronicle Broadcasting, told me that Kansas Senator Nancy Kassebaum kept a low profile. She would not turn Chronicle down if it had a legitimate request, but she was not a newshound and would go on television only if she felt she had something to say. And Edward Zorinsky of Nebraska was camera-shy, afraid of not looking good or of being quoted out of context. Newspapers were better able to follow him around, McDaniel continued. Chronicle had had to sit outside his office every day to get his reaction on an important farm bill. These are not isolated cases. Reporters' options may also be limited by the quality of legislators' press operations, although one should assume that politicians who want to be on television will eventually hire the staff necessary to facilitate their appearances. Mike Cozza, bureau chief for Jefferson-Pilot Communications, which has stations in Virginia and North Carolina, said in 1986, "There is a relationship between an aggressive media relations office and the coverage that a senator gets." He was making the point because Jesse Helms of North Carolina, who did not have a press secretary, was the exception to

25. The cases were Florida (Lawton Chiles, 29 percent; Paula Hawkins, 71 percent); Georgia (Sam Nunn, 67; Mack Mattingly, 33); North Carolina (Jesse Helms, 73; John East, 27); Wisconsin (William Proxmire, 29; Robert Kasten, 71); and Texas (Lloyd Bentsen, 28; Phil Gramm, 72). In tracking senators on the network news in 1981–82, Joe S. Foote and David J. Weber found that in 76 percent of the states there was an "intrastate visibility imbalance" of at least two-to-one. See "Network Evening News Visibility of Congressmen and Senators," paper submitted to the Radio and Television Division of the 1984 annual meeting of the Association for Education in Journalism and Mass Communication.

the principle. "You have to cover him even though he's not cooperative. . . . Wait outside his office and usually he will talk to you."

The frequency with which legislators appear on their local stations may
also depend on whether the story is done by a station's own bureau or an
independent news service. Because a Washington bureau often sends a
single story to more than one station, it must balance the needs of each
station against the constraints imposed by time and by the interests, expertise, and availability of the legislators. But freelancers are entrepreneurs who
seek business by thinking up stories that they hope they can sell to an individual station. The major users of these stories are stations in middle-size
cities—nearly half the stories produced by Potomac News in 1985, for
instance, were aimed at cities with 300,000 to 700,000 television households, market sizes approximated by Spokane and Kansas City. Because
congressional districts and television markets are apt to be congruent in cities
this size, freelancers' stories are more likely to focus on House members.
Newsfeed, which had about seventy-five clients in 1985, gave the House
about 60 percent of its attention.

Freelancers' stories are also more sharply tailored for specific local
markets. For instance, in the first four months of 1985, Potomac News
produced stories on the Supreme Court case of the Oklahoma City school
board vs. the Gay Task Force (for WWTV, Oklahoma City, January 14), on
the Weeping Watch high school band's visit to Washington for the president's inauguration (for KETV, Omaha, January 21), on the National
Science Foundation's award of $75 million to the University of Illinois (for
WCIA, Champaign, February 25), on Robert Smith's swearing in by the
House of Representatives (for WMUR, Manchester, New Hampshire,
March 3), and on Mayor Flynn's testimony before the House Budget
Committee (for WNEV, Boston, March 12). Potomac's ratio of local to
national topics during these months was 70 percent to 30 percent.

Even within a bureau the ratio of local to national stories may vary from
station to station, depending on the characteristics and competition of the
markets and the stations' personnel and clout within the organization.
Consider two Chronicle stations, KRON in San Francisco and KAKE in
Wichita. Robert Cohen, news director at KAKE in 1986, said he asked the
Washington bureau "to cover the congressional delegation, hearings and
agency developments affecting the local area, Washington visits by people
from the area, and other interesting stories." On the same day Bob
Hodierne, associate news director at KRON, said, "If [Wichita's] mayor goes
to Washington, [KAKE] will want a story. When the San Francisco mayor

goes, unless she ends up in the reflecting pool, the station is not very interested. If high school kids from Wichita go to Washington, the Wichita station will want that. In San Francisco, we're interested in offshore oil drilling, toxic waste legislation, AIDS." Tabulations for 1985 show that 76 percent of the stories Chronicle's Washington bureau prepared for Wichita were local; for San Francisco they were 46 percent national.

Just as members of Congress attract local attention, but in varying proportions, some congressional committees attract Washington regional reporters more strongly than others. From the number of local cameras that were at Senate hearings between February 1979 and June 1986, we determined that coverage of the Judiciary Committee was almost twice that of the next most popular committee, Labor, which was followed by Foreign Relations and Finance (appendix tables B-3 and B-4). The local broadcasters are as much drawn to the contentious "policy" committees as the networks are. The major exception is the Budget Committee, of interest to the networks but not to local stations; a Salt Lake City news director asserted that the committee produces "boring, talking-heads nonvisual stories." Local newscasters do, however, care more than the networks about "constituency" committees. Local stations gave nearly twice as much attention to the Committee on Environment and Public Works and the Committee on Commerce, Science, and Technology.

What could a Washington bureau mean to a station? For one year, 1985, we examined computer printouts of all stories that Jefferson-Pilot Communications sent to WBTV in Charlotte, North Carolina. Although the bureau also reported for WWBT, Richmond, our tabulations are of the stories produced exclusively for Charlotte. The bureau, consisting of a correspondent and a cameraman, had been opened in September 1981 by Mike Cozza, WBTV's assistant news director, a graduate of the University of North Carolina. In 1985 he was thirty-eight years old and had been a journalist for seventeen years and an employee of WBTV for a decade. Cozza sent Charlotte 15 stories a month, 182 for the year; 101 stories were local angles on national stories, 64 were local news from Washington, and three were on miscellaneous topics. Only 14 of the stories might have been produced for network television, one being on the death of Soviet leader Konstantin Chernenko.

About 20 percent of WBTV's audience lives in South Carolina, so Cozza's Congress consisted of four senators and eight representatives whose districts are within seventy-five miles of Charlotte. The following table compares the number of times these legislators appeared in the Washington reports for WBTV's local newscasts and the number of times they appeared on the "CBS Evening News," WBTV being a CBS affiliate.

Legislators	Local news	Network news
Senators		
John East	7	2
Jesse Helms	23	15
Ernest Hollings	13	2
Strom Thurmond	12	8
Total	55	27
Representatives		
James Broyhill	20	0
Carroll Campbell	7	0
William Cobey	0	0
Howard Coble	2	0
W. G. Hefner	11	1
J. Alex McMillan	21	0
Stephen Neal	2	0
John Spratt	9	1
Total	72	2

Senator Thurmond's chairmanship of the Judiciary Committee accounted for five of the eight times he appeared on CBS in 1985; Senator Hollings's two appearances related to the budget deficit reduction proposal known as Gramm-Rudman-Hollings; Senator East was mentioned incidentally because he missed a key vote while in the hospital and mentioned again (for twenty seconds) when he decided not to seek reelection. What was of most interest to CBS about Senator Helms was that he wanted to take over the network, the subject of nine of the fifteen stories in which he was a participant. It did not make any difference to CBS that these senators were from the Carolinas; they were part of national news. One national story in 1985 actually focused on the Charlotte area, where hundreds of textile mills are located. A bill attempting to protect the textile industry from imports, ultimately vetoed by President Reagan, was the subject of nine CBS stories, although only one included a Carolina legislator. But the bill was WBTV's top Washington story: Cozza covered it thirty-two times. Tobacco, another topic of special interest to the Carolinas, received more attention from the network: CBS produced twelve stories; Cozza, eleven. But on network news, tobacco is a health story. Many of these stories opened with an antismoking peg, such as a new scientific report, then provided a response from the tobacco industry. On the local news, the order may be reversed, and the story was more apt to focus on economics:

[*From CBS News, Vanderbilt abstract*] Senate subcommittee's consideration of extending deadline for dropping federal cigarette tax examined. Coalition on Smoking and Health spokesperson David Neumeyer compares death rates for airline disasters and smoking-related illnesses. Antismoking lobby's argument outlined on screen. Kenneth Warner [University of Michigan] claims lowering tax will result in higher death rate. Tobacco industry's position explained. Senator Wendell Ford opposes government dictating morality. Senator John Chafee responds.

[*From WBTV local news*] A coalition of 36 health and public interest groups called on Congress today to double the federal excise tax on cigarettes. The tobacco industry directly employs more than 70,000 people in North Carolina . . . and this issue is not taken lightly by the state's congressional delegation. Washington correspondent Mike Cozza reports.

The Carolinas' delegation in the House captured the attention of CBS only when South Carolina's John Spratt cast a last-minute vote against the MX missile and again during a story on military housing—North Carolina's W. G. Hefner was chairman of the Appropriations Subcommittee on Military Construction. Of least interest to the network was any freshman legislator from the minority party, such as Republican Alex McMillan of Charlotte, who was of greatest interest to WBTV in that his district most closely resembled its market area. After he was first elected in 1984 by 321 votes, McMillan commented for Cozza on a wide range of topics—the contras in Nicaragua, banning broadcast commercials for beer and wine, a proposed balanced budget amendment to the Constitution, tax reform, textiles, tobacco, Amtrak, nuclear power—but most often his comments directly related to representing Charlotte in Washington. A typical story from Cozza opened, "The federal Department of Transportation has agreed to speed up an $8 million grant to purchase land for Charlotte's long-awaited outer loop beltway. As a result, the state can begin immediately to acquire land for the first phase of the project, known as the Pineville Bypass, between US-51 and I-77. Congressman Alex McMillan announced the grant. . . ."

(Despite this publicity, McMillan was reelected with just 51 percent of the vote; he failed to carry Charlotte.)

Cozza's prime subjects, unlike the networks', were decidedly congressional; of his 347 sound bites, 56 percent were from members of Congress. The out-of-state legislators (18 percent of the total) tended to be House and Senate leaders—Speaker Thomas P. O'Neill commented four times, Senate Majority Leader Robert Dole five—or legislators prominent in national issues that concerned the Carolinas, such as Senator Daniel Evans of Washington, who filibustered against the textile bill. Executive branch offices made up 18 percent of Cozza's subjects. The president appeared nine times, followed by U.S. Trade Representative Clayton Yeutter, four times.

The people in Charlotte in 1985 who watched both local and network newscasts, then, were presented with complementary portraits of Washington: local and congressional on WBTV, national and executive on CBS.

Counting sound bites will not prove or disprove that legislators are "transforming themselves into virtual television stars back home . . . boosting their prospects for reelection," as the *Christian Science Monitor* claimed; but the absence of sound bites can show that the importance of television appearances has been overstated. Less than 10 percent of all stations have Washington bureaus, and few legislators are as fortunate as Alex McMillan with his 21 appearances on WBTV in 1985. Senator Robert Kasten of Wisconsin appeared in stories from the Washington bureau of WITI in Milwaukee roughly once a month: 12 times in 1983, 15 times in 1984, 14 times in 1985. Georgia Senator Mack Mattingly was part of a story from the Washington bureau of WAGA in Atlanta 10 times in each of those years; Senator Steve Symms of Idaho appeared in the Washington bureau stories of KTVB, Boise, 9 times a year between 1981 and 1985; Michigan Senator Carl Levin appeared in the Washington stories of WKBD, Detroit, once a month in 1984 and 1985; and Senator James Exon of Nebraska averaged 7 appearances a year from Washington for KOWT, Omaha. But sometimes, as in Seattle, where all three network-affiliated stations have Washington bureaus, the numbers can add up fast. Slade Gorton, elected to the Senate in 1980, produced 121 Washington bureau sound bites on KIRO (1981 to 1985), 93 on KOMO (1982 to 1985), and 157 on KING (1981 to 1985). And this was an incomplete survey. (Despite this attention, Gorton was defeated in 1986.)

Such coverage was always rare, however, and is growing more so. By 1990 three of the bureaus that participated in this study—Outlet Broadcasting, KUTV in Salt Lake City, and Jefferson-Pilot Communications—had closed shop in Washington. Mike Cozza returned to Charlotte in 1989 to be a weekend anchor. Chronicle, which some felt was the strongest Washington bureau, folded, leaving one correspondent to report for KRON. WCCO in Minneapolis-St. Paul, a pioneer in Washington reportage, also closed its bureau, as did Gannett. Although three new television bureaus were opened, notably Hearst Broadcasting, no one any longer claims the Seattle model as the wave of the future.

The reasons have little to do with the quality of the news from the Washington bureaus and a lot to do with economics. A *New York Times* headline on November 30, 1988, observed, "Glut of TV Stations for Sale Being Met by Buyer Apathy." Cable television, available to more than half the nation's homes, has eaten into the broadcast audience.[26] VCRs have multiplied amazingly, one more contender for people's attention. The excitement about the new video technology that Tim Hillard recalled had long gone. Some observers were even predicting that there would be "fewer local television stations" in the 1990s and "fewer local television stations doing news."[27] But even if all these trends could be reversed, the future of Washington bureaus is more precarious than anyone would have judged from the news accounts of the earlier 1980s.

In 1986 my assistants and I interviewed news directors from 102 television stations to find out what they anticipated their needs would be for Washington coverage, assuming that the desire for news from the capital was growing, as journalism journals kept asserting. We talked to top people at stations from New York City, Philadelphia, and Detroit to Presque Isle, Maine, Twin Falls, Idaho, and Anchorage, Alaska. To our surprise, very few wanted to expand Washington coverage. Only three claimed that national coverage improved their standing in the ratings, Charlotte's WBTV being one of them. The news manager at a large Texas station explained, "Our consultant says government news is boring to viewers. One thing Washington is full of is talking heads and meetings." Claims such as "Quietly, without fanfare, there is a new seriousness to local news," made in 1986, were based on anecdotal evidence from a few stations that seemed to turn up in all articles predicting that local newscasts would relegate network newscasts to "a mere memory by the century's end."[28]

26. James G. Webster, "Cable Television's Impact on Audience for Local News," *Journalism Quarterly*, vol. 61 (Summer 1984), p. 420, shows that "local news shares were significantly lower among cable subscribers than broadcast viewers."

27. Ron Handberg, "Broadcast News in the 1990s," address delivered at the first annual Dupont Awards Seminar, Columbia University Graduate School of Journalism, 1989, p. 6.

28. Desmond Smith, "Affiliates Usurping Networks' New Role," *Media Institute Forum*, vol. 3 (Spring 1986), p. 5; and Harry F. Waters, "The Future of Television," *Newsweek*, October 17, 1988, p. 85. Also see Barbara Matusow, "Learning to Do with Less," *Washington Journalism Review*, vol. 8 (June 1986),

Washington on the Local News

If local broadcasters' interest in Washington news is waning, what does appear on their newscasts? Imagine a leisurely trip around the United States. Each evening, usually at dinnertime, you turn on a local news broadcast. The tour takes you to thirty-five cities, from Los Angeles, the nation's second largest market, to Grand Junction, Colorado, population 30,000, which ranks 186th on Arbitron's scale of television households.[29] You stay a week in some places and watch competing stations; other stops are overnight. The journey starts in September 1987 and ends the next April.[30] This, in a sense, is what we did when we gathered tapes from fifty-seven stations.

Local newscasts, of course, are an amalgam of news, weather, and sports. The average news portion in the sample accounted for 68.4 percent of the broadcast, sports 17.8 percent, and weather 13.8 percent. But emphasis differed from station to station. News ranged from 94 percent of the evening broadcast to 36 percent. Two stations devoted more than a third of their newscasts to sports; three devoted more than a fourth to weather. The emphasis also differed according to market size.[31]

Content	Largest markets (1–25)	Middle markets (26–70)	Smallest markets (71–186)
Sports	16.7	17.2	20.3
Weather	10.0	14.2	19.3
News	73.3	68.7	60.4

The smaller the city, the lower the percentage of news and the more reporting on sports and weather.

Market size also affected the length and number of local newscasts. The larger the city, the more local news programming its stations provide. Of 102 stations sampled in 1986, those in the top 39 markets, New York City

pp. 23–25; and Rinker Buck, "What the Cutbacks Really Mean," *Channels*, vol. 6 (September 1986), pp. 67–69.

29. We are grateful to the good samaritans who taped local newscasts for this study, including Jim Bennett, Washington, North Carolina; Timothy Cook, Williamstown, Massachusetts; Julie Darnell, South Bend, Indiana; Martha Derthick, Charlottesville, Virginia; Morton Ellin, Baltimore; Joe S. Foote, Carbondale, Illinois; David Graves, Greenville, South Carolina; Marvin Kalb, Cambridge, Massachusetts; Spence Kinard, Salt Lake City; Heidi Levitt and Charles Hess, Los Angeles; Jan McDaniel, Chronicle Broadcasting; Alan Pasternak, Sacramento; James Smith, Geneva, New York; Steven Smith, Minneapolis; Ken Sneeden, Fort Myers, Florida; Clinton Stinger, Roanoke; Ellen Wartella and Charles Whitney, Champaign, Illinois; and Della Mae and Robert Weaver, Grand Junction, Colorado.

30. The dates have no special significance other than that Congress was in session.

31. The top market category consisted of 24 stations in 11 cities: 31 hours of broadcasting. The middle market category consisted of 18 stations in 14 cities: 15.5 hours of broadcasting. The small market category consisted of 15 stations in 10 cities: 13.5 hours of broadcasting.

through the Greenville-Spartanburg-Asheville region of the Carolinas, averaged 630 minutes of local newscasts each week; stations ranked 40-117,
Oklahoma City through Fort Myers, Florida, averaged 559 minutes; stations
in smaller cities, Montgomery, Alabama (119) through North Platte,
Nebraska (208), averaged 409 minutes.

In at least one respect, the fifty-seven stations in the survey do not represent a microcosm of all stations in the United States. This is a study of news
from Washington, and the intent is to contrast stations with and without
Washington representation, so stations with a Washington bureau made up
one-third of the total in the survey, although they made up only 10 percent
of all stations. It is reasonable to assume, then, that the total amount of
Washington news in the sample is substantially more than would be
"average" for the country.[32]

Most of the networks' national and international stories—other than news
of catastrophes—are tied to the doings of people who run or aspire to run
governments. But in our survey, fewer than one in five of the local people
who appeared were politicians or prominent government officials. Those
interviewed on network news are overwhelmingly officeholders and experts;
those on the local news are witnesses to crimes or fires, or have been
involved in accidents, or simply represent the so-called man on the street. In
a 1967 analysis Herbert J. Gans reported that 71 percent of the people in
network news stories were presidents, presidential candidates, members of
Congress, or other recognized figures. In 1987 Mark D. Harmon analyzed
local news from three Cincinnati television stations and found that 67
percent of the people seen and heard were "unknowns."[33]

Different, too, is the locale of stories. Unlike the globe hopping of the
network programs (and their anchors), more than three-quarters of the stories
on local newscasts originate locally. But, as mentioned earlier, the sample
still probably overrepresents national and international news.[34] By how

32. Of the 106 broadcasts in the survey, 96 occurred between 4:00 P.M. and 7:00 P.M., 6 at noon, and 4
between 10:00 P.M. and 11:00 P.M. Were we measuring the news at the wrong time? A study of ten
Pennsylvania stations in 1976 showed heavier emphasis on national and international stories on the late
evening broadcasts; see William C. Adams, "Local Public Affairs Content of TV News," *Journalism
Quarterly*, vol. 55 (Winter 1978), p. 693. So we asked stations, "During which broadcast(s) are you most
likely to run Washington stories (noon, evening, night)?" Of the twenty-one news directors we reached, three
were less likely to use national news in the 4:00 P.M. to 7:00 P.M. time slot, four were less likely in the 10:00
P.M. to 11:00 P.M. time slot, and the others indicated that it did not matter. All but one of the stations in the
survey were affiliated with a network, and four were owned by the networks.
33. Herbert J. Gans, *Deciding What's News* (Vintage, 1980), p. 9; and Mark D. Harmon, "Featured
Persons in Local Television News," paper prepared for the 1989 annual meeting of the Association for
Education in Journalism and Mass Communication.
34. National and international news is also probably overrepresented because 19 percent of the stations in
the sample were in the top ten markets, but only 12 percent of all U.S. stations fall into this category. Stations
in major markets tend to use more national and world news than stations in small markets.

much? A careful 1986 survey by Raymond L. Carroll has concluded that the national and world news portion of early evening local news programs amounts to 15 percent of the broadcast.[35] Green Bay listeners to WFRV's 5:00 P.M. news during three days in October 1987, for example, heard the following stories that were not local in origin:

—*International.* U.S. secretary of state meets with Gorbachev in Moscow (25 seconds), and Soviet citizen wins Nobel Prize (22 seconds).

—*Washington.* President Reagan to meet with congressional leaders to discuss deficit (27 seconds), and Senate rejects Robert Bork's nomination to the Supreme Court (95 seconds).

—*Other out-of-state locations.* Three stories about Wall Street (98 seconds), two about missing children (98 seconds), and one about a little girl in Texas recovering from having fallen down a well (26 seconds).

A modest menu of nonlocal news, yet from a station that is average—only 15 percent of its local newscast deals with national or international news.

Nor is it sufficient to describe the stations' own newscasts as 24 percent or 15 percent national and international. Compared with the networks' programs, a much larger proportion of these stories are nongovernmental: architect designs playground for pandas at national zoo (Washington story on a Minneapolis station), the search for the Loch Ness Monster continues (international story on a Detroit station).[36] In some cases, however, stories that are local in origin are national in context, as when WAGA, Atlanta, sought out area investors and stockbrokers to comment on Wall Street's "Black Monday" in October 1987.

Not only is there less national and international news on local newscasts than might have been expected, but there are differences in the lengths of the stories. The closer the story is to the site of its broadcast, the longer it turns out to be. International stories averaged 59 seconds, national stories 73 seconds, local stories 87 seconds (appendix table B-5).

Although local newscasts are not particularly interested in national and international affairs, our survey data form the usual bell-shaped curve. At one end, four stations broadcast only local stories; at the other, three stations

---

35. Raymond L. Carroll, "Market Size and TV News Values," *Journalism Quarterly*, vol. 66 (Spring 1989), p. 52. By coincidence, Carroll also surveyed fifty-seven stations. Another researcher, who measured local broadcasts on three stations in Cincinnati, recorded 10 percent of their news devoted to national and international news in 1978 and 25 percent in 1980. See Jung S. Ryu, "Public Affairs and Sensationalism in Local TV News Programs," *Journalism Quarterly*, vol. 59 (Spring 1982), pp. 76–77.

36. In an analysis that included coding news topics on Chicago local news programs and the networks for the same period, Doris A. Graber found that the local programs averaged nearly 22 percent less news on government or politics than the networks. See *Mass Media and American Politics*, 3d ed. (Washington: CQ Press, 1989), p. 88.

used local stories less than half the time. A San Francisco station sent a reporter to Miami to cover the visit of Pope John Paul II, and a Seattle station sent reporters to Seoul to do a series of features on Korea, including one story on the role of women. But far from heralding a brave new world of local newscasting, these kinds of stories are very few. Lawrence W. Lichty and Douglas Gomery are probably right that local stations cover such stories "to build the credibility of anchors and reporters. Virtually all of this effort is for promotional and personal reasons."[37] Clearly the intention of local stations is not to replicate the kind of reporting produced nightly by the networks.

What kind of government and political coverage do local newscasts provide then?

Our survey recorded 106 broadcasts or self-contained programs with their own anchors (the local evening news on KNBC, Los Angeles, which runs from 4:00 P.M. to 6:00 P.M., was thus considered two broadcasts). Including commercials, the 106 broadcasts amounted to 60 hours. We prepared a log on each segment, listing the locale of the story (international, national, Washington, or local), subject, and number of seconds. Typical notations of stories from Sacramento stations were:

—*International*. Sarah Ferguson [Duchess of York] pilots helicopter (17 seconds).

—*National*. Massive winter storm over southern Rockies buries parts of Colorado and New Mexico under deep snow (27 seconds).

—*Washington*. Gorbachev and Bush get out of limousine and shake hands of passersby (33 seconds).

—*Local*. School vandalism is on the increase, morning arson fire (137 seconds).

Because we did not tape the same number of broadcast hours for each station, we averaged this information so that we had one set of figures for each of the fifty-seven stations. News from Washington amounted to 7.5 percent of all local newscasts. We also arranged the data by market size and by whether the stations had a Washington bureau.

There were 1,419 total stories, 43 international, 397 national, and 979 local. Of the national stories, 125 came from Washington. Each of 249 stories about government or politics was summarized, noting the participants and whether they were seen and heard (*s,h*), seen (*s*), or simply mentioned (*m*). A 58-second report from WPXI in Pittsburgh thus reads, "*Summary:*

37. Lawrence W. Lichty and Douglas Gomery, "Why More and More is Less: The Future of Television News," paper presented at the Woodrow Wilson International Center for Scholars, Washington, May 4, 1989, p. 13.

Senate fails to override president's veto of trade bill. *Participants*: Senate—Howard Metzenbaum (s,h), Edward Kennedy (s,h), Orrin Hatch (s,h), Robert Dole (s); executive—Ronald Reagan (s)." Whenever possible we tried to track down the source for a story. The WPXI report, for instance, was prepared by Cox Broadcasting's Washington bureau. We also recorded whether a participant came from the state (none of the senators mentioned in this story was from Pennsylvania).

As expected, the president's domination of network news does not extend to local news. But counter to expectations, Congress does not dominate local news either. When the portion of the local news that is a report of national headlines (in these the president is the dominant figure) is combined with the rest of the local news (decidedly nongovernmental), the result for the fifty-seven stations as a group was a legislative-executive standoff (appendix table B-6). Instead of the new check-and-balance that the typical mix of network and local news might produce, local broadcasts covered executive and legislative branches of the national government in about equal proportions. President, vice president, and high administration appointees were mentioned ninety times; senators and representatives ninety-three times.

Seven out of ten times presidents are seen on local newscasts for the same reasons they are seen on network news: they address the UN General Assembly or ask Congress not to limit their actions in the Persian Gulf or veto a trade bill. Indeed, stations get these stories from the networks they are affiliated with or from Cable News Network (CNN) or the wire services. Two of ten times that presidents are mentioned they are in reports from stations' Washington bureaus or Washington freelancers. These stories usually relate legislators' reactions to presidential initiatives: Senator Donald Riegle comments on Reagan's Supreme Court nomination (Detroit); Georgia Representatives Ed Jenkins and Patrick Swindall comment on Reagan's news conference (Atlanta). The rest of the references come from the local stations: Reagan is mentioned in a commentary on the difficulty of approving Supreme Court nominees (Seattle); Reagan is to give a speech in the vicinity (Albany).

The "quality" of the legislators' appearances on local news is better, however, in that they are more often seen and heard, while the president is more often merely mentioned (appendix table B-7). On the other hand, a somewhat larger amount of the attention paid the president occurs in the top twenty-five markets.

Although the coverage of executive and legislative branches is balanced, when examining how much time local television news devotes to Congress, we might expect to find a natural affinity between members of the House of Representatives and local television newscasters. Both are supposed to be intimately connected with their communities, whereas members of the Senate, it could be said, fit more comfortably into the national orientation of network television. True, congressional districts do not always fit neatly into television markets, but most commentaries about the relation of Congress and local television focus on the energetic attention seeking of House members. Yet our survey shows that House members receive remarkably little coverage and senators dominate local news.

Of the 249 stories about government and politics, only 21 (8 percent) even incidentally concerned House members, who were seen, heard, or mentioned 26 times; senators appeared 67 times (appendix table B-6). Nine of the twenty-two House members who participated in these stories came from a locale other than that in which the station was located. They were newsmakers for the same reasons that they would have been on network programs: House Speaker Jim Wright of Texas was covered by a Seattle station as he commented on a possible Nicaraguan cease-fire; Armed Services Committee Chairman Les Aspin of Wisconsin was heard in Sacramento discussing a Reagan-Gorbachev summit; Beryl Anthony of Arkansas, chairman of the Democratic Congressional Campaign Committee, was mentioned on a station in Syracuse; and Lee Hamilton of Indiana, chairman of a committee investigating the Iran-contra affair, appeared on a Minneapolis station. Six representatives were covered because they held leadership positions; two more, Richard Gephardt of Missouri and Jack Kemp of New York, were running for president; and another, Henry Waxman of Los Angeles, was an expert, on health matters, in this case. (Ironically Waxman was not seen during the five and one-half hours of Los Angeles news we watched; it was a station in Roanoke, Virginia, that considered him newsworthy.) National congressional stories, like national presidency stories, are supplied by the networks or CNN, or are wire service copy that is read by the anchors.

Thirteen legislators made the local news in their districts in the sixty hours we were tuned in. Presumably this reflects Washington's congressional-media nexus. Few of these stories came from Washington, however. The origin of one remains a mystery, but of the others, two were from stations' Washington bureaus, one from a Washington freelancer, another excerpted from a floor speech carried on C-SPAN, and eight were locally produced.

Where are the legislators' video news releases that are so often described by print reporters? To find out, we called seventy-six House offices in August 1986, asking if they had produced any television tapes the previous week.

Sixty-nine said they had not, and seven had made one tape each. We repeated this exercise in October, reaching seventy-four of the same offices. It was now closer to elections and we expected the legislators to be more active. They were, but not much. Nine members had sent tapes to their local stations; five of the nine were the same people who had made tapes in August. Print reporters, it would seem, tend to write stories about legislators who produce video news releases, not about those who do not.

We also asked local news directors whether and how often they showed video news releases from members of Congress. The answers depended on the size of the market. For large cities the response of Randy Covington of KYW, Philadelphia, was typical: "We never use them. It's a waste of money for whoever sends them." The news director at KRON, San Francisco, also never used them, "unless we're doing a story making fun of them." KYW and KRON are network-affiliated stations, however. For independent stations, questions of news value may take a back seat to economic realities, and so may ethics. Kay Long, assistant news director at WTOG, Tampa, admitted, "We use them once or twice a week. We'd rather not get anything from the House or Senate, but with budget cuts in the TV industry you get it where you can." The smaller the city, the greater the enthusiasm for video news releases. In Roswell, New Mexico (Arbitron's 184th market), KBIM's news director said, "We use them as often as the offices send them." The absence of legislators' tapes in our survey may have partly reflected the underweighting of independent stations and stations in very small markets. But although there are tapes out there, it takes a lot of random watching to see one.[38]

Legislators' appearances on local television have been cited as one reason for the so-called incumbent advantage. If House members appeared on television in their districts often enough and long enough, and if they appeared in a positive light, some of the advantage in election campaigns that accrues to incumbents might be explained. But assuming our survey accurately reflected the state of their exposure, the proposition is dubious. Only seven legislators were both seen and heard on district stations; the others were merely mentioned, surely a lesser order of impact. The average length of these stories was 77 seconds. The shortest was 22 seconds, and six were less

---

38. From 1980 through 1986 the number of independent stations grew from 112 to 283. Their programming, however, is more noted for old movies than original news broadcasts. See Lisa Belkin, "New TV Stations Seek to Be Found by Viewers," New York Times, June 2, 1987, p. C18. Our survey also did not include the interview programs, usually a half hour in length, that legislators produce and distribute in their states or districts. See, for example, Jane Perlez, "Lautenberg Drops in, via Cable TV," New York Times, March 21, 1984, p. B1; and Esther B. Fein, "Senators as TV Hosts: Shows in Jersey Keep Voters Posted," New York Times, October 8, 1986, p. B6.

than one minute. Nor were the stories necessarily helpful to the legislator. Three were about a congressman's retirement and the race to succeed him. Three others covered opponents. This left five that could have been considered politically useful. For instance, Atlanta reported that Representative Newt Gingrich sought to expose "corruption" in Congress; in Rochester, New York, Representative Louise Slaughter gave a tribute to Terry Anderson, held hostage in Lebanon, on his fortieth birthday; in Green Bay, Representative Thomas Petri discussed the budget deficit. Five positive stories out of 15 from members' districts out of 21 about House members out of 249 about government and politics: less than 2 percent of the total, and a generous assessment at that because it does not consider other stories that might have been to the disadvantage of an incumbent.

Another way to judge local news as a factor in favoring incumbents' careers is to think of the entire survey as covering one big congressional district. In 60 hours of local newscasts, "positive" stories in which the House member figured in any way added to 7 minutes and 45 seconds. The actual time legislators were seen and heard, of course, was a fraction of this. Although sound bites on local news tend to run about two or three times as long as network sound bites, the result is still just 20 or 25 seconds each.[39] Of course, this is more attention than will be given to the House member's challenger.[40]

In *The Ultimate Insiders* I showed that the Senate has greater appeal to network cameras than the House because so many senators want to be president, certain senators are celebrities before they become senators, the Senate has some interesting constitutional duties that it does not share with the House, and the Senate is smaller and easier to explain: "The House of Representatives is too much like *War and Peace*; the Senate is more on the scale of *Crime and Punishment*."[41] What is true of network television is also true of local news operations.

In more than a fourth of the instances in the 1987–88 sample, when a senator was mentioned, it was because he was or might be running for pres-

---

39. William Edward Smith timed "the typical [network] newscast sound bite" in a 1988 sample at 10.3 seconds: "The Shrinking Sound Bite: Two Decades of Stylistic Evolution in Television News," paper prepared for the 1989 annual meeting of the Association for Education in Journalism and Mass Communication, pp. 7–8. Also see Kiku Adatto, "The Incredible Shrinking Sound Bite," *New Republic*, May 28, 1990, p. 20; and Daniel C. Hallin, "Whose Campaign Is It, Anyway?" *Columbia Journalism Review*, vol. 30 (January-February 1991), p. 43.

40. For differences in media attention given to incumbents and challengers in House elections, see Edie N. Goldenberg and Michael W. Traugott, *Campaigning for Congress* (Washington: CQ Press, 1984), pp. 127–29.

41. Stephen Hess, *Ultimate Insiders*, p. 91. Ross K. Baker, *House and Senate* (Norton, 1989), p. 113, also points out that the House receives less coverage because of its greater emphasis on "constituent problem-solving . . . not an inherently interesting process."

ident: Senator Dole announces candidacy (Seattle); charges of plagiarism made against Senator Biden (Boston); will Senator Nunn enter the race? (Los Angeles). As Nelson Polsby and others have pointed out, "the Senate is the main institutional source of presidential hopefuls."[42]

The top Washington event in the period covered by our survey, accounting for a third of all Senate stories, was Robert Bork's confirmation fight and the subsequent Supreme Court nominations of Douglas Ginsburg and Anthony Kennedy. Confirmation of Supreme Court justices is an "advice and consent" process that excludes the House of Representatives. For Senators Joseph Biden, Strom Thurmond, Edward Kennedy, Orrin Hatch, Howard Metzenbaum, Alan Simpson, Patrick Leahy, and Paul Simon, being on the Judiciary Committee during the Bork hearings provided a bonanza of local as well as network exposure.

To the degree that national headlines are incorporated in local newscasts, more senators than House members will always appear. Eleven of the forty stories involving senators were national in character, produced by the networks and simply passed along to their affiliates. But when local broadcasters, either at the stations or in their Washington bureaus, have the option of reporting on senators or House members, they too choose senators. Eleven of the Senate stories came from stations' Washington bureaus; only two of the House stories originated from the capital. C-SPAN II seems to have made a difference. From 1979 to 1985 Washington bureaus favored the House. After the Senate began to televise its floor proceedings in 1986, they focused on the Senate, and the 1987–88 survey reflected that decision. As a corollary, stations with Washington bureaus provide more news from Washington and emphasize the Senate more than those without bureaus (appendix tables B-6 and B-8).[43]

Senators not only get on local television three times for every time a House member makes the news, but they are more often both seen and heard, coverage that any politician prefers.

Nearly two-thirds of senators' appearances on stations in their states can be judged positive coverage. Just one-third of House members' appearances in their districts can be so considered. And senators' stories average a half minute longer than those of House members. The "all-encompassing pro-

42. Nelson W. Polsby, "Tracking Changes in the U.S. Senate," PS: Political Science and Politics, vol. 22 (December 1989), p. 789.
43. A third of the stations in the survey had Washington bureaus, but they accounted for nearly half (47 percent) of the times that senators and House members were mentioned.

senator bias on the part of the [national] media" that Richard Fenno has discerned applies to local newscasts as well.[44] Still, even Senate stories amounted to only 16 percent of all government and politics stories in the survey.

House members usually have to hold a leadership position to be seen on newscasts outside their districts, but being a senator often seems to be sufficient justification to be interviewed: a Detroit station features Senator Frank Lautenberg of New Jersey commenting on pollution, and a Seattle station shows Senator Steve Symms of Idaho talking about abortion, although neither Lautenberg nor Symms is a congressional powerhouse or celebrity beyond his state's borders. Consequently, three-quarters of the senators who turned up in the sample appeared on out-of-state stations, while only 42 percent of the House members were seen on stations not in their districts. In short, senators are more frequently on television but rarely on stations that do them much good in electoral terms unless they are running for president. House members seldom appear on television, but when they do it is apt to be in their own bailiwick.

When it comes to electoral advantage—assuming, as most politicians do, that being covered on the evening news is to be counted a blessing—a senator reaps little gain, but so too does his or her natural adversary, the state's governor. Senators were mentioned 67 times in the sample, 18 times in their own states; governors were mentioned 35 times, 26 times at home (Governors Michael Dukakis and Mario Cuomo also appeared as presidential contenders). In fact, the figures for governors were probably inflated because thirteen of the fifty-seven stations were within broadcast distance of a state capital. This finding is in keeping with other reports that local television stations shortchange the coverage of state government.[45]

Who wins? Who loses? At least as it relates to how local newscasts cover House and Senate, it depends on the size of the market. Urban coverage focuses on senators, small town stations on House members. The top ten markets devoted 95 percent of their congressional coverage to senators, the middle-sized markets 75 percent. In the smallest markets, House members

44. Richard F. Fenno, Jr., *The United States Senate: A Bicameral Perspective* (Washington: American Enterprise Institute for Public Policy Research, 1982), pp. 11–12.

45. Mark Harmon's study of Cincinnati stations, "Featured Persons in Local Television News," concludes, "State government . . . was nearly invisible" (p. 8). Also see William T. Gormley Jr., "Coverage of State Government in the Mass Media," *State Government*, vol. 52 (Spring 1979), pp. 46–51; Neal Koch, "Television Turns Its Back on the Statehouse," *Channels*, vol. 6 (April 1989), p. 12; and Rick Kushman, "Tuning Out the Capitol: Television News Abandons Sacramento," *California Journal*, vol. 6 (May 1989), pp. 221–23. Nor do states fare better on network news according to Doris A. Graber, who finds that state news constitutes 1 percent of early evening network newscasts and that only 24 percent of the stories deal with serious political events. See "Flashlight Coverage: State News on National Broadcasts," *American Politics Quarterly*, vol. 17 (July 1989), pp. 277–90.

got 75 percent of the congressional attention, although the figure is deceptive because these markets do so little congressional reporting that 75 percent means that House members were mentioned six times. One reason for the major metropolitan area stations' lack of interest in House members is obvious: fourteen congressional districts are folded into Los Angeles County, for example; thus each area House member, unlike California's U.S. senators, will be of direct interest to only a fraction of a station's viewers. One study illustrates that House incumbents win by larger margins in those areas where they receive least attention because so too do their opponents.[46] No news may be bad for a member's ego, policy position, and chances of challenging a senator, but it is good for being returned to a House seat every two years.

These soundings were not taken during a campaign period. Although political news and stories on national government activities are of modest interest at the stations, there is greater attention in the days before an election. But when Montague Kern examined news broadcasts for the final ten days before the 1984 elections from one area each in Indiana, California, North Carolina (where there was a particularly heated Senate contest between James Hunt and Jesse Helms), and Georgia, she found only eighteen stories related to Senate and House races. It is hardly surprising, then, that campaign ads overwhelm campaign news.[47] Congressional candidates do not have to buy much commercial time to get more air time than they will on local newscasts.

Yet paradoxically, the news-seeking efforts of legislators, rewarded with such trivial amounts of television attention, are neither irrational behavior nor irrelevant in terms of their electoral success. The more contacts candidates have with voters, the more likely they are to win.[48] In terms of name recognition, appearances on television are judged very good indeed. In an interview with Massachusetts Senator Paul Tsongas in 1986, Hedrick Smith heard what has been the experience of every legislator who becomes a sound bite on the evening news: "People would come up to me and say, 'I saw you on television last week,' and I'd say, 'Oh, what was it about?' and they'd say,

46. James E. Campbell, John R. Alford, and Keith Henry, "Television Markets and Congressional Elections," *Legislative Studies Quarterly*, vol. 9 (November 1984), pp. 665–78. Television markets also affect the relative news coverage of senators by stations that reach more than one state. See Charles Stewart III and Mark Reynolds, "Television Markets and U.S. Senate Elections," *Legislative Studies Quarterly*, vol. 15 (November 1990), pp. 495–523.

47. Montague Kern, *30-Second Politics: Political Advertising in the Eighties* (Praeger, 1989), pp. 47–69. "Astonishingly," according to Stephen Ansolabehere, Roy Behr, and Shanto Iyengar, "the 1988 senate race in California received fewer than five news stories from each of the Los Angeles-area television stations." See "Mass Media and Elections: An Overview," *American Politics Quarterly*, vol. 19 (January 1991), p. 113.

48. Gary C. Jacobson, *The Politics of Congressional Elections*, 2d ed. (Little, Brown, 1987), pp. 108–22.

'Well, I don't remember, but you looked tired,' or 'I liked your tie.' It was purely an impressionistic response."[49]

The Optical Phenomenon

A brief half-decade, 1980–85, probably will be recalled by those who were in Washington regional bureaus, and those who were reported on by them, as "the golden years," a time when the coming together of large profits and new technologies seemed to suggest that television stations were able and anxious to try to explain what Washington means to their communities. What the bureaus produced, a combination of reactions by local legislators to national events and stories of local importance that happened in Washington, was not at all like network news, and those who saw the bureaus as successors to the national broadcasters were wrong.[50] Whether reporting from Washington would have continued to expand if broadcast television had not stopped being able to afford it is a question that can never be answered. I think the answer would have been no. Too many broadcast groups that could have opened Washington bureaus chose not to. Ironically, these were often the great media conglomerates—the New York Times Company, Times-Mirror, Knight-Ridder, Scripps Howard—that would never think of conducting newspaper journalism without a Washington presence for their outlets.

What the Washington regional bureaus were (and still are) producing is heavily weighted toward Congress, although no longer focused especially on the House of Representatives. As such, the coverage offers some counterweight to the presidential emphasis of network news. There is some advantage to incumbents, of course, but it has never been as substantial as commentators have made it out to be.

When one turns to the gestalt of what actually appears on local newscasts rather than merely focusing on what the Washington bureaus send along, the picture changes. We are reminded forcefully that Washington reportage is a very small part of the whole and that the whole is decidedly ungovernmental and unpolitical. This helps explain much of the writing about the role of television from the Washington perspective. "Many members are . . . transforming themselves into virtual television stars back home" is how it

49. Hedrick Smith, *The Power Game: How Washington Works* (Random House, 1988), p. 127.
50. See William J. Drummond, "Is Time Running Out for Network News?" *Columbia Journalism Review*, vol. 25 (May–June 1986), pp. 50–52; and Ernest Leiser, "That's the Way It Was When Network News Died," *Washington Post*, July 13, 1986, p. B1.

may look from a congressional hearing room ablaze in lights for the benefit of the cameras or from the swampsite in front of the Capitol where legislators line up to talk into the mikes of channels 2, 4, and 7. It is not, however, the way it looks when sitting in front of a television set watching sixty hours of local newscasts, counting the occasional appearances of a House member. This is the optical phenomenon that I referred to, looking at an event alternately through both ends of the telescope.

Do Press Secretaries Change Light Bulbs?

CAPITOL HILL'S light bulb joke is "How many press secretaries does it take . . . ?" The answer is, "I don't have anything on that, but I'll get back to you." The humor, it seems to me, reflects the new importance of congressional media relations, and yet, at the same time, questions the output of all this laboring. "The press secretary, many times, may be the most important staff member a senator can employ," freshman senators were advised by the secretary of the Senate in a handbook prepared after the 1982 election. The pronouncement appears to have been heeded. Thirty-one senators employed press secretaries in 1960. Ninety-eight did so by the time I began my research in 1984.[1] A similar proliferation, called "the ascent of the press secretary" by Timothy Cook, occurred in the House of Representatives.[2] A look at press secretaries—who they are and what they do—seems an appropriate way to begin this inquiry into congressional press operations, to be followed in subsequent chapters by examinations of two of the offices' activities, press releases and op-ed pieces. Whereas the previous chapters focus on what the media produce about Congress, I now turn to what members of Congress produce for the media.

In the Senate

A press secretary, for those whose image of one may be formed largely by the White House model, is often thought of as a middle-aged confidant of his boss—President Eisenhower's Jim Hagerty or President Bush's Marlin

---

1. Only Jesse Helms of North Carolina and William Proxmire of Wisconsin claimed that they did not have a press secretary. Reporters at the press table in the Capitol dining room laughed knowingly about Proxmire's claim: "In his office everyone's a press secretary." But in Helms's office, calls from reporters were answered by a person whose title, according to a Senate document, was "file clerk." The comment on the importance of the press secretary is from *Congressional Handbook*, U.S. Senate ed. (Washington, November 1982), sec. 8, p. 1.

2. Cook noted, "Eighty-four percent of the House offices listed no person with press responsibilities in 1970; only 24 percent did so in 1986." See *Making Laws and Making New: Media Strategies in the U.S. House of Representatives* (Brookings, 1989), p. 72.

Fitzwater. But the reality we found in the Senate in 1984 was younger and less closely connected. If there had been a typical Senate press secretary in 1984, he would have been thirty-seven years old with a salary of $41,042, a strong tie to his senator's state, and some journalism experience, most likely as a reporter covering state politics.[3]

Of ninety-seven Senate press secretaries interviewed in 1984 (there was one vacancy), only nineteen were women. Ten worked for Republicans, nine for Democrats. On average, they received $6,377 a year less than their male counterparts. A high-level Senate aide, who said he often advised senators on choosing a press secretary, thought that the absence of women was not merely a matter of male chauvinism. "Being a press secretary entails traveling with the senator, and some [male] senators don't want to travel with a woman. It causes too many rumors." But a woman reporter who had been a press secretary commented that this had not been her experience. Rather, her senator "felt a press secretary should go drinking with the editors, should be 'one of the boys.' That was his stereotype of journalists."

By 1989, however, a third of all senators had employed a woman as press secretary at some time during the year. Again there was almost no difference in terms of party (Democrats fifteen, Republicans seventeen). The gender gap had narrowed without the aid of affirmative action legislation: Congress had exempted itself from the jurisdiction of these laws. (The two women senators employed men as press secretaries.) The most obvious reason for the change was that it mirrored the narrowing ratio of men to women in Washington journalism. Between 1978 and 1988 the proportion of female Washington reporters rose from 20 percent to 33 percent (appendix table B-26). During the same period the disparity in press secretaries' salaries was halved. Male press secretaries earned an average $49,148 in 1989 and women $45,365. And much of the remaining difference could be attributed to longevity. Eight of the ten press secretaries whose high salaries partly resulted from yearly increases over very long periods of Senate service were men.[4]

Press secretaries' salaries in 1984 ranged from $21,766 to $66,678. The span in 1989 was $27,500 to $84,958. In 1984, twelve earned less than $30,000 a year; only two earned less than that by 1989. Democratic senators paid their press aides more than Republicans—the 1989 average for Demo-

---

3. This section is based on a survey of Senate press secretaries conducted in 1984; it was updated for gender and salary in 1989. Salary information comes from the *Report of the Secretary of the Senate*, published twice a year by the Government Printing Office.

4. Also, by the mid-1980s two senators, a Democrat and a Republican, had black press secretaries, a man and a woman. See Karen Foerstel, "Cochran's Press Sec Is Second Black to Hold Post in Senate," *Roll Call*, July 19, 1990.

crats was $50,046, for Republicans $46,546. Senators from large states and those with leadership positions are given larger allowances for staff than their smaller-state and nonleader colleagues, and this too was generally reflected in press secretaries' salaries.

Salaries on Capitol Hill closely correlate with age. In 1984 the average age for women press secretaries was just over thirty-four; for men it was thirty-eight. Two were in their sixties, seven in their fifties, and seventeen in their twenties. Six were older than the senators they worked for, a situation with the potential to affect a relationship. Ken Thompson, who was press secretary to Steve Symms of Idaho and three years the senator's senior, told me, "I gave him unshirted hell for [his vote on] the tax bill a couple years ago." In contrast, Rex Buffington, Senator John Stennis's press secretary, said, "I'm always hesitant to advise him; he's been in the Senate longer than I've been on this earth."

Fifty-eight of ninety-seven press secretaries had journalism experience of at least three years; thirty-four said they had never worked as journalists. (We were unable to determine the previous occupations of six press secretaries.) Some may have left journalism for the same reason as Jim McQueeny, who worked for Frank Lautenberg of New Jersey: "I started to regret my passive role." The former journalists had usually worked for newspapers. Only fourteen had worked in radio or television; four had had both electronic and print media jobs. Yet those senators whose press secretaries came from broadcast journalism were rarely the ones who seemed to be partial to the publicity potential of television. Senators pick their press secretaries more on the basis of availability, friendship, happenstance, political knowledge, and perceived contacts than on a careful consideration of what skills would be most useful in the job. One press secretary described his boss, a Southern Republican, of whom he seemed quite fond, "as one of the many senators who don't understand the press."

Press secretaries with a journalism background most often had been reporters on newspapers in small cities—Ft. Wayne, Indiana; Midland, Texas—or for wire service bureaus in their senator's state, although there were several former reporters from the *Chicago Daily News* and the *Washington Star*, major papers that had gone out of business. Many had also worked in political campaigns or public relations. When we examined the work experiences of 125 press secretaries who were employed by 100 senators between 1983 and 1986, those from their senator's state had held 58 journalism jobs, 23 jobs in politics, and 11 public relations jobs (some had had more than one type of job). The résumés also included 34 other Senate jobs and 20 jobs in the House of Representatives; in some cases assistant press secretaries had been promoted or House press secretaries had moved to the other side of Capitol Hill.

What background is best? "Not all reporters make good press secretaries," said Linda Hill, press secretary to John Tower of Texas, "but all the good press secretaries I've known had been reporters." According to reporter Lee Bandy of the Columbia, South Carolina, *State*, "Not all reporters make bad press secretaries, but all the bad press secretaries I've known had been reporters." He thought that a public relations background was better training, although he may have been reflecting a view commonly held in the Senate Press Gallery that good journalists do not become press secretaries— or at least not for long. (The evidence is that only about half of the press secretaries who were former journalists had been deeply experienced news- people.)

A small cadre of Senate press secretaries, like employees who have served both Republican and Democratic presidents, consider themselves nonpar- tisan professionals. Eleven that we talked to in 1984 had worked for politi- cians of both parties. The communications director for Colorado conservative William Armstrong had previously been a special assistant to Connecticut liberal Abraham Ribicoff; another old pro went from an Idaho Democrat to a Rhode Island Republican. But in most cases they work for just one legislator and stay a short time. They are almost literally passing through the Senate on their way to something else. In fact, several were disdainful of the veterans. "I've a bias against them," said a press secretary who had come from a public relations background. "I assume they couldn't do better." Another press secretary, who was a former journalist, seemed apologetic for staying five years. He had delayed leaving because he had expected (incorrectly) that his boss would run for president, "and I didn't want to read about it in the papers."

It was almost always the old-timers—notably Murray Flander, who joined Alan Cranston of California in 1968, Jack Pridgen, who had been with Lawton Chiles of Florida since 1971, and Jack DeVore, with Lloyd Bentsen of Texas since 1972—who told me their jobs were "fun." But Roy Meyers, press secretary to Senator Howard Metzenbaum of Ohio for more than seven years, called being a press secretary "a burnout-prone profession."[5] The phrase has been used by others: Capitol Hill staffers like to promote the

5. Thomas J. Brazaitis, "Meyers Quits After 7-1/2 Years as Metzenbaum News Aide," *Cleveland Plain Dealer*, September 16, 1984, p. 6.

notion of being overworked. Only one *former* press secretary admitted that there were also "substantial periods of lull." Congressional jobs in general involve periods of stress followed by periods of inaction, creating an erratic schedule that is not easy on family life. But few press secretaries are around long enough to suffer from burnout. They rarely stay for a full six-year senatorial term. "Being a press secretary is not a lifetime career," commented Peter Loomis, aide to John Warner of Virginia. They drift away from Capitol Hill after four years or so, which is in line with figures on turnover for all congressional staff jobs.[6]

Of all the press secretaries who were in place at the start of the Ninety-eighth Congress (1983–84), one-third had left by the time the next Congress convened. Half those listed as Senate press secretaries in January 1982 were gone by the end of 1984. Some senators, of course, have a reputation of being difficult to work for: by September 1984, Iowa Senator Roger Jepsen was on his fifth press secretary in one term.[7] But the losses from senators' staffs have nothing to do with political party, leadership position, or publicity. Republicans and Democrats lose their press secretaries at the same rate; so do committee chairmen and rank-and-file members, and senators who are often or seldom on network news. Of Senate press secretaries who left in the Ninety-eighth Congress, sixteen worked for Democrats and seventeen for Republicans, sixteen for leaders and seventeen for nonleaders, thirteen for senators with high national media ratings in 1983, ten for those in the middle range, and ten for those in the bottom third.

Two-thirds of the press secretaries had some strong attachment to their senator's state. It was the place of their birth or where they went to college or the location of their most substantial previous employment. When Lance Morgan became Daniel Patrick Moynihan's press secretary in 1983, the *New York Times* reported that the New York senator "said he detected a rare qualification in Mr. Morgan. 'He's a New Yorker who knows where Buffalo is' " (Morgan had once worked for a Buffalo newspaper).[8] Given the press secretaries' primary audience, it may be surprising that a third had no significant local ties. "If I were the Senator, I wouldn't hire me," said one out-of-state press secretary after being unable to recall a particular county seat. Press secretaries who were known as the confidants of their senators sometimes attributed the close relationship to "chemistry," but most also had come to

6. See Robert H. Salisbury and Kenneth A. Shepsle, "Congressional Staff Turnover and the Ties-That-Bind," *American Political Science Review*, vol. 75 (June 1981), p. 383.

7. John Hyde, "Roger on the Run," *New Republic*, October 1, 1984, p. 18.

8. "Speaking for Moynihan," from the "Briefing" column of the "Washington Talk" page, *New York Times*, November 22, 1983, p. B6.

the Senate with their bosses. Otto Bos had been press secretary to San Diego Mayor Pete Wilson for six years and campaign director when Wilson ran for the Senate in 1982.[9]

Ties to their senator's state were apparent from where press aides went to college. Thirty-seven had degrees from in-state schools, and most of the schools (twenty-eight) were public institutions. Overall, however, almost as many graduated from private schools. There were forty-seven bachelor's degrees from public institutions and forty from private institutions, including Harvard, Yale, Princeton, Brown, University of Pennsylvania, Georgetown, Vassar, Middlebury, and the New England Conservatory of Music.[10] As a group, they had earned twenty-one master's degrees (including one in divinity and one in early childhood education) and two law degrees. Three of the M.A.'s were from the Journalism School at Columbia University. Two press secretaries said they were working on Ph.D.'s and one on a law degree.

The very model of a model press secretary, then, grows up in the senator's state, goes to the state university where he majors in journalism or political science, gets a job on a newspaper in the state, covers the senator's campaign or joins the campaign staff as press secretary, and goes to Washington when the senator is elected. He stays on the senator's staff for four years. A close approximation of this pattern is the career of Tom Griscom, thirty-four years old in 1984, a graduate of the University of Tennessee and a journalist for eight years on Chattanooga newspapers, who came to Washington after having served as Howard Baker's campaign press secretary in 1978.[11]

Another model would be the campaign volunteer or even college intern who goes to Washington to take a junior staff position, possibly as an assistant press secretary, and eventually moves up to the press secretary's job and perhaps beyond. Senator William Cohen's press secretary in 1984, Robert Tyrer, is one example; by 1990 he had risen to administrative assistant, the top job in the office. The out-of-state Senate press aide may come from a staff position in the House of Representatives, as did Liz Petten-gill, New Jersey Senator Bill Bradley's press secretary, or may have been a Washington journalist, as was Philip Shandler, who worked for Carl Levin of Michigan, or may have worked for a senator who was defeated or retired, as did Peter Smith, who joined Delaware Senator Joseph Biden's staff after

9. Otto Bos, "D.C. Diary," feed/back (Winter 1984), p. 16.
10. Six did not have a B.A.; and for four others, educational attainment could not be ascertained.
11. See Robert Timberg, "The Hill Handlers," Washington Journalism Review, vol. 7 (June 1985), pp. 39–40. Also see Martin Tolchin, "A Press Secretary Can Say Things a Senator Can't," New York Times, April 20, 1983, p. B6; and Will Scheltema, "In Focus: Tom Griscom," Roll Call, June 20, 1985, p. 1.

Iowa Senator John Culver lost in 1980. There are variations on all these themes as well as exceptions.[12]

Press secretaries leave, they say, to make more money or to take a more prestigious position in government or because they want to get back into journalism. There is a sort of Senate press secretaries' Hall of Fame, a small list of people such as Larry Speakes or Frank Mankiewicz who go on to prominence.[13] But a new job is usually just a modest step up the career ladder. Press secretaries do, however, often find it hard to go home again. Of fifteen former aides interviewed in the summer of 1985, ten had stayed in Washington. For Steven Allen, the job of being press secretary to Senator Jeremiah Denton was a means of relocating, from being an Alabama journalist to being an editor on *Conservative Digest* after a two-year stopover on Capitol Hill. Six of the fifteen worked for news organizations, a transition that is not as difficult as it once was. Three had gone into public relations for private organizations, five had taken other jobs in government, and one had retired. None regretted the time spent on a senator's staff. Those who went back to journalism invariably found the experience useful: "It's a political science education you'll never get from a book." One former press secretary, Kurt Burnett, who had been with Senator Jake Garn of Utah and did return to Salt Lake City, said, "My four years in the Senate will be the height of my professional career."

What They Do and Why They Do It

The typical Senate press office is a very small operation, most often just a press secretary and an assistant press secretary. Assistant press secretaries tended to be in their twenties, with an average salary, based on eighty-three cases in 1983, of $22,316. In a few instances the assistant was chosen because his or her television experience would complement the print orien-

---

12. Among those Senate press secretaries with more unusual backgrounds, William D. Livingstone, working for James McClure of Idaho and later Pete Wilson of California, was a filmmaker who had been the soundman on a movie called *Fraternity Row*; Ann Pincus (Charles McC. Mathias, Maryland) edited *The Kennedy Center Cookbook*; Richard Moore (Mack Mattingly, Georgia) wrote mystery novels, including *Death of a Source*; and Will Anthony (Gordon Humphrey, New Hampshire) wrote country music that has been recorded by Barbara Mandrell and Roy Clark, among others.

13. James Brady (William Roth, Delaware) and Speakes (James Eastland, Mississippi) became presidential press secretaries under Ronald Reagan. Tom Griscom was made White House director of communications when Howard Baker of Tennessee became Reagan's chief of staff. Mankiewicz (Robert Kennedy, New York) later became president of National Public Radio. Tim Russert (Daniel P. Moynihan, New York) became vice president and Washington bureau chief of NBC News; and Kathy Bushkin (Gary Hart, Colorado), director of editorial administration at *U.S. News & World Report*.

tation of the press secretary, but generally the job is entry level. A spot check of thirty-three senators in the summer of 1986 showed that six had one-person press operations, three a press secretary and a half-timer, and fifteen a press secretary and an assistant press secretary. Three offices employed two persons and a half-timer, and six had three persons (these figures do not include clerical personnel and interns). Only seven of these senators also had a full-time press relations person in their states.

Most senators spend 8 percent to 10 percent of their personnel budget on press relations. Using data filed with the secretary of the Senate for 1984–85, I made estimates for twenty-one senators: Daniel Patrick Moynihan, Arlen Specter, and John Warner spent 6 percent; Bill Bradley and Claiborne Pell, 7 percent; Dale Bumpers, Russell Long, James McClure, Jay Rockefeller, and Robert Stafford, 8 percent; Nancy Kassebaum, 9 percent; Lloyd Bentsen, John Kerry, and Don Nickles, 10 percent; Jeff Bingaman and Paula Hawkins, 11 percent; Barry Goldwater, Robert Kasten, Frank Lautenberg, and Pete Wilson, 12 percent; and Phil Gramm, 16 percent.

The relative importance of the press operation to a Senate office also can be estimated by comparing the salary paid the press secretary to the salaries of the other top aides. This may be an imperfect measure in that salaries tend to creep up with longevity. As Missouri Senator Thomas Eagleton told me in 1984, "I'm probably on the low side [in terms of paying a press secretary]. I've got a new person. If you had done this five or six years ago, I'd have been on the high side." (He was right. In 1984, seven staffers made more than his press secretary.) Still, relative salary levels are not arbitrary. In a six-month period one senator paid his press secretary $18,619.46 and an executive secretary $18,624.99; surely he meant the $5.53 difference to indicate to those who cared what the press secretary's standing was in his office.

The beginning hunch behind our survey was that the typical press secretary would rank third in the pecking order, after the administrative assistant and the legislative director. And the press secretary might rank even higher if the legislative director were not a lawyer (lawyers are much more highly paid than journalists on the open market). But in 1984 and again in 1989 the press secretary on average ranked fifth. There are, of course, nearly as many staffing patterns as there are senators, and in several cases the press secretary even ranked first, but most of the time, the press secretary earned less, and therefore ranked lower than the administrative assistant, the legislative director, and two others, who may include a state director, an office manager or executive assistant, or a second legal or legislative assistant. In several instances the low rank of the press secretary might be accounted for by the administrative assistant's having been a press secretary or a journalist who retained substantial supervisory responsibility for press relations.

At the start of a senator's career, when presumably the staff configuration is as the senator designs it, the mean rank of the press secretary is 5.4 (appendix table B-9). However, for senators who had served four or more terms by 1989 the mean rises to 4.0, which could suggest that veteran senators regard press secretaries' services more highly or could simply result from some press secretaries having stayed with their senators for a long time, gathering incremental raises along the way. Press secretaries of Senate leaders also rank higher.

Press secretaries see themselves as having more importance than their salaries indicate. When twenty-one of them were asked to state their place in the pecking order, their self-assessments averaged 2.6, although their average rank by salary was 5.5. Sixteen rated themselves too high in the pecking order, four gave self-assessments that accorded with their rank by salary, and one, Paul Lee of Senator Don Nickles's staff, judged himself lower in influence than his salary indicated.

Nor would the nature of their jobs support the notion of their being powerful figures on Capitol Hill. What might be called the Powerful Staff Theory of Congress argues that the tremendous growth in the number of staff assistants, supposedly designed to counterbalance the expansion of executive branch expertise, has produced a runaway situation in which many of the responsibilities of Congress are being shifted from the elected to the unelected.[14] Technically complex legislation is produced by negotiations between staff persons acting as surrogates for legislators who have neither time nor knowledge to understand the nuances of what is being decided in their names. One need not be a conspiracy theorist to worry about the problems that may be created by a legislative system that is beyond the grasp or attention span of its members. But this is not the world of the press secretary. The roles of legislative drafter and negotiator imply the power to give or withhold something of value. The role of press secretaries is one of supplication: they ask for favors on behalf of their bosses and the information that they give in return is modest by Washington standards. Moreover, they do not necessarily have a monopoly over the information that reporters get from

---

14. See Harrison W. Fox, Jr., and Susan Webb Hammond, *Congressional Staffs: The Invisible Force in American Lawmaking* (Free Press, 1977); Daniel P. Moynihan, "The Imperial Congress?" *Congressional Record*, June 15–26, 1978, pp. 17771–75; and Michael J. Malbin, *Unelected Representatives: Congressional Staffs and the Future of Representative Government* (Basic Books, 1980).

their offices. When we surveyed press secretaries in 1986, nineteen said they took all or almost all press calls, and six said that other staffers also talked with reporters. Then, too, reporters regularly interview Senate committee staff members, whom veteran journalist Eileen Shanahan calls "the explaining sources."[15]

Despite claims that Americans get much of their news from television, the medium of choice in press offices is print. This may reflect some generational drag: when one press secretary was asked whether his office did any teleconferences, he replied, "They're too high-tech for our senator." But Senate offices probably most often choose a print strategy because preparing material for newspapers and magazines is a *staff* activity. It involves very little of the senators' time, and is thus very efficient. For instance, when we asked twenty-seven press secretaries whether their senators personally approved draft press releases, only seven replied that they went over all or most of them; sixteen claimed that their senators seldom or never reviewed the drafts. Again, most press secretaries—and all of the veterans—said that they spoke for their bosses in answering calls from reporters, meaning that they had the authority to make up "quotes" that reporters could attribute to the senators. Obviously, press secretaries cannot stand in for their bosses on radio and television.[16]

Print also has an advantage over television because the stories can be clipped, duplicated, compiled, and presented to a senator as a measure of the staff's accomplishments. According to Charles Grassley's office, for instance, in 1983 the senator was mentioned in 3,200 Iowa newspaper stories comprising 24,760 column inches and including 352 photographs. Appearances on television can rarely be counted so accurately: district offices try to monitor local television news, but catching a senatorial sound bite is a hit-or-miss proposition. Weekly columns for small-circulation newspapers are probably the most certain and efficient products of all. A typical Grassley column about anticrime legislation appeared on February 23 or 24, 1983, in

15. In August 1983 we interviewed fourteen majority and ten minority staff members representing all Senate committees except Veterans' Affairs. In the preceding week they had received 95 telephone calls from media people, 8 from television reporters, 8 from radio, 8 from magazines, 55 from newspapers, 13 from trade publications, and 3 from other questioners. One staff member had 15 calls, several had none; the average was 4. Ten staffers said this was a typical week, eight that they received more calls than usual, five that they received fewer than usual, and one could not remember because his first child was born the week before.

16. When this idea was offered to a meeting of Republican senators' press secretaries in 1987, they agreed and volunteered other reasons as well: small states have limited television markets; TV stations do not editorialize, so there are more opportunities in newpapers for taking a position; and stations do not specialize in politics, whereas newspapers have political reporters and political editors who are receptive to their information. Of course, most press secretaries also still come from print journalism; it may be that senators will lean more to television when they get press secretaries with an appropriate background.

the Parkersburg *Eclipse-News-Review*, Hudson *Herald*, Manson *Journal*, Scranton *Journal*, Dayton *Review*, *Guthrie County Vedette* of Panora, Tripoli *Leader*, Humeston *New Era*, Glidden *Graphic*, and other Iowa papers, most with circulations between 1,200 and 2,200.

Although press offices are responsible for producing newspaper columns and the newsletters that are sent to constituents, they tend not to write their boss's speeches. Of twenty-nine press secretaries interviewed in 1986, fifteen said that they did no speechwriting and only three said that they did substantial speechwriting.

During October 1988 we asked seventy-nine press secretaries about the activities they initiated the previous week and discovered that the average Senate office sent out three or four press releases and made one radio recording and one television tape. It also produced a newspaper column every other week and held a press conference every third week (appendix table B-10). The most active press operations were for senators from the Northeast, Republicans, veteran legislators, and those about to face the voters. Indeed, the offices that produced the most were those of senators who were either leaders or were running for reelection. Adding up the five media activities yielded a mean score of 6.6 products for the week. Of those who were campaigning for reelection, John Heinz scored 22, Pete Wilson 16, and Don Riegle 13. Republican leader Dole, who was not up for reelection, had 11 and Democratic leader Byrd, who was campaigning, 10. The figures for senators, as for House members, do not suggest that the younger legislators are more public-relations conscious than their elders.

The overwhelming opinion among press aides was that the media is most useful in helping a senator be reelected, and the vehicle to get from here to there is local. One press secretary did talk about a media strategy to help his senator win a leadership post. Another, whose senator was about to retire, said he concentrated on national topics. Yet these were exceptions. "This office focuses on the local press, and the national reporters could keel over for all I care," said Mary Lahr, press secretary for Rudy Boschwitz of Minnesota. And Peter Lincoln, who worked for Dan Quayle of Indiana, said, "The state news media is the most important market as far as I'm concerned. The senator wouldn't have a job if we did it any other way." Although local media and local news need not be synonymous—some outlets carry little political news at all and a few carry more national than local news—most press secretaries implicitly make the connection. "Nearly all of our news has a local focus," said Timothy Gay, press secretary for Jay Rockefeller of West Virginia. This does not mean, of course, that senators' offices do not deal with issues beyond the immediate concern of their states. What it does mean is that their press operations, far from being designed to catapult the senators to national fame or promote the legislation they endorse, are looked upon through a lens that focuses on winning campaigns and serving constituents.

In the House

In 1989 the popular "Hill Climber" column in *Roll Call* guessed that Ken Levitt of Senator David Boren's office, twenty-three years old, was the youngest congressional press secretary. The next week the newspaper published a correction: Lisa Greene, press secretary to Representative Ron Machtley of Rhode Island, was twenty-two. A week later, in another correction, it noted that Representative Mel Hancock of Missouri had a twenty-year old press secretary, Sam Coring.[17]

Despite averaging five years younger, House press secretaries are much like their counterparts in the Senate. In a survey of eighty-seven House press secretaries (forty-nine Democrats and thirty-eight Republicans) that we conducted in 1988, one-fifth were twenty-six years old or younger and one-third were twenty-seven or younger (appendix table B-11). One quarter were women. One-third had held their jobs for a year or less, two-thirds for two years or less. There was a handful of old-timers, the most senior being age sixty-two. The longest service was twenty-two years. One-third had majored in journalism, another third in political science. One in five had a master's degree. Half had journalism experience, and a third had worked in public relations. Half claimed a connection with their legislator's state, but only a third called it meaningful.

Although press secretaries in the House earn less than those in the Senate, 12 of the 87 had annual salaries exceeding $44,000, with the highest paid receiving $60,000. A 1990 study of 212 House offices concluded that the average salary was $34,455.[18] House press secretaries hold the same rank in the pecking order as those in Senate offices—fifth—except that this is a less accurate index of their importance in House offices because some legislators assign press duties to their administrative assistants, others resist the temptation to have a press secretary, and many staff members with the title of press secretary also perform duties unrelated to press relations. When inter-

---

17. *Roll Call*, January 15, 22, and 29, 1990.
18. The study by the Congressional Management Foundation also found that 50 percent of the House press secretaries had been in their job for a year or less, 69 percent for two years or less. See Karen Foerstel, "Staff Turnover Rises Sharply with Half of All House Aides in Jobs Year or Less," *Roll Call*, October 22, 1990, pp. 1, 18.

viewing 116 press secretaries in 1989, we found that 80 percent had some regular nonpress assignments that consumed nearly a third of their time. This work was most often doing research of the type performed by legislative assistants, although one did the congressman's scheduling, another was in charge of the office payroll, and others were involved in district casework, immigration problems, patronage appointments, passport applications, and appointments to the military academies. A typical House member's press operation, then, consists of one person or less than one person, without the full-time use of a secretary. Only 15 percent of the press secretaries said that someone in the district also handled press relations for their representative. Still, the percentage of the House offices' budget spent on press operations was in line with our estimates for Senate offices.[19]

We also checked on House offices' media contacts, just as we had for Senate offices. When surveying the House, however, we asked the same questions of the same offices in July 1988 and again in October. Did you initiate any press releases last week? Any radio actualities? Any newspaper columns? Any press conferences? Any video tapes? As we suspected, House offices became busier the closer they came to election day. The mean score for the five media activities in the July week was 3.1, and in October, 4.2 (appendix table B-12). The comparable October figure for senators was 6.6.

Journalists and scholars have often portrayed Congress as a beehive of media courtship, noting the ever-increasing number of House members' media activities. "It is 10 P.M. in Wichita, Kansas, and the day ends like most others," an article in *Congressional Quarterly* begins. "The cat is out, the children are tucked in bed, and Democratic Rep. Dan Glickman is on the local television news."[20] Glickman happened to turn up in our random sample; but rather than being typical—the implication of the reporter's lead—he was one of four (out of seventy-three) legislators to make a television tape in both weeks surveyed. Many House members use the media only rarely to call attention to themselves (indeed, they may have concluded that a low profile is a small target). During the week in July, for example, one-third of the House offices issued no press releases and one-quarter put out only one. Two-thirds of the House members did not record a radio actuality, 84 percent did not hold a press conference, half did not write a column for

19. See Steven H. Schiff and Steven S. Smith, "Generational Change and the Allocation of Staff in the U.S. Congress," *Legislative Studies Quarterly*, vol. 8 (August 1983), p. 464. Their table, "Time Devoted to Various Functions . . . ," shows that the mean percentage of time used for publicity and speechwriting is 12.0 percent in the House member's Washington office and 5.3 percent in the district office.

20. Bob Benenson, "Savvy 'Stars' Making Local TV a Potent Tool," *Congressional Quarterly Weekly Report*, vol. 45 (July 18, 1987), p. 1551.

their districts' newspapers, and 90 percent did not make a tape for their districts' television stations.[21]

That during a July week in 1988 only 10 percent of House members made television tapes and during a week in October only 15 percent did so seems to controvert both scholarship and conventional wisdom. Floyd McKay surveyed 218 House offices and concluded that nearly 90 percent reported making "some use of satellite transmission, cable television or videocassette recordings during 1988 or 1989." But a closer look at his data shows that in 1988 "the mean use of satellite for transmission of news material to local stations" was 4.6 transmissions. In other words, the average was fewer than five tapes produced in fifty-two weeks. Heavy users (twelve to fifty transmissions during 1989) constitute only 17.9 percent of his large sample.[22]

In the House, as in the Senate, Republicans appear to be more active in using the media, but merely because they put out more press releases than House Democrats. Also, as in the Senate, veteran legislators initiate more media activities than newcomers, reaching a peak during their second decade in office when, presumably as subcommittee chairmen or ranking members, they hold the most press conferences (appendix table B-13). The offices of the youngest members produce the most press releases, but counterintuitively are not heavier users of television.[23] Legislators with the narrowest winning margins in their previous elections, as expected, are above average in the number of their media activities—but only slightly— and are not as active as those who record the biggest victories.

The explanation for why some House members in our survey were so active in using the media seems obvious. Republicans William Clinger of Pennsylvania and Bill Emerson of Missouri come from closely contested districts and always have to fight to stay in Congress. Jack Kemp, on the other hand, wanted to get out of Congress in 1988 to become president of the United States. Rod Chandler, a Seattle Republican, had been an anchorman on KOMO-TV and must know the value of publicity. And the

---

21. For the week in October, 19 percent had no press releases and 22 percent had one; 63 percent did not record a radio actuality, 75 percent held no press conferences, 41 percent wrote no newspaper columns, and 85 percent made no television tape.

22. Floyd John McKay, "The Electronic Congress: Use of Electronic Media by Members of the U.S. House of Representatives in 1988 and 1989," M.A. thesis, University of Maryland, 1990, pp. 74, 81. I prefer to use questionnaires measuring "last week's" activities partly because of the tremendous turnover of press secretaries and partly because the responses are less pure guess. I always ask, however, whether the week was typical and factor the answer into conclusions.

23. For a study that does correlate one type of television activity positively with the age of House members, see Michael J. Robinson, "Three Faces of Congressional Media," in Thomas E. Mann and Norman J. Ornstein, eds., The New Congress (Washington: American Enterprise Institute for Public Policy Research, 1981), p. 63.

late Silvio Conte, a Massachusetts representative from 1959 until his death in 1991, never had trouble getting reelected, but apparently had a "craving for attention."[24] Still, how does one explain the media enterprise of Virginia Smith? The Nebraska Republican was seventy-seven years old in 1988, held one of the safest seats in Congress, and was not interested in higher office. She was not a crusader for special causes nor did the press seek her out as a colorful character. Yet among her activities were a weekly satellite feed for all Nebraska television stations, a weekly five-minute radio program that went to 35 stations, and a weekly column, "For the Record," that was sent to 120 weekly newspapers and 8 dailies. When asked why, her press secretary replied, "Due to an economic crunch in the Nebraska area, local stations have cut back on newsgathering from Washington. So Mrs. Smith considers it part of her role to be a news source in Washington for her district." At the other end of the scale, one press secretary said of his inactive boss, "The press is not interested in the same things he's interested in." Another commented, "He doesn't have the drive to be anything more than he is." A third press secretary, who had been on the job for three months, explained an unexpected burst of publicity: "I really wanted to get him on the wires."

The local press, of course, is what consumes most House offices' attention. Press secretaries claim that more than 60 percent of their time is spent on the media in their congressional districts (appendix table B-14). The figure is lower for the House leaders (52 percent) but higher for those members who won narrowly (73 percent), are in their first three terms (68 percent), and are younger than forty years of age (65 percent).

What should we conclude from data that show an average House office just before an election produces two press releases a week, one radio actuality every other week, and a television tape once a month? Given journalists' accounts of extensive media efforts by members of Congress, is this a case of the Lake Wobegon factor at work? In that mythical town, according to its creator Garrison Keillor, all the children are above average. So, perhaps, all legislators' media activities are also above average. Clearly, legislators spend more time cultivating the media than they once did. But press operations are small and press secretaries are not considered especially important. From the legislators' point of view, if the results are modest, so too is the price.

24. David Rogers, "House Republicans Face a Transition Following Death of Liberal Rep. Conte," *Wall Street Journal*, February 11, 1991, p. B5. In 1983 Conte wore a pig's snout during a House floor speech denouncing colleagues for having "their noses right in the trough . . . at the expense of all the taxpayers." See Tom Kenworthy, "Rep. Silvio O. Conte Dies," *Washington Post*, February 9, 1991, pp. A1, A5.

The Lowly
Press Release

WHEN I WADED through stacks of handouts from five federal executive agencies in 1982 for a study of government press offices' routine activities, the main obstacle to careful research was staying awake. Press releases from the Department of Transportation, for example, are best described as layers of information, dull, unimaginative. They do not tell the whole story, of course; they are the agency's side of the story. But the facts they give are bankable. At the Food and Drug Administration the releases go through three writing stages—initial drafting, technical editing, and copy editing—and five internal clearance steps. Dependable, if limited, and again dull. There is a generic resemblance to other agency press announcements in a typical Pentagon release of this period, which opens,

> The Department of the Navy announced today that OHIO (SSBN-726), first of a new class of nuclear powered ballistic missile submarines, will be commissioned at 11:00 A.M., November 11. . . . OHIO class submarines are 560 feet long, have a beam of 42 feet and displace 18,700 tons when submerged. OHIO will initially carry 24 TRIDENT-1 (C-4) missiles as compared to the 16 POSEIDON or TRIDENT-1 missiles carried by today's ballistic missile submarines.[1]

Such statements might almost substitute for objective wire service copy. Not so, however, for many Capitol Hill handouts. In a release of September 21, 1989, Representative Tom Petri of Wisconsin opens, "I think it's nuts," referring to a Senate proposal to shoot down aircraft suspected of smuggling drugs. And a release of September 20 from Maine Representative Joe Brennan opens, "Nice try, New Hampshire, but it won't work. . . . Pay your taxes," referring to a dispute over whether New Hampshire residents working at the Portsmouth Naval Shipyard should pay taxes in Maine. But the handiwork of other press secretaries may not be even this staid. The office of

---

1. See Stephen Hess, *The Government/Press Connection: Press Officers and Their Offices* (Brookings, 1984), p. 47.

Wisconsin Representative Les Aspin issued "a nine-paragraph press release to announce the death of his dog, Junket."[2] And on February 1, 1984, Representative William F. Clinger, Jr., whose rural Pennsylvania district included the community of Punxsutawney, "invited the famous groundhog from that borough to come to Washington to explain his forecasting techniques to the experts at the National Weather Service."

SENTIMENTAL, sententious, or snide, the lowly congressional press release constitutes legislators' most common means of indicating to news outlets what they want reported about them. On September 28, 1984, Representative Dale Kildee of Michigan wanted it known that he had met with Patricia Paschal, a teacher at the Flint Community Schools' Special Education Services Center, "to discuss a handicapped education bill being considered by Congress." On September 13 Iowa Representative Jim Leach wanted it known that after "nearly a decade of uncertainty, aggravation and inconvenience" a new post office was to be built in Keokuk. But despite their interest in reaching constituents, most legislators are "not too involved" in the production of their press releases—the typical judgment of a congressional press secretary. A press aide, who said he checked with his boss on quotations, did note, "We don't like making up words that haven't come out of his mouth," but otherwise, press releases are largely a staff product. They are written by press secretaries after consulting with legislative assistants or caseworkers or the district office, and their ubiquity reflects the growth of staff. Collectively, however, as an indicator of what legislators care about, press releases deserve more serious study than they have received, and to rectify the omission, my assistants and I gathered all the handouts (2,576) produced by twenty-three senators' offices in 1984 and a month's supply of press releases (321) from sixty House members in 1989, as well as daily handfuls of releases picked off the racks in the Senate Press Gallery.[3]

As products mostly of staff efforts, do press releases indicate more about a legislator's staff than a legislator's publicity goals? One way to judge might be to compare the number of releases with the rank of the press secretary that we calculated in the last chapter. We can do this for twenty-two senators (having to exclude William Proxmire, who in 1984 did not have a press secretary).

2. Rich Jaroslovsky, "Washington Wire," *Wall Street Journal*, September 1, 1989, p. 1.
3. Unless otherwise noted, all Senate press releases cited are from 1984 and all House press releases from 1989. For a list of the senators and House members in this study, see appendix table B-15. That 1984 was an election year had virtually no effect on the analysis because only two of the twenty-three senators were running for reelection.

—*High-ranked press secretary, high press release productivity*. This description fits five senators, most of whom seemed to have a precise reason for wanting to generate publicity and, apparently, were willing to pay the price. For example, Senators Dole and McClure were running against each other to succeed Howard Baker as majority leader in 1984. Dole also wanted to be the presidential nominee, if Ronald Reagan chose to step down, and McClure had to stand for reelection in Idaho that year.

—*High-ranked press secretary, low press release productivity*. Five senators had press secretaries who were older and had been with them longer than average; the aides seemed more likely to be used as political advisers than as hands-on flacks.

—*Low-ranked press secretary, high press release productivity*. These seven senators' press relations are harder to characterize as a group. What common denominator fits Fritz Hollings and Quentin Burdick, John Heinz and Paul Laxalt? The answer, perhaps, is that all had press secretaries who were young (twenty-seven or twenty-eight years old) and had held the press job for a relatively short time. Presumably if they stayed with their senators, they would rise in rank, but it was the senators' needs more than the press secretaries' energy that defined output.

—*Low-ranked press secretary, low press release productivity*. Five senators, including Daniel Inouye and Nancy Kassebaum, were clearly low-key legislators who did not put a premium on personal publicity.

In short, legislators may not devote much time to producing press releases (or to not producing press releases), but the result reflects the individuality of the legislators.

FOR CONGRESSIONAL reporters, press releases form a smorgasbord of subjects competing for attention. On just a few average days, September 18–20, 1984, Colorado Senator Gary Hart comments on "the tragic events in Lebanon," John Chafee of Rhode Island praises the president's decision on steel imports, Pete Wilson of California announces Senate approval of his "Wine Equity Act" as part of "the tariff reciprocity bill," Chris Dodd of Connecticut "urges action on the genocide convention before adjournment," South Carolina's Ernest F. Hollings tells "the executive board of the United States Jaycees that government is 'cheating our young,' " and Jeff Bingaman of New Mexico holds hearings "to explore ways to increase productivity and manage the federal government more efficiently."

Most of the releases are written as ersatz news stories, are rarely as detailed as the Pentagon announcements, and are usually a page in length. A typical one begins, "Forty-five years after he was wounded in battle, a Yonkers man was awarded a Purple Heart today by Congressman Eliot L. Engel." But reporters browsing through the racks in the congressional press galleries will also find some press releases that are the text of a legislator's speech or committee statement. The formats of the releases are sometimes simple and functional, headed merely by an office address and phone number; but more often there is eye-catching color, bold type, and photographs of the legislators, suggesting that they want to be thought of as friendly (smiling) or attentive to business (serious, even pensive), as well as patriotic (with flag) and important (with Capitol dome). They do not, however, wish to be stuffed shirts: the releases say that they come from the offices of Bob (Dole, Packwood) and Bill (Armstrong, Bradley, Roth) and Jim (Abdnor, McClure, Sasser). The 1984 Senate also had a Tom (Eagleton) and a Dick (Lugar) but no Harry. Rarely do the releases mention whether the legislators are Democrats or Republicans, although obviously they are one or the other. Informality is in? Partisanship is out? Presumably there are some marketing principles at work in these designs.

AN ILLUMINATING way to think about press releases is in the context of David Mayhew's typology "of the kinds of activities congressmen find it electorally useful to engage in," namely advertising, credit claiming, and position taking. Advertising is "any effort to disseminate one's name among constituents in such a fashion as to create a favorable image but in messages having little or no issue content." In credit claiming the legislator tries "to generate a belief . . . that [he or she] is personally responsible for causing the government . . . to do something that the [constituent] considers desirable." Position taking is "the public enunciation of a judgmental statement."[4] All press releases are a form of advertising, of course, and many have more than one purpose, but it is still possible to describe the message of each in terms of one of these categories.

The advertising quotient of press releases is obvious and continual. Roger Jepsen of Iowa "today received the Golden Gavel Award from Vice President George Bush for presiding over the Senate for 100 hours" (September 29); Indiana Senator Richard Lugar "raced by the rest of his colleagues today to become the fastest Senator in a 3-mile road race around East Potomac Park" (September 13); "In what is considered a rare accomplishment for any elected

4. David R. Mayhew, *Congress: The Electoral Connection* (Yale University Press, 1974), pp. 49, 52–53, 61.

official," Senator Strom Thurmond of South Carolina "cast his 10,000th recordedvote as a United States Senator" (September 14); Senator Bill Bradley of New Jersey "was named 'National Father of the Year' today by the National Father's Day Committee" (May 16); and Senator Carl Levin was "To Honor Winner of Michigan Bean Soup Contest" (June 19). On the other side of the Capitol, House press releases announce that Sherwood Boehlert of New York "received the American Fire Sprinkler Association first annual Legislator of the Year Award" (September 29) and Richard Ray was named " 'Man of the Year' by the Air Force Association of the State of Georgia" (September 19).

Some releases recapitulate exotic travels, suggesting that important people take important trips. Representatives Mickey Edwards (Oklahoma), Howard Coble (North Carolina), and Tim Penny (Minnesota) tell of separate visits to Latin America (September 9, 15, 20). Representative Hamilton Fish, Jr., of New York and his wife, Mary Ann, "greet Polish Solidarity Leader Lech Walesa in Gdansk, Poland" (September 19). Representative Eliot L. Engel of New York briefs "Irish-American leaders" on his "recent fact-finding trip to Northern Ireland" (September 9).

Not all such press releases are limited to relentless self-promotion. Just as newspaper advertisements list the day's specials at the supermarket or the starting times of movies, some legislators' advertising also provides useful information: "Senator Jesse Helms, Chairman of the Senate Committee on Agriculture, Nutrition, and Forestry, today reminded farmers that this Friday, March 16, is the signup deadline for the feed grains, cotton, and rice programs" (March 12). Indiana Senator Dan Quayle releases a list of witnesses who will appear at a "December 13 hearing on the career development of procurement managers at the Department of Defense" (December 11). And Bob Dole discloses that "he and Mrs. Dole paid a total of $194,650 in federal and state income taxes and self-employment taxes for calendar year 1983 on a joint taxable income of $351,151." The press release gives a summary of the Doles' tax returns from 1979 to 1983 and a list of all "honoraria contributed to charity" (undated).

Many legislators use press releases to announce procedures for applying to the U.S. service academies. "The service academies aren't for everyone," Representative Joe Skeen of New Mexico is quoted as saying. "Academy students are expected to meet high academic standards, be physically fit, and be prepared for the rigors of military training. If that sounds like you, I hope you'll submit your application to my office" (September 27). Other standard fare is to provide itineraries for local appearances: "Congressman Don Sundquist will hold another in his series of community days Friday, September 29, in NcNairy County. The congressman plans stops in Ramer, Adamsville, Rosecreek, and Finger. 'Community days give me a chance to meet and talk with people in an informal setting and find out what's on their minds,' Sundquist explained" (undated). Identical press releases announce that he will be in other Tennessee counties on September 30, October 7, and October 9. On the day that Sundquist plans to be in Hickman County, Representative Don J. Pease of Ohio will be at the Ashland County Courthouse Assembly Room ("use the entrance on Third Street, Pease advised"), and a "Media Advisory" from Representative Tom McMillen of Maryland notifies the press that he will be at the Fire Hall in Gambrills from 9:00 A.M. to 10:30 A.M. and the North County Library in Glen Burnie from 11:00 A.M. to 12:30 P.M. Some legislators' press releases announce staff visits to their districts.

Another form of the advertising press release is the questionnaire: Representative Benjamin A. Gilman "has distributed his 1989 Congressional Questionnaire to households throughout his 22nd Congressional District of New York. 'Your response to this questionnaire is of great help to me in tackling the complex issues before the 101st Congress,' Rep. Gilman stated" (September 18). Survey results are later announced by press release. "First District Congressman Pat Roberts, announcing results of this year's 'Big First District Questionnaire,' said the overriding concern of western Kansas continues to be federal spending and the huge federal deficit Congress rings up every year" (August 24). And "Crime, drugs and growth management are Florida's greatest problems, according to most 12th Congressional District residents answering U.S. Rep. Tom Lewis' 1989 district-wide survey" (September 15).

The most common type of credit claiming in congressional press releases is the announcement of grants, loans, and other forms of Washington largess: "More federal money is heading for Lorain County, Congressman Don J. Pease (D-13 Ohio) announced today" (September 11). From Representative Joe Barton of Texas comes word of conference committee agreement "to spend $225 million on the Superconducting Super Collider, the world's largest high energy particle accelerator, to be built in Ellis County" (September 7). But small sums also deserve a press release. Representative Bill Dickinson of Alabama is pleased that the Eufaula City School System is to get "a $5,378 federal grant for the adoption and installation of energy saving measures" (September 1), and John J. Duncan, Jr., of Tennessee is enthusiastic about an award of $10,191 to the University of Tennessee's

College of Veterinary Medicine. It confirms "the fact that Tennessee is a strong educational institution in this nation" (September 14).

Credit claiming may become the most common type of press release as a legislator approaches an election. During September 1984 Senator Roger Jepsen's releases declared that the Hawkeye Tri-County Electric Cooperative in Cresco would receive a loan from the U.S. Department of Agriculture Rural Electrification Administration, that the U.S. Environmental Protection Agency was to give a construction grant to the city of Fredericksburg, and that the University of Iowa would get $128,419 "for studying swine," as well as other grants from the National Institute of Arthritis, Diabetes, Digestive and Kidney Diseases and the National Institute on Alcohol Abuse and Alcoholism. The Federal Aviation Administration, he announced, would support "runway improvements" at the Ames and Ottumwa airports, and there would be "an additional $3.5 million in funding for Iowa's highways" from the Federal Highway Administration. The Department of Housing and Urban Development would provide "rent subsidies" for "about 5,000 lower-income, single parent families" in Dubuque and Linn Counties, there would be loans for "elderly and handicapped housing in eight locations," including Des Moines, Davenport, and Iowa City, and the Veterans Administration had "awarded a $383,466 grant to the Iowa Veterans Home in Marshalltown."

Many federal grants are awarded on the basis of formulas and do not require legislators' involvement, although congressional press releases imply otherwise. In 1989 Representative Robert Wise of West Virginia informed editors in his state that he would no longer bombard them with notices of routine grants. In the future his announcements would be limited to projects "in which we are actively involved." The Associated Press thought this was newsworthy, and it was even reported in *Editor & Publisher*.[5]

Although subtlety is not a necessary ingredient, some grant announcements require a certain delicacy. When Representative Charles W. Stenholm of Texas proclaimed how proud he was that four hospitals had been given "seed money" by the Health Care Financing Administration, his press release added, "My only disappointment is that all 17 of the hospitals in our district who applied for grant money did not get it" (September 15).

A dependable subcategory of credit claiming is the announcement of commemorative legislation: "Congress Approves Quayle's Resolution Designating November 11–17 'National Blood Pressure Awareness Week'" (October 3). Representative Sundquist proposes "designating the week of

---

5. "Congressman Cuts Number of Releases," *Editor & Publisher*, vol. 122 (November 18, 1989), p. 46.

October 1, 1989, as 'National 4-H Awareness Week' " (undated). But championing such proclamations has its detractors. On September 25, 1989, a press release from Representative Bill Dickinson commented, "Congress—you might think—would have more important matters at hand than voting on National Prune Day or National Dairy Goat Awareness Week."

Claiming credit for commemorative legislation requires a certain imagination, but claiming credit when nothing tangible has happened is an art. In 1984 Senator Pete Wilson of California announced that he had urged the Department of Labor to approve a grant to retain tuna cannery workers (June 19), that he would offer an amendment to compel the International Trade Commission "to consider the plight of farmers" (September 18), that he "applauded the decision of the Federal Communications Commission to allocate a new, much needed communications channel to the Los Angeles Sheriff's Department" (September 26), that he had written a letter to the secretary of the navy asking that the aircraft carrier *Nimitz* be based in San Francisco Bay (April 5), and that he had "strongly recommended the appointment of a Los Angeles woman to a key position in the U.S. Department of Health and Human Services" (July 31).

Occasionally a trace of humility can be glimpsed in congressional efforts to claim credit. When South Carolina Representative John Spratt introduced a bill to provide federal tax relief for timber growers who had suffered losses from Hurricane Hugo, his press release concluded, "I do not want to raise false hopes by claiming we can pass every bill we file" (October 11). Still, credits are wondrously claimable on Capitol Hill, as this July 23, 1984, release illustrates:

> Senator Ernest F. Hollings, D-S.C., today recommended in a letter to President Reagan that Federal District Judge Matthew J. Perry of South Carolina be appointed to the United States Fourth Circuit Court of Appeals. Perry is the first black to serve as a federal district judge in the south.

What the release does not bother to include is that, unlike appointments of district judges, appointments of circuit judges are not based on recommendations from senators; President Reagan, a Republican, was not especially beholden to Senator Hollings, who in 1984 wanted to be his Democratic opponent; and the Senate Judiciary Committee, through which appointments must pass, was chaired by another South Carolina senator, Republican Strom Thurmond. Hollings's press release might be viewed as grandstanding to the third degree. (The nomination was given to a former administrative assistant to Senator Thurmond.)

More straightforward than advertising or credit claiming is the position-taking press release: New Jersey Senator Frank Lautenberg wants President Reagan to rehire the dismissed PATCO air controllers (September 7); Senator Howard Metzenbaum of Ohio tries to block a proposed "balance the budget" constitutional amendment (August 9); Senator Edward Kennedy of Massachusetts deplores U.S. mining of Nicaraguan ports (April 9); New Hampshire Senator Gordon Humphrey wishes to abolish the U.S. Synthetic Fuels Corporation (May 9); Senator Mark Hatfield of Oregon opposes the death penalty (February 8); Senator Jeremiah Denton of Alabama introduces right-to-work legislation (April 5). Press releases are also used to explain votes. When the House considered a cut in the capital gains tax, Maine Representative Joseph Brennan opposed it because "80% of the benefits would go to the 3.3% of Americans with incomes over $100,000" (September 22). Tennessee Representative John Duncan, Jr., favored it because "over 70% of this tax cut will go to families making less than $50,000 a year" (undated).

Not all positions need be about cosmic issues, of course. Senator William Proxmire of Wisconsin noted that "The President set a sterling example for the federal government when he visited the Capitol for a January 24th luncheon. He handed Senator Baker a $5 bill to show that there is no such thing as a free lunch. That principle, enunciated so well by the President, should be applied to exclusive dining rooms operated by executive agencies but subsidized by the taxpayer" (January 29).

Many position-taking press releases represent a legislator's reaction to an event and are often an attempt to place a quotation or sound bite in a national story. After the House voted on the so-called Flag Protection Act in September 1989, Virginia Representative Stan Parris's press release declared, "In my view . . . the flag represents far more than the simple material it is made out of. The American flag is a tangible representation of the values and spirit this country stands for." And when President Bush gave a televised speech that month outlining his war on drugs, South Carolina Representative Floyd Spence put out a press release that read in its entirety,

I am pleased that the federal government is going to undertake greater initiative to attack the drug scourge head on.

This problem has been festering for far too long and time is past due to act with as much zeal and determination as the drug pushers themselves.

I applaud the President's efforts. We must now get to work to insure that our children are no longer bombarded by this plague.

Other House members announced their "support" (John Duncan of Tennessee), "full support" (Richard Ray of Georgia), "total support" (Tim Johnson of South Dakota), "whole-hearted support" (Raymond McGrath of New York), and "thorough support" (Dean Gallo of New Jersey). In this case, then, the me-tooism lapped over into advertising and credit claiming.

Another technique is to find positions that represent unassailable virtue, an exercise akin to pushing against an open door. In 1984 Senator Bill Bradley announced his disapproval of the 1932–33 famine caused by the Soviet government in the Ukraine: "It is shocking that the pre-meditated deaths of so many innocent people have been hidden from the consciousness of the world" (October 4). Senator Lloyd Bentsen favored tough penalties on "persons who misuse benefits intended for elderly or disabled Social Security recipients" (May 15). Senator Arlen Specter introduced the Pornography Victims Protection Act (October 4). Senators William Roth and Paul Tsongas condemned "the recent arbitrary arrests and indefinite detention of peaceful opponents of the government in South Africa" (September 12). And Alfonse D'Amato wanted to strike "a heavy blow at the laundering of drug money" (April 10). Position taking can thus become analogous to the more specious forms of credit claiming.

THE PROPORTIONS of the various types of House and Senate press releases in our survey were almost identical. Advertising accounted for 21 percent of House releases and 17 percent of Senate releases. Nearly half of all releases came under the heading of credit claiming and about a third were position taking. This similarity should not, however, be taken as a sign that House and Senate are converging, as some have claimed; Ross K. Baker is right to remind us of important differences between the two bodies, including a more authoritative style of leadership in the House.[6] Still, the Senate is usually thought of as more august, emphasizing unlimited debate on matters of national and international import, and filled with members who are household names. Moreover, political scientists have noted that issues are more

---

6. Ross K. Baker, *House and Senate* (Norton, 1989), pp. 199–209.

important in Senate campaigns than in those for House seats.[7] The percentage of Senate releases devoted to position taking, then, might have been expected to be higher and the percentage of credit claiming lower than for House releases. Why weren't they?

There are no special factors relating to the particular mix of legislators included in the sample that would account for the results.[8] It is true, of course, that since credit-claiming releases often announce grants, senators will have more opportunities to make these sorts of announcements. Yet there is another difference that may explain why half of all senators' press releases claim credit for one thing or another: senators are more often unseated. The average percentage of the vote that our House members received in their previous election was a very comfortable 74.2, thirteen points higher than the average for the senators. More than half the senators—but only 12 percent of the House members—received less than 60 percent of the vote. As Everett Carll Ladd has pointed out, the 1988 House elections were the least competitive in U.S. history: more than 98 percent of the incumbents seeking reelection won.[9] Of those who served in the Senate in 1984, however, twelve had been defeated by 1990 and nineteen had retired, in some cases hurried off by the difficulty of winning again.

These conditions are reflected in the quantity as well as the content of press releases. Senators put out two and one-half times as many press releases as House members. Not all senators have the same publicity imperatives, of course; in September 1984 one office produced three press releases, another sixty-four. Yet on average, they tried harder than House members, a point to which I shall return.[10]

Credit claiming is the most electorally useful type of press release and a special favorite of first-term senators, 56.7 percent of whose announcements can be classified under that heading. In contrast, press releases of House

7. See Gerald C. Wright, Jr., and Michael B. Berkman, "Candidates and Policy in United States Senate Elections," *American Political Science Review*, vol. 80 (June 1986), pp. 567–88; and Alan I. Abramowitz, "Explaining Senate Election Outcomes," *American Political Science Review*, vol. 82 (June 1988), pp. 385–403.

8. House members and senators in the sample were about the same age, had been in office for the same number of years, and were almost equally divided between Democrats and Republicans, liberals and conservatives. The mean age of the survey's House members was 54.2 years, and for senators 56.4 years. The mean number of years of service in both the House and Senate was thirteen. The House survey included 31 Democrats and 29 Republicans, the Senate survey 11 Democrats and 12 Republicans. According to *National Journal* ratings, House members and senators voted 26 percent liberal on social issues; on foreign policy issues the House was 28 percent conservative and the Senate was 26 percent conservative.

9. Everett Carll Ladd, "Public Opinion and the 'Congress Problem,' " *Public Interest* (Summer 1990), pp. 58–61.

10. The mean number of senators' press releases was 12.4; the House figure for those putting out press releases was 5.4. (September was an above-average month for press releases in the Senate. I do not know whether this was also the case in the House).

members who have served six years or less use credit claiming 42.7 percent of the time (appendix table B-15). For senators in their second and third terms, credit claiming drops to 45 percent. There is not a great deal of difference among senators by age, although those younger than fifty are much more likely to use credit claiming than are House members of the same age. Within the House, leaders do less advertising and more position taking than nonleaders. In the Senate there are no real differences on this scale. House Republicans do more credit claiming, House Democrats more advertising; there is little difference between the parties in the Senate. House liberals are more likely to advertise themselves than Senate liberals are. House conservatives are somewhat more apt to claim credit than Senate conservatives.

When press releases were sorted by whether their contents were local, national, or international, the results for House and Senate were once more virtually identical. Both focused on local issues in 43 to 45 percent of the releases, national issues in 45 to 47 percent, and international issues in less than 10 percent (appendix table B-16).[11] This similarity, too, suggests that senators may be using press releases as a campaign weapon to a greater degree than might be expected. The handouts reinforce the stereotype of a provincial House of Representatives, the localizers of the capital city: "In testimony presented before the New York City Council today, Congressman Eliot L. Engel supported a Transportation Committee resolution opposing a proposed fare increase on express bus service to Manhattan" (September 15); "Congressman Dale E. Kildee visited with a youth group sponsored by the Holly Seventh Day Adventist Church, who came to Washington, D.C., to tour the nation's capital on their way to a national campout in Pennsylvania" (September 6); "U.S. Rep. Robert T. Matsui, in a letter to Los Angeles Raider owner Al Davis, has urged Davis to move his successful football franchise to Sacramento" (September 21). Yet the press releases from the Senate turn out to be equally provincial. House press releases address international topics as often as Senate releases—about 9 percent of the time—but neither House nor Senate sees much political payoff in press releases about international affairs. All politics is local, as Tip O'Neill said.

Yet press releases focus less often on local issues as House members get older and stay longer in Congress. House leaders also are less local and more national in their releases than nonleaders (appendix table B-16). For those

---

11. Diana Evans Yiannakis, "House Members' Communication Styles: Newsletters and Press Releases," *Journal of Politics*, vol. 44 (November 1982), pp. 1049–71, who also uses Mayhew's categories but modifies them to allow for "consideration of geographic focus," has concluded that "the distinction between nationally oriented and locally oriented position taking was . . . particularly important" (p. 1049).

legislators who stray too far into international concerns, however, the press release is one way to remind constituents that their thoughts are never far removed from their home towns. Thus the House Armed Services Committee chairman's press releases included "Aspin Welcomes Helwig as Janesville Office Intern" (August 15) and "Marquette Graduate Interns in Aspin's Racine Office" (August 8), while Representative Stephen Solarz, a foreign affairs maven, put out a September 20 press release urging public hearings on the proposed expansion of the Newton Creek Pollution Plant in the Greenpoint section of Brooklyn.

Legislators vary considerable as to when and how often they issue press releases. Eleven of the House members in the survey (18 percent) did not issue a release during September 1989; three members (13 percent) issued 15 each. Among twenty-three senators whose 1984 releases were counted, Bob Dole produced 260 and Warren Rudman 34. When all legislators in the survey are arranged by how often they put out press releases, the prolific producers are in the Senate—Senate leaders, Republicans, younger senators and those older than age sixty, conservatives, and veteran senators. This result recalls earlier studies showing that the news media pay more attention to senators than to House members.[12]

Richard F. Fenno has suggested some likely reasons why the Senate is favored, including the sizes of House and Senate—"each senator's share of legislative power is four times as great as each representative's share"—and the fact that "a few potential presidential candidates live in the Senate."[13] But examining the lowly press release, the basic unit of congressional publicity, suggests an additional reason: if the media are more interested in covering senators, so too are senators more interested in attracting the media.

12. See Stephen Hess, *The Washington Reporters* (Brookings, 1981), pp. 101–02; and Tracy White, ed., *Power in Congress* (Washington: Congressional Quarterly, 1987), p. 90.
13. See Richard F. Fenno, Jr., *The United States Senate: A Bicameral Perspective* (Washington: American Enterprise Institute for Public Policy Research, 1982), pp. 10–11.

The Lordly
Op-Ed Piece

ON SEPTEMBER 21, 1970, a Monday, the page across from the editorial page
of the *New York Times*—where the obituaries used to be—featured three
essays by people who were not employees of the paper: W. W. Rostow,
writing about the United States and Asia, commented, "the net cost of the
war in Vietnam . . . is less than 2 percent of GNP" and "is declining, not
rising." Han Suyin, in "Peking in Autumn," wrote, "the cultural revolution
has been a success," and that there is a "new sense of freedom, a real grass-
roots democratic spirit, which is evident everywhere." Under the headline
"S. T. Agnew Is No H. L. Mencken," Gerald W. Johnson discussed
different purposes of the American language as used by the vice president
and the Baltimore writer. These articles launched an innovation, seven years
in gestation, according to Harrison E. Salisbury, the paper's first editor of the
opposite-the-editorial page. In his memoirs he wrote that the idea was to
"present an alternate opinion [by outsiders] to those expressed by *Times*
editorials and columnists. . . . Within a year every paper of consequence in
the country had adopted Op-Ed."[1]

A future senator, Daniel Patrick Moynihan, wrote his first op-ed piece,
"Above Thy Darkling Plain," for the *Times* of September 22, 1970; a former
senator, Pierre Salinger, wrote "Exposing the President" two days later; but
it was not until "The Politics of Despair" appeared on October 3 that a sitting
senator, Ernest F. Hollings, made use of the *Times* op-ed page. "Op-ed"
then quickly became a noun, as in "I'm going to write an op-ed," and legislators on Capitol Hill were quick to adopt this new opportunity to publicize
their ideas. By its twentieth year, Senate Republican leader Bob Dole, who
certainly did not lack platforms for his opinions, proposed cutting U.S. aid
to Israel in an op-ed; Moynihan, now New York's Democratic senator, wrote

---

1. Harrison E. Salisbury, *A Time of Change: A Reporter's Tale of Our Time* (Harper and Row, 1988), pp.
316–17. See also Robert B. Semple, Jr., "Op-Ed at 20: All the Views That Are Fit to Print," *New York Times*,
September 30, 1990, sec. 4A, p.1.

one to further his battle to reduce social security tax rates and was opposed by Democratic economists Henry J. Aaron and Charles L. Schultze.[2] As Ken Bode commented, also in an op-ed, "Democrats have become a party of policy freelancers who communicate with each other through Op-Ed pages."[3]

During the first half of 1989, senators and House members contributed thirty-eight articles to the *New York Times*, thirty-seven to the *Washington Post*, twenty-three to *USA Today*, twenty-two to the *Los Angeles Times*, twenty-one to the *Washington Times*, twenty to the *Christian Science Monitor*, and seven to the *Wall Street Journal*, the seven newspapers in which most national op-eds appear.[4]

"Op-ed" has become generic, referring to a type of article regardless of where it is placed in a newspaper. It is similar to the traditional letter to the editor, only longer. The typical op-ed is 750 words; a letter may be as long as 400 words, as short as 100, and averages 250. Indeed, congressional offices often must decide whether to submit a piece as an op-ed or a letter. When we interviewed staff members whose bosses had letters published in 1989, an assistant to Representative Bill Archer of Texas said, "Some thought was given to writing this as an op-ed column. However, we figured that it would be easier and more expeditious to send it in as a letter [to the *Washington Post*]. This would insure that the publication would coincide with the House debate." But as pointed out by an aide to Representative Michael Andrews of Texas, the decision is not always the legislator's. "He might send it in as a column and the op-ed editor says they cannot run it as is but could stick it in the letter section. The congressman can then adjust it to letter format and resubmit it." Legislators who write op-eds also tend to write letters, but legislators who write letters do not necessarily write op-eds.[5] Legislators who write op-eds also get paid for their labor, the standard fee

2. Bob Dole, "To Help New Democracies, Cut Aid to Israel, 4 Others," *New York Times*, January 16, 1990, p. A27; Daniel Patrick Moynihan, "To My Social Security Critics . . ." *New York Times*, February 9, 1990, p. A31; and Henry J. Aaron and Charles L. Schultze, "Moynihan's Right, but . . ." *New York Times*, January 18, 1990, p. A27.

3. Ken Bode, "Senate Control: Who Cares?" *New York Times*, May 17, 1990, p. A29.

4. The 1988 weekday circulations of leading op-ed papers were *Wall Street Journal*, 1,931,410; *USA Today*, 1,341,811; *Los Angeles Times*, 1,119,840; *New York Times*, 1,117,376; *Washington Post*, 812,419; *Christian Science Monitor*, 177,504; and *Washington Times*, 103,652.

5. Some legislators' letters are written for a reason that does not apply to op-eds—to correct error. "Your May 4 editorial . . . misses the mark in many respects. Perhaps the most glaring is the description of an amendment I offered," wrote Representative Bruce F. Vento of Minnesota to the *Wall Street Journal*, on June 2, 1989. When asked why he wrote the letter, his press secretary replied, "If the *Journal's* presentation was left uncorrected, it could disaffect supporters for the bill. However, the central purpose was not to push legislation but to correct mistakes."

being between $100 (*Christian Science Monitor*) and $250 (*Los Angeles Times*).[6]

Unlike the press release, with its accent on self-advertising or credit claiming, the op-ed is not usually part of a congressional electoral strategy. If winning reelection were the primary aim, surely the most threatened legislators would be the most prolific writers. But they are not. In terms of winning margins in their last elections, op-ed writers are among the most secure members of Congress (appendix table B-18). As an electoral strategy, an exception of sorts must be made when legislators write for national newspapers that are also their local papers. Thus Representative Norman F. Lent of New York warned in the *New York Times* that "Long Island Faces a Financial Meltdown" (June 8, 1988), a comment on closing the Shoreham nuclear power plant; Representative Stan Parris of Fairfax, Virginia, asked "What Good Is D.C.'s Residency Requirement?" in the *Washington Post* (June 26, 1988); and five of the fifteen House members who wrote for the *Los Angeles Times* in 1988 represented districts in the paper's circulation area. For a self-chosen few the op-ed can also be part of a national electoral strategy: Richard Gephardt, Jack Kemp, and Pat Schroeder, the three House members who aspired in 1988 to be president, were op-ed writers.

The main reason most of these essays are written, however, is to try to influence policy. When we interviewed staff members immediately after their bosses had published op-eds, we were offered variations on the same motive.

The defense authorization bill is coming to the floor next week. The congressman [Charles Bennett of Florida] has an amendment on the bill to reduce SDI [strategic defense initiative] spending.

He [Dave McCurdy of Oklahoma] wrote this piece at this time in order to regenerate the debate. He introduced legislation in January and it received a great deal of media attention. After a month, however, discussion died down. He wants now to keep people talking about the idea.

6. Other standard fees paid for op-ed pieces in 1989 were $200 by the *Washington Post*, $150 by the *New York Times*, $125 by *USA Today*, and $100 by the *Wall Street Journal* and *Washington Times*. Reports called "Honoraria Scorecard," which listed fees paid members of Congress and ran weekly in the *Washington Post* in 1989 and 1990. Fees for op-eds occasionally showed up from other papers, such as *Newsday*, $150, reported by Representative Pat Schroeder of Colorado; *Miami Herald*, $150, reported by Representative William Gray of Pennsylvania; and *Atlanta Constitution*, $100, reported by Representative Mervyn Dymally of California.

The column was sent before the White House announcement of its plan for environmental cleanup. However, the paper would not run it in advance. He [Philip R. Sharp of Indiana] had hoped to influence the president's proposal, since Indiana is one of the states suffering from demands for unequal emissions reduction.

In light of the past presidential elections and the lack of success of the Democratic party, he [William O. Lipinski of Illinois] thought it would be appropriate since the party is considering a rules change.

The column was written [by Henry Hyde of Illinois] to coincide with the confirmation hearings of Donald Gregg as ambassador to South Korea.

ASIDE, THEN, from presidential hopefuls, who else are the op-ed writers who want to influence national policy, and how do they differ from their colleagues who do not publish their opinions in such a formal way?

Op-ed writers in the House tend to be slightly younger, yet have served in Congress longer, than nonwriters. A "typical" 1988 essayist was elected in 1974 when he was thirty-eight years old. His district is fairly safe, but so too is the nonwriter's district.[7] The writers include the group of House members described by Burdett Loomis in *The New American Politician* that are distinguished from their predecessors by "their use of writing to establish credentials as intellectuals and as serious participants in national policy debates."[8]

Among those who came close to matching this profile in 1988 were Representatives James Florio of New Jersey, Mickey Edwards of Oklahoma, and Don Bonker of Washington. They are ambitious, even by congressional standards. Florio was elected governor of New Jersey in 1989, defeating another congressional op-ed writer, Jim Courter. Edwards became chairman of the House Republican Policy Committee, the third-ranking party post, when Dick Cheney, also an op-ed writer, resigned to become secretary of defense in 1989. Bonker sought a seat in the Senate and lost in a Democratic primary; but four members of the "class of '74," Max Baucus, Christopher Dodd, Paul Simon, and Timothy Wirth, are now senators, and they too wrote op-eds in 1988 or 1989.

7. The mean age of House op-ed writers is 51.4 years; of nonwriters, 53 years. The mean number of terms in office of the op-ed writer is 6.5, or 13 years, and 5.2 terms for the nonwriter. Writers averaged 73 percent of the vote in 1986; nonwriters 72 percent.

8. Burdett Loomis, *The New American Politician: Ambition, Entrepreneurship, and the Changing Face of Political Life* (Basic Books, 1988), pp. 55–56.

Occasionally junior legislators see the op-ed page as a means of shoe-horning themselves into policy debate, a tactic used in 1988, for instance, by two House members in their third term. In *Christian Science Monitor* articles, Barbara Boxer of California proposed reforming Pentagon procurement practices and Robert Mrazek of New York faulted U.S. military operations in the Persian Gulf. (Both would later eye Senate seats.)

Op-ed writers are more apt than nonwriters to be party leaders, especially in the minority party (appendix table B-18). However, the House Speaker, who holds a daily press briefing when Congress is in session, does not need the op-ed page to make news. Neither are writers usually found among the chairmen of House standing committees. Only eight of twenty-two wrote op-eds in the 1988 sample, and several of them, California Representatives Ron Dellums (Committee on the District of Columbia) and Julian Dixon (Committee on Standards of Official Conduct), were concerned with matters unrelated to their committees' jurisdictions, while two others, Kika de la Garza of Texas (Agriculture Committee) and Sonny Montgomery of Mississippi (Veterans' Affairs Committee), wrote pieces that were more akin to letters to the editor, protesting previous articles that they felt were unfair to their committees' positions: "If only agricultural policy were as simple as it appears to be on newspaper editorial pages," de la Garza lamented in the *Washington Post* (October 1, 1988).[9] Nor are op-eds likely to come from the thirteen chairmen of the appropriations subcommittees, who exercise vast power over federal spending and thus are already formidable policymakers. Known on Capitol Hill as the college of cardinals, these legislators produced only one op-ed piece, jointly written by Californians Dixon and Edward Roybal for the *Los Angeles Times* (November 4, 1988), in which they opposed a state ballot proposition that would allow Occidental Petroleum to drill in Pacific Palisades.

Constituency committees, such as Agriculture and Veterans' Affairs, may wish to defend themselves in print from time to time and, of course, members have interests beyond their committees, but to the degree that specialization still dominates the House, those who choose membership on Foreign Affairs, Ways and Means, Energy and Commerce, Armed Services,

9. Our survey codes all articles that the *Washington Post Index* labels as "commentary." It should be noted, however, that this includes pieces by ten House members from "Free for All," a page that runs each Saturday immediately before the editorial page, on which some entries are as long as op-eds but are always written in response to something that has appeared in the paper. An example by Michigan's Howard Wolpe on July 9, 1988, begins, "I take strong exception to the *Post* editorial celebrating the apparent demise of what are derisively referred to as 'playthings called Urban Development Action Grants.' "

and Judiciary are the ones most often published. Basically, then, the op-ed page is the domain of the policy committee member.

More than half of House members' articles in the *Christian Science Monitor* in 1988 and more than a third of those in the *Los Angeles Times* concerned foreign policy. For members of the Foreign Affairs Committee the year's production was especially significant.

Legislator	Position	Newspaper
Dante B. Fascell	Chairman	*Washington Post*
Howard Wolpe	Chairman, Africa Subcommittee	*Washington Post* (2)
Stephen J. Solarz	Chairman, Asian and Pacific Affairs Subcommittee	*New York Times* (2) *Christian Science Monitor* (2) *Los Angeles Times* (3) *Wall Street Journal*
Lee H. Hamilton	Chairman, Europe and Middle East Subcommittee	*Christian Science Monitor* (5) *Washington Post*
Don Bonker	Chairman, International Economic Policy and Trade Subcommittee	*Washington Post*
Jim Leach	Ranking Minority, Asian Subcommittee	*Los Angeles Times*
Toby Roth	Ranking Minority, International Economic Policy Subcommittee	*Christian Science Monitor*
Howard L. Berman		*Wall Street Journal*
Gerry E. Studds		*Christian Science Monitor*
Henry J. Hyde		*Los Angeles Times* (2) *Washington Post*
Mel Levine		*New York Times* *Washington Post* *Los Angeles Times* (4)
Edward F. Feighan		*Washington Post* (2)

Most, but not all, of the articles were about foreign policy, as might be expected. Lee Hamilton, for instance, wrote "Why the U.S. Must Remain a Key World Player" (June 14), "U.S. Bases in Europe: Renegotiating Access Amid New Realities" (March 17), and "Time for a New American Relationship with Vietnam" (December 12), for the *Christian Science Monitor*. The sheer number of op-eds from members of the Foreign Affairs Committee—thirty-three—is striking when compared with the output from members of such committees as Public Works and Transportation (fifty-two members, two articles) or Small Business (forty-three members, four articles) and underscores where those who wish to be policy players can be found.

Moreover, the example of op-eds from the legislators on Foreign Affairs also suggests that specialization remains the House members' path to power. Rare are those such as Charles E. Schumer of New York who chose to comment on such disparate subjects as debt relief for third world countries, *Washington Post*, May 26, 1987), the homeless in America (*New York Times*, March 9, 1988), and journalism's failure "to look inward" and report on itself (*New York Times*, July 18, 1988).

Additionally, in the course of a year a couple of legislators will become "accidental" authors because of an energetic assistant or a pushy lobbyist or because they happen to catch a cause—tearing down the bugged U.S. embassy in Moscow or shooting the Yellowstone bison. And finally, there is a small group of former college professors in Congress who simply love to write. Aside from their academic origins, they do not have much in common. Some are powerful (Wisconsin's Les Aspin is chairman of the Armed Services Committee), others are not (Paul Henry of Michigan and Dick Armey of Texas were first elected in 1984). Ideologically, they are liberal (Michigan's Howard Wolpe and Wisconsin's Jim Moody), moderate (Henry and Philip Sharp of Indiana), and conservative (Newt Gingrich, Armey, and Pennsylvania's Don Ritter). Bill Thomas of California is a conservative on economic and foreign policy issues, a moderate on social issues; Aspin is a liberal on social issues, a moderate on the economy and foreign policy.

Exceptions aside, op-eds are the best indicators of which legislators use the media for legislative purposes. Indeed, they are the purest form of outside strategy: no nine-second sound bite adjusted to the needs of a television package, no ten-word quotation in the fifth paragraph of a reporter's story. Rather, op-eds are the chance for those seriously interested in policymaking to state their cases in prestigious forums. Using these articles as an index of how many House members employ a media strategy to try to influence the passage of legislation suggests that some previous analyses are overstatements.[10] My study found that sixty-eight representatives wrote op-eds in the five leading outlets during 1988 (appendix table B-19). In another year some names would be added, others deleted. But 16 percent of House members seems a responsible estimate of the number of players in this game.

10. See Timothy E. Cook, *Making Laws and Making News: Media Strategies in the U.S. House of Representatives* (Brookings, 1989), pp. 124–25.

IF WRITING op-eds defines the elite group in the House of Representatives who use an outside media strategy to promote their policy goals, in the Senate this activity has become so widespread as to call into question its legislative usefulness. In the House, according to a staff aide, "when members see someone who has written a column, they will give that person a slap on the back." Not so among senators. A third of the Senate published articles in the *New York Times, Washington Post,* or *Wall Street Journal* during 1988, three times the percentage for the House (appendix table B-18). And when these findings are tacked on to what appeared in the seven papers studied from January through June 1989, making an eighteen-month period in which there were 111 senators, almost half the Senate wrote op-eds (appendix table B-20).

Op-ed pages, then, represent another example of the media's bias toward the Senate. One reason is that senators are much more likely to be celebrities. Of those who wrote five or more articles in the eighteen months—Bradley, Biden, Kennedy, Moynihan, and Gordon J. Humphrey of New Hampshire— only Humphrey need have his first name spelled out for attentive newspaper readers. The Senate also draws greater attention because it has exclusive domain over the confirmation of presidential appointees and the ratification of treaties. The nomination of John Tower as secretary of defense in 1989, for instance, inspired pro and con op-eds in the *New York Times* by Republican leader Bob Dole (March 17) and Democrat J. James Exon of Nebraska (March 7), while Jesse Helms, who had challenged various State Department nominees, wrote "Blame the System, Not the Senate" (March 7), and Gordon Humphrey challenged the role of the American Bar Association in the confirmation of federal judges (*Wall Street Journal,* March 22).

As in the House, specialization can produce op-eds: New Mexico's Jeff Bingaman, a member of the Armed Services Committee, wrote "New Threat: Poison Tipped Missiles" (*New York Times,* March 29, 1989); Bob Packwood of Oregon, former chairman of the Finance Committee, wrote "What Tax-Increasers Really Want" (*Washington Times,* March 17, 1989); and Frank Murkowski, a senator from Alaska, wrote "Save the Salmon from Poachers" (*New York Times,* March 4, 1989), "The USA Needs Arctic Refuge Oil" (*USA Today,* March 21, 1989), and "The Tongass National Forest—At Risk?" (*Christian Science Monitor,* March 14, 1989). But unlike the opinions of House members, those of senators are welcome regardless of their committee expertise.[11] Senators who are not members of the Foreign

11. During the first six months of 1989 there were a dozen or more op-eds produced by senators from fourteen standing committees.

Relations Committee analyze international events; senators who are not on Armed Services discuss defense. Others choose to argue that Congress must fight violence on television (Paul Simon of Illinois) or to speculate on whether the United States should federalize the police (Alfonse D'Amato of New York). In short, as op-ed writers senators are increasingly indistinguishable from professional columnists—George Will or Tom Wicker or others who have political points of view.

This variety and apparent resistance to a restricted expertise suggests that senators consider op-eds much more a part of their electoral strategies than House members do. Indeed, considering senators' output in 1989, the closer they are to a reelection campaign, the more apt they are to publish an article: of those having to run in the 1990 election, 45 percent wrote op-eds; for senators who would not have to run again until 1992 the figure was 29 percent, and for those who had just been elected or reelected in 1988, it was 27 percent.

Perhaps senators also get more op-eds published than House members do because—as we found when comparing press releases from the two chambers—they work harder at generating attention. One measure that could reflect this is the rank of the press secretaries in Senate offices: Is the press secretary's salary among the top four in the pecking order? Press secretaries of op-ed writers in the House do not rank higher than those of nonwriter House members, but in the Senate they have a somewhat higher status (appendix table B-18). This should not necessarily imply greater skill on the part of the better-paid press secretaries but merely that their services are more valued.

Otherwise, the Senate's 1988 op-ed writers tend to follow the same pattern as their House counterparts. They are more likely to hold a leadership position than the nonwriters (excluding the majority leader, but not the minority leader) and they have been more comfortably elected: only seven of the thirty-three writers had less than 55 percent of the vote. They are younger members, but ones who also have been elected at least twice. The mean age of the Senate writers was fifty-four years, of nonwriters, fifty-eight. Senators older than seventy rarely wrote op-eds. The most prolific writers in the Senate and the House conform to this mold even more closely than those who wrote only one piece, the major difference being that the prolific senators were in their third term.

There are, however, distinct differences in ideology between the op-ed writers in the House and Senate. Using three scales devised by the *National Journal*—the legislators' positions on economic, social, and foreign policy matters—House members are proportionally similar to their percentage in that body only on economic issues. In the following table, 25 percent of the House members are economic conservatives and 27 percent of the op-ed writers are conservative; 24 percent of the members are liberals and 25 percent of the writers are liberal. On social issues, liberals are more apt to be the writers; on foreign policy issues, both liberals and conservatives are better represented than their percentages in the House would suggest. On all scales, Senate op-ed writers are consistently more liberal.[12]

	House		Senate	
Ideology	All legislators	Op-ed writers	All legislators	Op-ed writers
Economic policy				
Conservative	25.2	27.1	25.3	21.9
Liberal	24.2	25.0	19.2	24.4
Social policy				
Conservative	25.6	19.1	25.3	21.9
Liberal	24.9	36.2	24.2	37.5
Foreign policy				
Conservative	25.7	33.3	25.3	18.8
Liberal	23.1	31.3	25.3	31.3

Why are op-ed writers more often liberals? Partly, of course, it is the slant of the newspapers that choose the stories, but it may also reflect divided government. If the president is a Republican, the editors of op-ed pages seek out Democratic members of Congress for opposing opinions. Although this observation does not explain why the editors more often choose their liberals from the Senate, the choice may again merely reflect Senate celebrity status: a Bradley, Moynihan, or Kennedy will add a certain glitter to the page that their counterparts in the House do not provide.

How DO congressional offices decide to which newspapers they should offer the articles they write? "The group targeted was an 'inside the beltway' crowd, so the Washington Post is best suited for reaching such an audience," a press assistant to Lee Hamilton commented, thus confirming what Michael J. Robinson and Maura E. Clancey discovered in 1983 when they polled senior congressional aides about their news habits. "More than 60 percent of the staffers named the Post, among all possible sources, as their main supplier of news and political information."[13] On deciding where to

12. These figures combine op-ed output in the New York Times, Washington Post, and Wall Street Journal.
13. Michael J. Robinson and Maura E. Clancey, "King of the Hill: When It Comes to News, Congress Turns to the Washington Post," Washington Journalism Review, vol. 5 (July-August 1983), p. 47.

send an article analyzing the "Panama policy vacuum," an aide to Representative Sam Gejdenson of Connecticut observed, "the battles between a Republican administration and a Democratic Congress take place on the pages of the *Washington Post*."

To reach a broader elite audience, the forum of choice is the *New York Times*. "Choosing the *Times* was consistent with the 'outside the beltway' thrust of [this particular] column," said Dave McCurdy's press secretary. Beyond this basic rule of the road, if the op-ed piece is rejected by the *Post* and the *Times* (or if it seems likely to be rejected), press secretaries simply send their wares to other leading papers. "The column was initially submitted to the *New York Times*. They didn't run it so it was sent to the *Monitor*." It is a buyer's market.

A simpler means of getting published is for legislators to send op-eds to the paper that most closely supports their position. Harrison Salisbury wrote that the *New York Times* op-ed was designed to be opposite in the true sense: "If the *Times* was liberal, the Op-Ed articles would be reactionary or conservative or radical or eccentric."[14] But op-ed pages are now ideologically supplemental, not opposite (appendix tables B-23 and B-24). The *New York Times, Christian Science Monitor,* and *Los Angeles Times*, which take liberal editorial positions, print much more material from liberal legislators than from conservatives. The *Wall Street Journal* and *Washington Times* choose the writings of conservatives. (During the first six months of 1989, for instance, the *Washington Times* ran ten pieces by House members, eight of whom were conservatives). An exception is the *Washington Post*, a liberal paper, whose editorial pages editor, Meg Greenfield, told a meeting of Republican senatorial press secretaries in 1984 that she looks for op-ed pieces "where a senator takes an unusual, unexpected, surprising position on an issue, almost without regard for what side he is on." On social issues in 1988 liberals and conservatives each made up a quarter of the House of Representatives. *Post* op-ed writers came closest to matching these proportions.

Liberal		Conservative	
Newspaper	Percentage of op-ed writers	Newspaper	Percentage of op-ed writers
Los Angeles Times	72.7	Wall Street Journal	38.5
New York Times	63.6	Washington Post	24.0
Christian Science Monitor	41.7	Los Angeles Times	18.2
Wall Street Journal	30.8	Christian Science Monitor	12.5
Washington Post	28.0	New York Times	4.5

14. Salisbury, *A Time of Change,* p. 317.

All newspapers seek a certain amount of "balance" on their op-ed pages—Ted Kennedy gets published in the *Washington Times* and Jesse Helms in the *New York Times*. The editorial page of *USA Today* follows a tape-measure definition of balance, with its own editorial in the upper left of the page and "an opposing view" in the upper right. When a *USA Today* editorial of August 23, 1990, argued against forcing states to cancel driver's licenses of convicted drug users, Representative Gerald Solomon of New York countered, "Yank Highway Funds If Licenses Aren't Lifted." Across the bottom of the editorial page, *USA Today* also runs "Face-Off," two opinions, side-by-side, exactly the same number of words. On August 2, 1990, Representatives Ronald Dellums of California argued against funding the B-2 bomber and Representative Ike Skelton of Missouri argued in its favor.

The ideal piece for an ideological op-ed page is the "mea culpa" in which an adversary admits error and joins your side. "Red flags went up all over Western Europe last week when I introduced a resolution in the House calling for the withdrawal of American personnel assigned to the intermediate-range nuclear forces in Britain, West Germany, Belgium, Italy and the Netherlands," Representative Andy Ireland of Florida began in "A Hawk Says: Pull Our Troops Out" (March 7, 1989). "The fact that I'm a conservative Republican with a strong pro-defense record also has our allies and some people at the Pentagon worried. . . ." The article topped the op-ed page of the *New York Times*. Why did the congressman choose the *Times*? According to his aide, "The *Times* asked him to write the piece."

As Salisbury has concluded, "with the passage of time, Op-Ed has lost most of its Op quality."[15]

15. Salisbury, A *Time of Change*, p. 317.

I Am on TV Therefore I Am: A Postscript

DURING THE 1980s, for a variety of reasons, including television's need to fill airtime with relatively inexpensive programming, some reporters in Washington became household names.[1] Although celebrity was conferred upon only a handful—the Sam Donaldsons and Ted Koppels—it added an aura of power to all those who had once been lumped together as "working press" (so as to separate them from the capitalists in the front offices). That apparent power, combined with the seeming pervasiveness of the media in American life, stimulated the activities of groups with acronyms such as FAIR and AIM who were dedicated to the proposition that the biases and inaccuracies of the media are of overriding concern to the nation and must be vigorously corrected.[2] Such organizations surely would not devote attention to a product that is unimportant. Thus by 1988 Mark Hertsgaard could assert with confidence, "The news media has become the single most influential actor on the stage of American politics."[3]

Yet, in many ways, this has been a book about the unimportance of the press.

The unimportance stems from the focus of these studies: the relations between Congress and press rather than White House and press. The press is important to presidents, and hence to the presidency.[4] Even if most Americans—and most news organizations—did not believe that the president is more important than Congress, the oneness of the presidency would give its coverage a unitary character. The nature of White House reporting is to act as a concave reflector, narrowing and maximizing attention. But Congress is

1. See James Fallows, "The New Celebrities of Washington," *New York Review*, June 12, 1986, pp. 41–49.

2. Fairness and Accuracy in Reporting (FAIR) is on the political left; Accuracy in Media (AIM) is on the right.

3. Mark Hertsgaard, *On Bended Knee: The Press and the Reagan Presidency* (Farrar Straus Giroux, 1988), p. 348.

4. See Elmer E. Cornwell, Jr., *Presidential Leadership of Public Opinion* (Indiana University Press, 1965); Michael Baruch Grossman and Martha Joynt Kumar, *Portraying the President: The White House and the News Media* (Johns Hopkins University Press, 1981); and Richard L. Rubin, *Press, Party, and Presidency* (Norton, 1981).

535 individuals with a jumble of interests, and reporting from Capitol Hill has the effect of atomizing the institution, separating particles of information to fit the diverse needs of legislators and news organizations. One reporter writes of legislation to regulate commodity markets, another on funding for repaving a highway through Altoona, others on other subjects.

Congress, of course, demands a fair share of media attention. Borrowing from a theory of political scientist James Q. Wilson—"organizations come to resemble the organizations they are in conflict with"—Senator Daniel Patrick Moynihan invented the Iron Law of Emulation: "Whenever any branch of the government acquires a new technique which enhances its power in relations to the other branches, that technique will soon be adopted by those other branches as well."[5] At least since Franklin D. Roosevelt invented the fireside chat, presidents have attempted to exploit technical advances provided by the news media. Which helps explain why legislators have hired press secretaries, allowed television cameras into committee rooms, supported the creation of C-SPAN, and expanded House and Senate recording studios. A great deal of information gets transmitted by means of these innovations. But in the end, partly because of the principle that dissemination is also dispersion, legislators can rarely concentrate enough video time or command enough newspaper space to make a difference in promoting a policy or even getting themselves reelected.

Still, not all legislators are equal. From the vantage point of the press, the House Speaker and the Senate majority leader can be handy institutional counterweights to the president. During Ronald Reagan's first term, with the Republicans in control of the Senate, Thomas P. "Tip" O'Neill suddenly became "the most televised Speaker in history."[6] His visibility was further enhanced by his imposing physical stature, by skillful public relations help, and by Republican attempts to turn him into a campaign issue—a confluence of circumstances not likely to occur very often. Yet he appeared on less than 7 percent of the network evening news programs—whereas a president almost always gets at least one story a day (97 percent of the time, by one count) and usually two or three.[7] And such differences in coverage are not

5. Daniel Patrick Moynihan, *Counting Our Blessings: Reflections on the Future of America* (Little, Brown, 1980), pp. 117–18.

6. Joe S. Foote, *Television Access and Political Power: The Networks, the Presidency, and the "Loyal Opposition"* (Praeger, 1990), p. 129.

7. Speaker O'Neill was seen on the network evening news programs 184 times in 1981, 146 times in 1982, 159 times in 1983, and 168 times in 1984. See Timothy E. Cook, *Making Laws and Making News: Media Strategies in the U.S. House of Representatives* (Brookings, 1989), pp. 196–97. For presidential appearances, see Fred Smoller, "The Six O'Clock Presidency: Patterns of Network News Coverage of the President," *Presidential Studies Quarterly*, vol. 16 (Winter 1986), p. 46. Doris A. Graber, *Mass Media and American Politics*, 3d ed. (Washington: CQ Press, 1989), who charted all network evening news broadcasts from July

simply quantitative. Presidents can be certain that everything they want reported will be reported. This allows them to use the media to semaphore political friends and foes. Legislators, even the leaders, have no guarantees that the press will play this game.

Nor, in terms of press coverage, are all issues equal. An investigation of a Watergate or Iran-contra scandal, a debate on a Panama Canal Treaty or a resolution to go to war in the Persian Gulf, a confirmation fight over a pivotal Supreme Court appointment—all can galvanize and focus the attentions of correspondents covering Congress, although the issue is usually framed as "Will the President Win or Lose?"[8] There are, of course, exceptions. A modest issue such as the members of Congress voting themselves a pay raise can have "talk radio" resonance. And sometimes there are rare legislators, a Phil Gramm or Newt Gingrich, without seniority or previous celebrity status or even the physical attributes that are supposed to attract television cameras, who have been able to exploit the media to advance themselves and their causes. "No camera, microphone, or notebook could be too inconveniently located for Phil Gramm," recalled National Public Radio's Cokie Roberts of the Texas senator, who was ninety-ninth in seniority when he brought into being the deficit reduction law that bears his name.[9] And Gingrich, then a junior Republican House member in an overwhelmingly Democratic body, is supposed to have said, "We are engaged in reshaping a whole nation through the news media."[10] So far, his campaign has contributed significantly to the unseating of House Speaker Jim Wright and to his own election as minority whip.

That Congress does not get all the television attention it might want partly results from the nature of legislative activity: it represents the quintessential talking-heads story. The president can take the cameras to China as he walks along the Great Wall or to the beaches of Normandy for the fortieth anniversary of D-Day. Even a presidential candidate can make his point from a boat in a polluted harbor. But the best a legislator can usually offer the cameras is a finger pointed at a recalcitrant committee witness. This lack of visual drama has meant that even the regional television bureaus in Washington, once exclusively moored on Capitol Hill, are more and more

---

1986 to June 1987, found that "the president received roughly seven and one-half hours of television news coverage each month from the networks, compared with slightly over one hour for Congress" (pp. 236–37).

8. See Denis Steven Rutkus, *Newspaper and Television Network News Coverage of Congress during the Summers of 1979 and 1989: A Content Analysis* (Congressional Research Service, 1991), pp. 35–40.

9. Cokie Roberts, "Leadership and the Media in the 101st Congress," in John J. Kornacki, ed., *Leading Congress: New Styles, New Strategies* (Washington: CQ Press, 1990), p. 91.

10. Quoted in John M. Barry, *The Ambition and the Power* (Viking, 1989), p. 166.

focusing their attention away from Congress as new technology has given them greater flexibility.[11] But perhaps a deeper reason for the lack of attention is that Congress moves too slowly for the dailiness of American journalism or, for that matter, for the action-now psyches of most reporters. This is the pace I recorded in my Senate diary of October 5, 1984:

> Floor debate on deficit reduction plans continues. . . . Clearly everyone has already said everything, yet it drones on. It is obvious that the reporters have become bored, and, more important, that they do not have front page stories until something passes. So the impression lingers that the Senate isn't doing much. Yet it's a question of time frame. Is several weeks really too much time for cutting the budget by $149 billion over three years?

Since the studies of Joe S. Foote early in the 1980s, it has been confirmed that most legislators are seldom seen on network news. As I showed in *The Ultimate Insiders*, for example, during 1983 one-third of the members of the Senate appeared only one time or not at all on the ABC, CBS, or NBC evening news programs.[12] According to Timothy E. Cook in *Making Laws and Making News*, 53 percent of the members of the House of Representatives were never mentioned on these programs during 1986.[13] But at the same time, virtually every journalist's and scholar's account of Congress-media relations has asserted that the situation is otherwise on local television news, where legislators have been turned into "media stars in [their] home towns."[14] So I looked at who appears on local television news, a strangely ignored area of inquiry, and discovered that most members of Congress also rarely get seen on these programs. Congress remains largely a print story, and as newspapers lose out to television as the news purveyor of choice for Americans, Congress loses out to the president.[15]

THE CONUNDRUM, then, is why television appears to be so important to the life of Congress. As researchers are finally figuring out how to measure the place of television in the political process, television's importance for Congress is best measured by the degree to which House and Senate are not covered.[16] But members of Congress and congressional reporters do not seem

---

11. See Larry Makinson, *Dateline: Capitol Hill* (Washington: Center for Responsive Politics, 1990), p. 62.

12. Stephen Hess, *The Ultimate Insiders: U.S. Senators in the National Media* (Brookings, 1986), p. 16.

13. Cook, *Making Laws and Making News*, p. 60.

14. See Roger H. Davidson and Walter J. Oleszek, *Congress and Its Members*, 3d ed. (Washington: CQ Press, 1990), p. 147.

15. For the case that more coverage does not lead to more power, see Stephanie Greco Larson, "The President and Congress in the Media," *Annal*, vol. 499 (September 1988), pp. 64–74.

16. For some studies that have measured television's political effect, see Thomas E. Patterson, *The Mass*

to have noticed. Quite the contrary, in fact: they tend to overestimate the extent of television coverage and hence its importance in the legislative and electoral processes.[17] Partly this stems from the journalist's habit of ignoring the average, the typical, and the routine. When Hedrick Smith in *The Power Game: How Washington Works* made the case for media politics as a staple of the House of Representatives by citing the activities of Stephen Solarz, Les Aspin, Richard Gephardt, and Newt Gingrich, it was as if he had chosen Larry Bird, Patrick Ewing, Michael Jordan, and Magic Johnson as representative players in the National Basketball Association.[18] But a more important explanation is the solipsistic view of the world that permeates Capitol Hill. Reality to reporters is what they can see, to politicians what they can touch. And Capitol Hill is always crammed with cameras, lights, sound equipment, tape recorders, news conferences, handouts, stakeouts. This is their reality. This also contributes to the myth of television's power as they react to its presence rather than to its output.

The output, as I have demonstrated, is often small. Timothy Cook has told the affecting story of Don J. Pease, a staid and hardworking backbench congressman, who wanted to extend a program of unemployment benefits that was about to expire in 1985. His staff convinced him that a visual aid was just what he needed to get himself on television:

> When his turn came up [at a rally], Pease vigorously deplored official Washington's callousness toward unemployed workers: "If you want to know the truth, the Reagan administration acts as if you don't exist." Then raising the spatula in his right hand, he shouted, "Do you know what this is? *This* is a burger flipper. *This* is the Reagan administration's answer to unemployment. And *you* can flip burgers all day, and *your spouse* can flip burgers all day, and you *still* won't get above the poverty line!"

The results of this exercise, according to Cook, were that the "network

---

Media Election: How Americans Choose Their President (Praeger, 1980); George Gerbner and others, "Charting the Mainstream: Television's Contributions to Political Orientations," *Journal of Communication*, vol. 32 (Spring 1982), pp. 100–27; Larry M. Bartels, "Expectations and Preferences in Presidential Nominating Campaigns," *American Political Science Review*, vol. 79 (September 1985), pp. 804–15; Benjamin I. Page, Robert Y. Shapiro, and Glenn R. Dempsey, "What Moves Public Opinion?" *American Political Science Review*, vol. 81 (March 1987), pp. 23–43; and Shanto Iyengar and Donald R. Kinder, *News That Matters* (University of Chicago Press, 1987).

17. See, for example, Michael D. Wormser, ed., *Guide to Congress*, 3d ed. (Washington: CQ Press, 1982), p. 744. Scholars, however, have been less likely to fall into the journalists' trap. A number of studies have noted the modest television coverage of congressional campaigns. See, for example, Mark C. Westlye, *Senate Elections and Campaign Intensity* (Johns Hopkins University Press, 1991), pp. 39, 41. John W. Kingdon, *Agendas, Alternatives, and Public Policies* (Little, Brown, 1984), pp. 61–64, also describes a more limited role for the media in setting congressional agendas.

18. See Hedrick Smith, *The Power Game: How Washington Works* (Random House, 1988), pp. 139–46.

evening news programs ignored the story . . . and the next morning neither the *New York Times* nor the *Washington Post* mentioned it. The staff's one consolation was a color photograph in the *Baltimore Sun*, although the caption neglected to explain why Pease was waving the spatula." The legislation did not get out of committee.[19]

Nevertheless, Congress and its members are spending more each year trying to influence news media coverage.[20] But the interest is not as pervasive as I had expected after reading some accounts of Capitol Hill activities, and data in the surveys in this book may serve as a midcourse correction. Electronic news releases, for instance, are far more rare than is suggested by the newspaper and magazine stories that focus on legislators who produce the tapes and ignore those who do not. Press secretaries by my calculations rank a lowly fifth in the pecking order of both House and Senate offices; in the House they also spend a fair amount of time on activities that have nothing to do with the media. And perhaps one House member in five feels virtually no need to seek publicity. Jamie Whitten, chairman of the House Appropriations Committee, in nearly a half-century of being a member of Congress, is said never to have held a press conference: "You do your job best when you do it quietly," he summarized.[21]

Indeed, legislators should know that sound bites on the evening news will not get them reelected. Other avenues of publicity in which they can target the audience and control the message are infinitely more effective and involve less risk of losing voters. The odds of being able to move a policy debate by using television news are very long for the average member of Congress. Why then do they devote such energy to this pursuit?

One answer could be that legislators do not know of television's limited impact because it does not appear limited from their vantage point. It is limited only if the question is framed: How many impressions of me, for how long, how positively, is a voter likely to get from my effort? Rather, staff and friends collect and comment upon their appearances, thus magnifying them. (It is similar to what I witnessed a few years ago when I watched a cabinet officer reading his daily press clippings. His senses told him that an awful lot was being written about him. It was harder for him to recall that he was the

---

19. See Cook, *Making Laws and Making News*, pp. 132–46. Cook's point, however, is that Pease's media campaign, of which the spatula incident was a part, is what allowed his bill to get within two votes of passage. My interpretation of his case study is that the bill did as well as it did because Pease convinced Speaker O'Neill to support him.

20. See Walter Pincus, "TV Staff for House May Grow," *Washington Post*, April 25, 1990, p. A26, and "House TV Expansion Deferred," *Washington Post*, April 26, 1990, p. A21.

21. Quoted in Peter Osterlund, "Media-Savvy Congress Turns to TV," *Christian Science Monitor*, June 3, 1988, p. 3.

only one reading all of it). Under this closed system, even an obscure cable program at an obscene hour can produce a reenforcing feedback.

Another answer could be that legislators are cockeyed optimists. Is there not some of this quality in everyone who seeks elective office? Senator William S. Cohen believed that the politicians' common denominator is ambition. "Whether it is noble or ignoble," he wrote, "it is an all-consuming passion which refuses to acknowledge the folly of its relentless pursuit."[22] In pursuit of the elusive sound bite, surely each member of Congress thinks he is as energetic, articulate, and intelligent as Phil Gramm and Newt Gingrich. Moreover, sound-bite journalism protects legislators from themselves. Although television and newspapers work off the same definition of news, their needs differ—TV needs nine seconds, and thus must edit out redundancy and even the awkward pauses of conversational speech. This will not necessarily make legislators look good, but it keeps them from looking bad.

Add to Senator Cohen's definition of political ambition Joseph A. Schlesinger's theory of progressive ambition: "The politician aspires to attain an office more important than the one he now seeks or is holding."[23] More than a third of the Senate once served in the House. How many senators would rather be president? On December 30, 1971, Jim Wright wrote in his diary, "In two days, a New Year will begin. It is my 50th, will be my 18th in Congress. . . . Maybe just in the past year have I really acknowledged that I won't ever be president."[24] For some legislators, perhaps, being on television has less to do with the next election than with some future election that may only be a dream.

So, as the members of Congress supposedly rush to recording studios to tape instant reactions to the president's State of the Union message, the political pluses outweigh the minuses. Getting on the air is an advantage, even if an exaggerated one. The costs are small, both in time and money, and the money is provided by taxpayers or campaign contributors anyway. Also,

22. William S. Cohen, *Roll Call: One Year in the United States Senate* (Simon and Schuster, 1981), p. 165.

23. Joseph A. Schlesinger, *Ambition and Politics* (Rand McNally, 1966), p. 10. Articles relating ambition theory to Congress include Michael L. Mezey, "Ambition Theory and the Office of Congressman," *Journal of Politics*, vol. 32 (August 1970), pp. 563–79; Jeff Fishel, "Ambition and the Political Vocation: Congressional Challengers in American Politics," *Journal of Politics*, vol. 33 (February 1971), pp. 25–56; David W. Rohde, "Risk-Bearing and Progressive Ambition: The Case of Members of the United States House of Representatives," *American Journal of Political Science*, vol. 23 (February 1979), pp. 1–26; Paul Brace, "Progressive Ambition in the House: A Probabilistic Approach," *Journal of Politics*, vol. 46 (May 1984), pp. 556–71; and Paul R. Abramson, John H. Aldrich, and David W. Rohde, "Progressive Ambition among United States Senators: 1972–1988," *Journal of Politics*, vol. 49 (February 1987), pp. 3–35.

24. David J. Montgomery, "Jim Wright, The Speaker of the House for the 100th Congress," *Fort Worth Star-Telegram*, December 9, 1986, p. 1.

because most legislators sincerely wish to be noticed, there is no longer a stigma—the "show horse" label—attached to those who are exceedingly good at getting themselves on television.[25]

Yet there is still something else. It is August 1, 1984, and I am sitting next to Senator Alan Dixon in a screening room in the basement of the Capitol. This is part of the Senate's television complex, a railroad flat of a place carved out of long and narrow space that had once been the path of the capitol subway. There are two television studios with a control room between them, two radio studios with a control room between them, and two TV editing rooms in addition to the room where we are now watching a tape of the town meeting that the senator has recently broadcast from a cable station in Peoria. A question put to him requires a delicate answer. Dixon listens to his response. He smiles, then issues a laugh that comes from deep inside him. "I got out of that pretty good," he says. Watching a man so thoroughly enjoy watching himself is an exquisite experience. Few senators—only Moynihan and Cohen come to mind—get the same satisfaction from the printed word.

For the legislators of Capitol Hill, television is not primarily about politics at all, I realize. Or rather, without elections to be won and legislation to be passed, there would still be the rush to television. For television is about being a celebrity. Television appearances are analogues of the decor of their offices, which are filled with cartoonists' impressions of them and photographs of them taken with famous people at important events. *"The celebrity is a person who is known for his well-knownness,"* said Daniel J. Boorstin. In his brilliant essay, *The Image*, he concluded, "The hero created himself; the celebrity is created by the media."[26] I am on TV therefore I am.

25. See John R. Hibbing and Sue Thomas, "The Modern United States Senate: What Is Accorded Respect," *Journal of Politics*, vol. 52 (February 1990), pp. 126–45.
26. Daniel J. Boorstin, *The Image: or What Happened to the American Dream* (Atheneum, 1962), pp. 57, 61.

Appendix A

The Washington Reporters Ten Years Later

IN 1978 John J. Curley, Washington bureau chief of the Gannett newspapers, told me, "Management is my bag." I wrote it down, of course, but I needn't have. The line would stick in my memory. Of the hundreds of reporters I interviewed, he was the only one to make this claim. More typical was Richard Dudman, bureau chief of the *St. Louis Post-Dispatch*. From behind a desk piled high with books, magazines, letters, old press releases, he stated flatly, "I have a fear of filing. Administration bores the hell out of me." Curley and Dudman were among the journalists I surveyed for a book to be called *The Washington Reporters* that was published in 1981.

Ten years later Dudman had retired to Maine where he and his wife Helen own a radio station. Curley had also left downtown Washington, but only to relocate across the Potomac River in Arlington, Virginia, at the Gannett Company's headquarters. He is chairman, president, and chief executive officer, whose salary and bonus for 1988 was $1,500,000.

Besides Dudman and Curely, what has happened to Lynch and Bandy and Aukofer and the others? Have they changed? And do the changes add up to a different Washington press corps?

When I first met David Lynch he worked for the *Buffalo Courier-Express*, one of the metropolitan newspapers that did not survive through the 1980s. But I find he is still in the press galleries in 1988, reporting for several smaller papers from Iowa and Nebraska. Lee Bandy is still there too, only the *Columbia State* is now owned by the Knight-Ridder chain. Frank Aukofer of the *Milwaukee Journal* continues to work out of the gallery, even though he has become bureau chief. Regional reporter Mary Kay Quinlan, who told me that despite what folks in Omaha thought, Washington reporting was not constant "hobnobbing with the great and the near-great," has been elected president of the National Press Club. Joan McKinney, *Baton Rouge Advocate*, is a member of the prestigious Gridiron Club, which did not admit women in 1978. Bill Keller has advanced from regional reporting for the Newhouse papers to Moscow bureau chief of the *New York*

Times and has just won a Pulitzer Prize. Kathleen Patterson of the *Kansas City Star* now works for the American Public Welfare Association, and Arthur Wiese of the *Houston Post* for the American Petroleum Institute. Robert Maitlin of the Newhouse chain has joined a congressional staff. Doug Underwood of Gannett is a journalism educator at the University of Washington. Ferrel Guillory of the *News and Observer* is back in Raleigh as the editor of the editorial page. Richard L. Strout died in 1990 at the age of ninety-two.

"In terms of demographics," I wrote a decade ago, "if there is an average Washington reporter and an average American, they do not look much like each other."[1] Neither did the average Washington reporter look much like the average reporter in the rest of the United States. Based on conventional measures of status—schools attended, educational attainment, prestige of their news organizations—Washington reporters were an elite. Richard Strout, for instance, had two Harvard degrees. At a time when 10 percent of all American journalists had graduate degrees, a third of the Washington reporters had them.[2]

A decade after the original research, a new survey of 190 regional reporters based in Washington suggests that the gap between Washington journalists and other American journalists has narrowed significantly. Although regional reporters are not absolutely representative of all Washington reporters, the differences are such that a comparison of 1978 and 1988 data reflects the direction of change in Washington journalism. If, for example, there have been changes in the age pattern of the regional reporters during the decade, it is likely that similar changes have also occurred in the entire Washington press corps.[3]

1. Stephen Hess, *The Washington Reporters* (Brookings, 1981), p. 117.
2. The goundbreaking works on the U. S. journalism population are John W. C. Johnstone, Edward J. Slawski, and William W. Bowman, *The News People: A Sociological Portrait of American Journalists and Their Work* (University of Illinois Press, 1976), reflecting a 1971 survey; and David H. Weaver and G. Cleveland Wilhoit, *The American Journalist: A Portrait of U.S. News People and Their Work* (Indiana University Press, 1986), reflecting 1982–83 data. The figures for graduate degrees and college degrees in 1978, midway between the two studies, come from averaging their percentages.
3. The figures on regional reporters in 1978 differ from those presented in *The Washington Reporters* (pp. 156–57 and elsewhere) because the earlier data have been recoded to conform with the definition of regional reporters used here. Comparing reporters on the regional beat and all Washington reporters in 1978 exposed similarities and dissimilarities. The similarities were in gender, a male-female ratio of four to one; race, overwhelmingly white; age, except among young reporters, where a fifth of all reporters and a third of the regional reporters were in their twenties; the region of the country they came from; and the prestige of the colleges they attended. The dissimilarities were primarily in education. The regional reporters were more likely to have majored in journalism, 37 percent, compared with 24 percent for all Washington reporters. At the graduate level, more than 70 percent of the regional reporters but fewer than half of all reporters studied journalism.

Region

One unexpected development is where reporters have grown up. Washington journalism has always been suspected of an East Coast slant: former Harvard professor Daniel Patrick Moynihan even accused Washington reporters of being Ivy Leaguers.[4] Although a quarter of the American population lived in the Northeast in 1978, more than a third of the Washington reporters came from there, while the western states were underrepresented.[5] Ten years later these imbalances had evened out considerably. The percentages of reporters from the Northeast and West were much closer to the percentages of all Americans living in these regions.[6]

One of the reasons given in 1978 for why so few reporters were from the West was that westerners, according to westerners, resisted transfer to Washington. Even now, they still talk longingly of what they left behind: *Life in Utah is more laid back, not as crowded or hectic. . . . I grew up in Denver. There's importance to living in a community where you have roots. It's a question of stability and family.* (These are not the types of comments about home regions that I heard from nonwesterner reporters in Washington.) Yet they keep coming. Among the new arrivals, those who had been in Washington for a year or less, the percentage from the West (24.6) exceeded the region's share of the population (20.4). Part of the explanation is an increase in the number or size of western-based news organizations with Washington bureaus.[7]

Education

The differences in educational background also became more modest. By 1988 Washington reporters had almost reached the saturation point (98 percent) for college degrees, but other journalists were catching up. On daily newspapers across the United States, for example, 85 percent of all reporters

4. Daniel Patrick Moynihan, *Coping: Essays on the Practice of Government* (Random House, 1973), p. 319.

5. These discrepancies were somewhat more pronounced for the entire press corps than among the regional reporters. See Hess, *Washington Reporters*, p. 165.

6. The disparity between Washington regional reporters coming from the Northeast and the U.S. population from that region in 1978 was 11.9 percentage points, reduced to 4.2 points by 1988; in the West the disparity was down to 2.9 points from 6.1. The percentage of regional reporters from the North Central region increased 2.9 points and from the South 1.6 points between 1978 and 1988. For U.S. population projections by region, see Department of Commerce, 1989 *Statistical Abstract of the United States*, p. 20. Reporters' regions were determined by where they spent their childhood and where they were college undergraduates, with twice the weighting given to the former.

7. These include Bonneville, Chronicle, Donrey, Fisher, King, and KUTV (Salt Lake City).

were college graduates. In 1971 the figure was 63 percent, and in 1982 it was 74 percent.[8]

In 1978 there also had been a difference in what journalists inside and outside the Washington beltway had chosen to study. Although the academic major of choice throughout the rest of the United States was journalism, 62 percent of all Washington reporters and 54 percent of the capital's regional reporters had studied humanities or liberal arts. Nationwide, the figures became more lopsided over the next decade, largely because of the growth of television news, whose reporters were even more preponderantly journalism majors.[9] And the trend was now mirrored in Washington: 49 percent of Washington regional reporters had majored in journalism, a figure that combines 45 percent for those who worked for newspapers with 60 percent for the television reporters (appendix table B-25). Moreover, 60 percent of the regional reporters' graduate degrees were in journalism. Three-quarters of the undergraduate journalism majors who went on to graduate school studied journalism (but journalism majors were less likely to do graduate work than those who had majored in humanities and liberal arts or science and technology).

The changing educational backgrounds of Washington reporters can be seen most graphically in the youngest and oldest cohorts, those in their twenties and those fifty and older.

Undergraduate majors	Age 20–29	Age 50 and older
Humanities and liberal arts	41.9	58.3
Journalism	48.4	33.3
Science and technology	9.7	8.3

Majors in journalism education would be even more common had not so many of the younger Washington reporters attended highly selective colleges that do not have journalism departments. Fewer than one in ten of those who went to the most prestigious universities were journalism majors; but more than half of those from the least selective schools were.

The education of Washington reporters reflects that of the group from which they are drawn. Because it is rare for a journalist to begin a career in the capital, more Washington journalists have studied journalism because more journalists someplace else had studied journalism. More than 80 percent of the applications for entry-level news jobs nationwide now come

8. Data for 1988 are from Lee Stinnett, ed., *The Changing Face of the Newsroom* (Washington: American Society of Newspaper Editors, 1989), p. 119.
9. See Lee B. Becker, Jeffrey W. Fruit, and Susan L. Caudill, *The Training and Hiring of Journalists* (Norwood, N.J.: Ablex, 1987), p. 185.

from journalism majors.[10] Bachelor's degrees granted in the communications fields increased from 28,000 to 43,000 a year between 1980 and 1986, a rate of growth exceeded only by computer sciences.[11]

It is possible, of course, to be a journalist without having studied journalism, and some reporters in 1988 had unusual academic credentials. One who wrote for several small newspapers in Indiana had done graduate work in molecular biology. A television freelancer had earned a degree from Cornell in industrial and labor relations, and another television reporter, working for a chain of western stations, had a master's degree in business administration from Columbia. A wire service regional reporter had been an electrical engineering student at Duke as an undergraduate.

In 1978, news organizations had broadly hinted that they might go outside the ranks of journalists to staff their Washington bureaus. The need was for specialists, reporters whose training was not in interviewing sources and writing stories—those skills could be learned on the job, said editors— but in analyzing Supreme Court decisions or directions in health care policy or the sources of the national debt. Filling these needs is expensive, however, not necessarily because the reporters cost more (although they may) but because they cannot easily be transferred to other assignments when the demands of events call for reallocating resources.[12] Apparently sometime between the 1978 and 1988 studies, the desire for specialization slowed down, perhaps even stopped. The increased proportion of reporters who have majored in journalism may be one result. The journalism major, so out of fashion in 1978, would be 1988's ultimate generalist.

The dramatic proliferation of undergraduate and graduate backgrounds in journalism by the 1980s exemplifies what Everette Dennis has called a love-hate relationship between the news business and journalism educators.[13] The universities can supply the industry with a steady stream of workers, whose training it has not paid for, but the industry cannot agree on what training

10. For figures on radio and television reporters, see Vernon A. Stone, "J-Grad Quality and Entry-Level Hiring Surveyed," *Communicator*, vol. 43 (September 1989), p. 58; for newspaper reporters, see Christine Reid Veronis, "J-Curriculum Still in Debate," *presstime*, vol. 11 (September 1989), p. 49. Stone's survey showed that liberal arts majors were hired at the same rates as those who had studied some form of journalism.

11. Department of Commerce, 1989 *Statistical Abstract*, p. 157.

12. Stephen Hess, "A Washington Perspective: On the Rise of the Professional Specialist," *Communication*, vol. 8 (1985), pp. 165–81.

13. Everette E. Dennis, "Journalism Education," *presstime*, vol. 5 (September 1983), p. 7. For a useful brief history of journalism education in the United States, see David H. Weaver and Richard G. Gray, *Journalism and Mass Communication Research in the United States* (School of Journalism, Indiana University, 1979).

it wants the universities to supply. Still, most journalists aspire to professional status, and university training is one of the criteria that define professional standing.[14] The value of the training received, however, is in dispute.
One television reporter argued that studying TV journalism was a waste of
time because the technology changes so rapidly and its use varies greatly
depending on the size of the market. A journalism educator countered that
in the best academic programs the equipment and facilities are better than
tyro reporters would find at most of the smaller stations where they would
begin their careers. The journalism major thus has a headstart of up to a year
over the competing nonjournalism major. In a 1988 survey, two-thirds of
television and radio news directors claimed that journalism education had
provided their staffs with "solid training in basics"; the other third
complained that journalism education was "not much help."[15]

So in the course of a decade it became less common for Washington
reporters to have backgrounds in humanities and liberal arts and more
common to find vocationally oriented training, a development experienced
by the rest of the nation's journalists. In part this may reflect an increased
emphasis on professional education for Americans in all fields and in part
the special drive of women and minorities to get into journalism. And, of
course, as journalism becomes more technologically complex, there is more
to be taught. A humanities or liberal arts background was in keeping with
journalism as an occupation that was easy to get in to and out of. *The Washington Reporters* documented the drift of talented journalists away from journalism. Some of those interviewed contended that this was simply a
characteristic of a low-paying business. Reporters are better paid now. But
does the trend toward a major in journalism mean that reporters are likely to
remain longer in a profession than they did in a craft? Of the regional
reporters sampled in 1978, those who went to the most elite universities were
slightly less likely (3 percentage points) to have stayed in journalism than
those who went to the least selective universities, but humanities and liberal
arts majors were 2 percentage points more likely than journalism majors to
stay. Even more surprising, those who earned graduate degrees in humanities or liberal arts were much more likely to remain journalists (by 14.5
points) than those with graduate degrees in journalism.

---

14. An exception is a group of *Washington Post* employees who sued their paper not to be considered
professionals: as nonprofessionals they would be entitled to overtime pay. See *Sherwood* v. *Washington Post*,
U.S. District Court for the District of Columbia.
15. Stone, "J-Grad Quality," p. 58.

Gender

At the start of the 1970s, women made up just 20 percent of the employees of American news businesses. One woman for every four men. A decade later, women were a third of the work force. Two men, one woman. Obviously there are all sorts of differences disguised in these statistics. A third of the work force in broadcasting, for instance, included a lot of women in sales and very few women technicians.[16] There were also fewer women working for wire services and more working for weekly newspapers.[17] Yet in the two premier categories, television and daily newspapers, the ratio of men to women was two to one.

Indeed, by the mid–1980s, a University of Maryland study commenting on the increased number of women majoring in journalism caused a minor furor by suggesting that "journalism and related communications fields may become 'pink-collar ghettos.' "[18] Women became a majority of journalism majors for the first time in 1977 and made up 59 percent of the majors by 1985. By 1986 women comprised 64 percent of white journalism school graduates and 77 percent of minority graduates.

But the employment spurt of the 1970s stopped, and the number of women in both newspaper and television journalism stuck at a third throughout the 1980s. Although women were being hired at a proportionately higher rate, the male-female ratio held constant, suggesting that the turnover rate was higher for women than for men.[19] Whether women will

16. In 1988, women made up 13 percent of the technicians and 49 percent of the sales employees in broadcasting according to data supplied by Dwight M. Ellis, vice president, Department of Minority and Special Services, National Association of Broadcasters, 1989.

17. A 1982–83 survey shows that women comprise 19 percent of the work force at wire services and 42 percent at weekly newspapers. See Weaver and Wilhoit, *American Journalist*, p. 21. Since a group of women employees sued the Associated Press in 1978, however, settling five years later for more than $800,000 in back pay, women have made up 44 percent of AP's new hires, although they are still only a fourth of its work force. See Kay Mills, *A Place in the News: From the Women's Pages to the Front Page* (Dodd, Mead, 1988), pp. 151, 155.

18. Maurine H. Beasley and Kathryn T. Theus, *The New Majority* (University Press of America, 1988), p. 140. For the controversy caused by this report, see Susan H. Miller, "Was 'Pink Collar' Ghetto Study Deliberate Sensationalism?" *Editor & Publisher*, vol. 117 (November 23, 1984); Maurine H. Beasley, "In Defense of the 'Women in Journalism' Study," *Editor & Publisher*, vol. 118 (December 14, 1985); David Lawrence, "The Myth of the Pink Collar Ghetto," *Washington Journalism Review*, vol. 8 (January 1986) pp. 21–23; and Stephen Hess, "The Sex Test," *Columbia Journalism Review*, vol. 25 (March-April 1986) p. 45.

19. In a substantial 1988 survey, 28 percent of women newspaper journalists said they would "leave newspapering before they are 40, compared with 15 percent of the men." See Stinnett, ed., *Changing Face of the Newsroom*, p. 19. At the same time, however, there were modest improvements in the types of jobs women held. Eighteen percent of television operations and 26 percent of radio operations had women news directors in 1987, a significant increase from previous years. Women also gained forty-two more "directing editorships" of daily newspapers in 1988, although they filled less than 14 percent of all these jobs. See Lois Lauer Wolfe, "Women's Share of Directing Editor Jobs Increased Slightly in 1988," *ASNE Bulletin* (January 1989), p. 10–11; and Vernon A. Stone, "Minorities Gain in TV News, Lose in Radio," *Communicator*, vol. 43 (August 1989), p. 32.

reach numerical parity probably depends most on factors beyond the control of the news business. Between 1980 and 1987, men gained 8 percentage points in the U.S. labor force participation rate and women 18 points, yet the 1987 rate for men was 76 percent and only 56 percent for women.[20]

It is more difficult to measure statistically the progress that women journalists have made in Washington. An estimate can be made by counting first names of those accredited to the congressional press galleries, if one remains alert for women who have been given names such as Elder. But such a count must be used with caution because it would include some part-time journalists. Its value is to allow comparisons over time and measures of the relative permeability of the various news organizations or types of media. Judging, then, by the names of those who are entitled to use the congressional galleries, the number of women in the Washington press corps nearly doubled from 1979 to 1989, from 690 to 1,231, compared with a nationwide growth rate among women journalists of slightly more than 50 percent.[21]

Women made up a third of the galleries' members in 1989. A decade earlier, when they had made up a fourth, I wrote, "It can be assumed that the hiring of female reporters in Washington lags behind the rest of the United States by seven years."[22] It can now be assumed that Washington has caught up with the rest of the news industry, but the industry's population of women professionals lags behind the employment of women professionals in the rest of the nation by about 10 percent.

The subtotals for Washington journalism, however, continue to tell a story of some inequalities. Women in the Radio and Television Correspondents' Galleries increased from 24 percent of the members in 1979 to 29 percent in 1989. In the Press Galleries, where the daily newspaper reporters roam, the increase was from 23 percent to 26 percent, and in the Periodical Press Galleries, from 30 percent to 41 percent. However, aside from those working for the weekly newsmagazines, members of the periodical galleries represent newsletters and specialized publications, which suggests that women continue to make their greatest gains in the least prestigious branch of the news business.

Among other ten-year comparisons that can be gleaned from examining congressional gallery accreditation, women reporters at *Time*, *Newsweek*, and *U.S. News & World Report* have increased from 29 percent of the work

20. Department of Commerce, 1989 *Statistical Abstract*, pp. 376, 379.

21. These figures include journalists working for foreign news organizations, most of whom are not Americans. Foreign correspondents make up 9 percent of the women in the Senate and House Television Correspondents' Galleries and 8 percent of the women in the Senate and House Press Galleries.

22. Hess, *Washington Reporters*, p. 67.

force to 38 percent. At Associated Press and United Press International the increase has been 4 points, to 24 percent. At CBS, ABC, and NBC television the gain has been 2 points, to 26 percent, but women have become a majority in the newer CNN bureau. At National Public Radio they also do well (41 percent), prompting Nina Totenberg, its legal affairs correspondent, to credit an old-girl network, and evening news anchor Robert Siegel to explain that there are more women partly because "we are a low-paying news organization."[23]

One does, then, get an impression of progress. Partially it is "compared to what," in that gains have been less pronounced in other fields. Six percent of the members of the U.S. House of Representatives are women, two of one hundred U.S. senators, and less than 24 percent of the country's career diplomats.[24]

In moving from a consideration of women in U.S. journalism to women in Washington journalism to the gender of Washington regional reporters, it is well to recall a rule of the road from the earlier study: the more prestigious the beat, the smaller the percentage of women. Thus diplomacy, the premier assignment, had the fewest women in 1978 (2.6 percent) and the low-prestige domestic agencies the most (37.5 percent).

There were two exceptions. The Supreme Court was a high-prestige beat with a substantial number of women in its press corps. The assignment was understood to be important, but it was not fun because it relied on research in documents rather than interviews. Male reporters, unless they happened to have law degrees, would perhaps as soon let it be woman's work. The other exception was regional reporting, the beat lowest in prestige of the thirteen measured, which had a relatively small number of women (18.2 percent), probably because it was dominated by noninfluential independent newspapers. The influentials, such as the *New York Times* and the *Los Angeles Times*, had a national perspective; not many reporters were assigned to cover local angles. One wire service, UPI, had withdrawn from the regional news business, and chains were smaller—the McClatchy group, for instance, which now owns six papers and has five reporters in the capital, had three papers and a one-person bureau. But at most noninfluential independent newspapers, the Washington correspondent ranked high in the organization's pecking order. A job of such worth likely would be held by a man,

---

23. Quoted in Jean Gaddy Wilson, "Where Women Have a Real Voice," *Ms.*, December 1984, p. 46.
24. See Barbara Gamarekian, "Women Gain, but Slowly, in the Foreign Service," *New York Times*, July 28, 1989, p. B5; and E. J. Dionne, Jr., "Women Make Gains in Attaining Office," *New York Times*, August 8, 1989, p. A12.

perhaps a future editor or a senior employee who had lost out in the competition for editor.[25]

By 1988, women made up 26.8 percent of all regional reporters, still well below their representation in the journalism work force nationwide and in Washington. And the percentage was only as high as it was because of television. Before the advent of communications satellites the regional press corps consisted almost entirely of print reporters: of the eighty-eight Washington regional reporters surveyed in 1978, only four men and two women were in broadcast news. In 1988, a fourth of the reporters worked in radio or television and almost 40 percent of them were women. The percentage of women working for newspapers rose from 14.3 to 19.5 percent. The increase was so limited because the smaller papers, those with circulations of less than 100,000, employed Washington work forces in which just 15.6 percent of the reporters were women.[26]

Most women regional reporters in 1978 were in their twenties; in 1988 most were in their thirties. Were they the same people? To find out we located nine of the ten women who were originally surveyed. Two were no longer journalists: one was sailing in the South Pacific (a former colleague said she might return to journalism), and the other worked in Washington for a trade association. Two journalists now practice their craft in other cities. Five remained Washington journalists: one works for a specialized publication, one covers the White House for the *Washington Post*, and three are still regional reporters, two of whom have changed jobs.

The record reflects commitment in an industry with the reputation of having a high dropout rate. But with one exception, their record is not one of notable achievement, a point made in my earlier study: those who become superstars tend to come to Washington in their thirties after considerable seasoning at other posts. Thus the age distribution for women in 1988 more closely resembles the male pattern than it did in 1978, with both sexes now having the largest number of reporters in their thirties, which suggests that women now hold a higher place in journalism (appendix table B-26).

For men and women, Washington reporting is still a calling without senior citizens. Seven percent of the 1988 respondents were age fifty or older;

25. There was tradition here. In 1935, Leo C. Rosten found three women in the Washington press corps, one of whom was the correspondent for the *Daily Worker*. He also found that the 127 people he interviewed had held 74 editorships of various descriptions before coming to Washington. See *The Washington Correspondents* (1937; rprt. by Arno Press, 1974), pp. 312–23, 332.

26. Yet a 1989 national survey found that "ordinarily, the smaller the newspaper, the higher percentage of women employed." Press release, Women, Men, and Media Conference, Washington, D.C., April 10, 1989.

16 percent were in 1978. Most striking is the almost total absence of older women. Of the thirteen persons who were older than fifty, only one was a woman, a print reporter. Although nearly 40 percent of the television reporters were women, the oldest was forty-two. Only three of nineteen were older than forty, compared with 28 percent of the men. "There is no doubt that women face more pressure than men do on television in terms of appearance, age, and demeanor," Marlene Sanders, a former network correspondent, has commented. In *Waiting for Prime Time*, she and coauthor Marcia Rock calculated that although a third of local television news anchors are women, only 3 percent are older than forty. Half the male anchors are older than forty, and 16 percent are older than fifty.[27] The contrast between television and print journalism is striking: nearly half the women television reporters in our sample were in their twenties but only a quarter of the women newspaper reporters.

The men and women of regional reporting are college graduates, and a fourth have graduate degrees, most often M.A. degrees in journalism (appendix table B-26). They attended the nation's elite schools in equal numbers, one in five, the women going to such institutions as Harvard, Georgetown, Smith, University of Virginia, Wesleyan, Bryn Mawr, and the University of Pennsylvania. Generally, the women went to better schools, a statistic in keeping with that in the 1978 study. That almost half the men and women attended private colleges suggests that journalists, at least in Washington, often come from wealthier families.

Although majoring in journalism clearly has been an undergraduate trend, men and women are choosing this career-centered education at different rates. A decade ago 53 percent of women reporters but only 33 percent of the men had majored in journalism. By 1989, some 57 percent of the women had chosen journalism and 46 percent of the men. Women and men are equally uninterested in studying science and technology. Among print journalists there is now virtually no difference between the undergraduate majors of women and men (appendix table B-27). The 60 percent of television reporters who have been journalism majors is a compound of 52 percent for men and 74 percent for women. Otherwise the educational profiles of men and women seem to be blending, and distinc-

27. Marlene Sanders and Marcia Rock, *Waiting for Prime Time: The Women of Television News* (University of Illinois Press, 1988), pp. 147–48. For a history of women in broadcast journalism told largely through biography, see David H. Hosley and Gayle K. Yamada, *Hard News: Women in Broadcast Journalism* (Greenwood Press, 1987).

tions can be more accurately defined by whether they work in print or electronic media than by gender.

Men in 1988 had the same number of years of journalism experience as they had had in the 1978 survey; women were more experienced in 1988 by two and one-half years. An experience gap between the sexes was more pronounced in television than in newspaper journalism. Women usually had worked in journalism for five years before arriving in Washington, men nine years. On average, male regional reporters had been journalists for thirteen years, women for nine.

Race

On the professional level, minorities are doing better than women in the news business. Women made up 44 percent of the country's professional work force in 1987, yet remained a third of the journalism population. Minorities in 1987 accounted for 10 percent of U.S. professional workers.[28] The American Society of Newspaper Editors has stated that 7.5 percent of employees on daily newspapers in 1989 were members of minority groups (up from 4 percent in 1978).[29] The National Association of Broadcasters computed minority professional employment in radio and television in 1988 at 13 percent (up from 12 percent in 1980).[30] The NAB's figure for total minority employment, including technicians, salespersons, and others, is 17 percent, about a percentage point below the 1987 level of minorities in the U.S. civilian labor force (sixteen years and older).[31]

Unlike their record for hiring women—about the same for newspapers and television—print and electronic media show notable differences in employing minorities. Television employs nearly twice the percentage of minority professionals that newspapers do, apparently in part because significantly more black journalism students are interested in radio or television

28. Department of Commerce, 1989 *Statistical Abstract*, p. 388, includes subtotals for blacks (6.2 percent) and Hispanics (3.7 percent).

29. American Society of Newspaper Editors press release, April 12, 1989, which also states that minority figures contain "a slight overstatement" of about 0.3 percent. The survey includes supervisors, copy editors, reporters, and photographers.

30. National Association of Broadcasters, "1980 to 1988 Percentage Growth Analysis of Minority and White Female Employment in Total Commercial and Non-Commercial Broadcasting," n.d., p. 2. The survey is based on Federal Communications Commission data. Another survey, prepared for the Radio-Television News Directors Association, gives 1988 minority employment as 16 percent for commercial television stations, 8 percent for commercial radio stations, and 17 percent for public radio. These data reflect a 3-percentage-point increase in television and a 5-point decline in radio since 1972. See Stone, "Minorities Gain in TV News, Lose in Radio," p. 32.

31. Department of Commerce, 1989 *Statistical Abstract*, p. 38.

careers (nearly 35 percent) than in working for daily newspapers (5 percent).[32] But the bigger the operation—television station or newspaper—the higher the percentage of minority journalists. Papers with circulations higher than 500,000 had 7 percent minority work forces in 1980 and 12.5 percent by 1989. Papers with circulations lower than 5,000 had 2.8 percent in 1980 and 4.7 percent in 1989 In the top twenty-five television markets, 1988 minority employment was 20 percent of the work force for network affiliates, 29 percent for independent stations.

Supervisory personnel at newspapers rose from 4 percent to 14 percent of the minority work force between 1978 and 1989; white supervisors increased from 13 percent to 24 percent of the white work force. About 8 percent of television news directors in 1988 were from minority groups, nearly half Hispanic men.

The Washington national reporters in 1978 were 96 percent white. Of the eighty-eight regional reporters surveyed, there was one minority respondent, a black woman. Minority employment on the regional beat lagged behind the overall level of minority employment in the Washington press corps because regional news at the time was dominated by smaller newspapers. (The best records for minority hiring were in television and at prestige organizations.) When resurveyed in 1988, minorities made up 5 percent of the regional reporters, but that was still below the national average. The gain was largely from television, whose 8 percent minority employment was twice that of newspapers, and the movement to group-owned newspapers, which performed slightly better than independent newspapers.[33]

Generalizing on the basis of modest numbers is a risky proposition. The 1988 sample included five black men, two black women, one Hispanic man, and two Hispanic women. Still, the figures are in line with national statistics, which show that 44 percent of minority newspaper journalists are women, compared with 34 percent women among nonminority journalists; 39 percent of all minority journalists are women and 29 percent of the nonminority journalists.[34] The same trend emerges for Washington regional reporters: 40 percent in the minority population are women but only 26

32. See Weaver and Wilhoit, *American Journalist*, p. 22. Also see Becker, Fruit, and Caudill, *Training and Hiring of Journalists*, p. 56.

33. The improvement at chains, however, is mainly from one organization, Gannett, the employer of two of the sample's ten minority journalists, one print reporter and one television reporter. Gannett now has the reputation of being the media company that is most aggressive in hiring minorities, with its managers' annual bonuses linked to their success at meeting equal opportunity goals. See Johnnie L. Roberts, "Gannett Surpasses Other Newspaper Firms in the Hiring and Promotion of Minorities," *Wall Street Journal*, May 11, 1988, p, 23.

34. Sandra D. Petykiewicz, "Love the Job! Like the Newspaper!" *ASNE Bulletin*, (July-August 1989), p. 9.

percent among whites. All of which suggests that there is still a "two-fer" phenomenon in the news business. Organizations prefer women to men when they hire minorities because they can take credit for two appointments with one job. This is especially true of on-camera positions where the color and gender are most obvious: minority women are more likely to be reporters or anchors, causing one media scholar to talk about "the vanishing minority man."[35] Nevertheless, the plight of the minority male journalist in Washington is much improved since 1978, when 53 percent of minority journalists were women.

The 1988 data also reflect the emergence in mainstream journalism of Hispanic reporters, invisible in the 1978 study. Nationally, Hispanics now represent a quarter of the minority population in both radio and television; on daily newspapers they represent a third. Combining blacks and Hispanics in the 1988 figures may veil the degree to which blacks are falling further behind (7 persons in a survey of 190). A caveat is that Washington regional reporting is least important at those national news outlets that are most under pressure to hire minorities.

The educational profiles of minority and majority journalists in Washington were similar in 1988, as they had been in 1978: nearly all were college graduates, with about the same amount of graduate training, and had attended public or private institutions in the same ratio (only one respondent went to a black college). The level of the colleges was now the same, whereas in 1978 more whites went to "highly selective" schools and 53 percent of blacks went to schools that were "not selective."

Minority journalists have become considerably more vocationally oriented in their schooling than they were in 1978 and are now much more likely than their white counterparts to have been journalism majors. Seven of ten minority reporters majored in journalism as undergraduates and the two graduate degrees were in journalism. The accent on journalism education was not a product of the greater interest in television among minority journalists.

One notable difference among minority journalists is that the newspaper reporters were sent to Washington by their organizations, but television reporters found their own jobs in Washington. Five of the six newspaper reporters appeared to be on fast tracks. Mike Frisbee of the *Boston Globe*, for example, was covering presidential campaign politics, a prime assignment.

35. See Ernie Schultz, "The FCC EEO Conference: Building the Right Mirror to Reflect Our Society," *Communicator*, vol. 43 (April 1989), p. 42. Also see "Ellis Reports Hiring Shifts," *Broadcasting*, February 17, 1986, pp. 72–73.

The sixth print reporter was in Washington as part of a training program for minority journalists and has since joined a good newspaper in another city. The four television reporters, on the other hand, had résumés similar in degree to that of the woman who, at age thirty-five, had worked for five outlets in four cities in thirteen years. Each move was into a bigger market. For minority newspaper journalists, and perhaps for newspaper reporters regardless of race, Washington is often an important rung on an ascending ladder, whereas in television the reporters are more often on their own, changing employers and even cities to get ahead.

Half the newspaper journalists in the survey worked for papers that rank among the country's one hundred largest, with circulations of 115,000 or more. In line with national figures, the percentage of minority Washington journalists on large papers was double what it was for minorities on small papers.

The minority reporters in 1988 were mostly in their thirties, those in 1978 mostly in their twenties. (Just as we discovered with women reporters, these are not the same journalists merely a decade older.) The oldest was age 38, while nearly a quarter of the white reporters were older than 40; but the gap was small, a mean age of 36.4 years for whites, 32.7 for minorities. Whites and minorities had the same amount of pre-Washington journalism experience, nearly 8 years; women had 5 years.

Logic might dictate that employment of minorities and women would rise in tandem because similar arguments for catch-up hiring and promotion apply. Yet women made gains nationally and in Washington in the first half of the 1980s, then stopped. Minorities' gains seem to have followed. The two movements may be unrelated. Or it may be that the news industry, as one president of the United States is supposed to have said of another president of the United States, can't chew gum and walk at the same time.

Television and Print Journalists

What was notable about newspaper and television reporters in Washington in 1978 was how much they resembled one another. Most television journalists were network correspondents; only 1 percent of the national press corps then worked for television stations. Thirty-five percent of network reporters and 38 percent of the newspaper reporters held graduate degrees, attendance at highly selective universities was about the same, and majors were in humanities and liberal arts and journalism with almost identical frequency. Network people were not especially young: nearly 20 percent

were age fifty or older, compared with 15 percent of their newspaper counterparts. The older generation of reporters seemed alike because they were
alike. Television journalists had learned their trade at newspapers and wire
services. All were equally and overwhelmingly white and male.

The new television reporters in Washington, on the other hand, the journalists who work for or service local stations throughout the United States,
are significantly different from those who cover the same stories for newspapers. Although the average age of television and newspaper reporters is
nearly the same, 35.1 and 36.6 years, the figures come from adding up very
different columns of numbers.[36] Television has twice the percentage of
reporters in their twenties and half the percentage of reporters older than fifty
(appendix table B-29). The so-called pretty face syndrome, which was not
reflected in the 1978 count of national reporters, is now clearly evident from
the proportion of younger persons among those who work for local television.

Almost all reporters are college graduates, but about twice the percentage
of newspaper reporters have earned graduate degrees, which is explained
perhaps by the larger number of young people among video reporters who
may yet go back to school. Young television reporters are now more likely to
have majored in journalism; and newspaper reporters in the humanities and
liberal arts. Nor is there any longer a similarity among schools attended:
newspaper reporters went to much better and much worse institutions.

In short, there are two distinct profiles, two career tracks. For the forty-
eight broadcast reporters interviewed for the 1988 survey, radio and television jobs were relatively interchangeable early in their careers. A number of
reporters also had brief experiences in politics, working in a campaign or as
press secretary to a public official. But only five indicated that they had ever
worked in print journalism, and they were older. There would be no replace-
ment generation for the Eric Sevareids, David Brinkleys, Daniel Schorrs,
and John Chancellors, who were nurtured in print journalism before
switching to radio and television.[37]

Yet, of course, all television reporters are not from the same mold.
Reporters in the Washington bureaus of broadcast groups—Cox or King or

36. The closeness of the ages may be partly attributed to the fact that the survey included eighteen TV
reporters who were also bureau chiefs (mean age 39.1 years).

37. Having to admit error in expecting in 1980 that the future would hold markedly increased levels of
subject specialization in the Washington press corps, I can take some comfort in having correctly predicted
that "the demarcation between print and television will become more pronounced, and reporters' skills [will
be] less transferable." See *Washington Reporters*, p. 31.

other collections of stations with the same ownership—are statistically different from those employed by the services that have freelance arrangements with a shifting clientele of stations. The freelancers are younger and more apt to have been journalism majors; they have less experience and are twice as likely to be women. In the pecking order of Washington broadcast journalism, reporters try to move from freelance work to positions with stations, although there is also a small cadre of highly entrepreneurial permanent freelancers and some others (mostly in radio) who have personal reasons for preferring a more flexible work schedule. There are even reporters who do freelance work for freelance reporters.

The desired career pattern among Washington newspaper journalists, to move from regional to national reporting, from home office to capital, is not necessarily the pattern desired by broadcast journalists. Not every television reporter wants to go from local news to the networks or from a station to a Washington bureau. When asked about their aspirations, less than a fifth of the print reporters wished to leave Washington, but almost a third of the television reporters saw their futures elsewhere. The responses need to be put in context: this was a time of considerable turmoil at the networks: *There's no security there. . . . The networks are not a happy place to be.* Even in the best of times, however, some regional reporters would have expressed reservations about working for the networks. *Involuntary transfers, too much travel. I don't want to live out of a suitcase. . . . Only a select few get on the air. What do the others do all day? Sit there vegetating?* The trade-off was frequently stated: *I get on the air all the time.* Two reporters moved from the Washington bureaus of local stations to the networks during the period of this study; five of the regional broadcast reporters surveyed had worked in network television. Jan McDaniel, for example went from news assignment manager for the Washington bureau of CBS News in 1984 to Washington bureau chief of Chronicle Broadcasting (owner of stations in San Francisco, Wichita, and Omaha), to news director of KAKE-TV, Chronicle's Wichita station in 1988. Jim Compton, Washington bureau chief of King Broadcasting (owner of stations in Seattle, Portland, Spokane, and Boise) from 1976 to 1979, commented, "I went to NBC because of bigger challenges, more money, and travel. I worked in Egypt for six or seven years. Then I came to Seattle because I was fed up with being on the road and waking up in hotels in Africa." He now does political commentary for King's Seattle station. Clearly there is no single or simple hierarchy of jobs.

Independent Newspapers and Newspaper Groups

In 1978 there were significant differences in the profiles of print journalists employed in the Washington bureaus of independent newspapers and those who worked for newspaper chains.[38] The reporters at the chains, for instance, had gone to much less prestigious universities and were much more likely to have attended public institutions (appendix table B-30). When asked about their employment preferences, Washington reporters had very different feelings about whether they wanted to work for independents or chains.[39] Perhaps because only 30 percent of daily newspapers were still independently owned by 1986 (down from 68 percent in 1960), the reporters of 1988 were no longer as interested in this distinction.[40] At any rate, in the second survey the only major differences between reporters at the chains and at the independent bureaus were that more reporters in their twenties worked for the chains and more reporters older than age fifty for the independents. Even these differences seem to result more from the size of the newspapers than from their corporate ownership. When reporters are grouped by the circulation of the papers they write for, regardless of whether the papers are independents or part of a chain, there is the same age-distribution pattern: the papers with large circulations have fewer young and more old reporters (appendix table B-31). Otherwise, differences in the profiles—undergraduate majors, graduate degrees, selectivity of universities attended, whether they were public or private institutions—for chain and independent newspapers have nearly disappeared. In 1978, for instance, 21 percent of the independents' reporters and 41 percent of the chains' reporters had gone to schools that were not selective, but ten years later the comparable percentages were 39 for the independents and 31 for the chains.

Regional Reporters

Newspaper reporters on Washington's regional beat vary from a twenty-three-year-old working at one of the smallest and least prestigious chain bureaus to Edgar Poe, called Mr. Poe by other reporters, now in his eighties,

---

38. This study does not use the standard definition of groups or chains, which is "two or more daily newspapers in different cities under the same principal ownership or control"; see *Editor & Publisher's Yearbook* 1988, p. I-375. Rather, I use Washington bureaus as the unit of measurement: for example, *Newsday, Baltimore Sun, Hartford Courant,* and *Los Angeles Times* are counted as independents because they have separate operations, even though they are owned by the Times-Mirror Company.

39. Hess, *Washington Reporters*, pp. 155–56.

40. See John C. Busterna, "Trends in Daily Newspaper Ownership," *Journalism Quarterly,* vol. 65 (Winter 1988), p. 834.

who wrote his first story from Washington on Easter Sunday 1930, and now writes a column of regional news for the *New Orleans Times-Picayune*. Between these two extremes are the regional reporters working for elite chains, ambitious to become national correspondents, at which time other ambitious reporters will be sent to Washington to take over their regional beats. There are also those who will become frustrated and drift out of journalism, perhaps to better-paying jobs in public relations; those who will return to their home papers as editors, or go to some other paper if they work for a chain; and a small number, like Mr. Poe, who love Washington regional reporting and cannot think of a better way to spend a lifetime.

The regional reporter of 1978 and the regional reporter of 1988 would be recognized on sight as of the same parentage. Ten years after the initial study the "average" reporter was a white male, thirty-six years old, more likely to have grown up in the Middle West than in another region of the country, and the graduate of a good (though not great) university (appendix table B-25). He was more likely than his 1978 counterpart to have gone to a public school, to have majored in journalism, and to have an advanced degree. He was still not interested in science. Yet subtle distinctions suggest that regional reporters—who sometimes think of themselves as the Rodney Dangerfields of the Washington press corps—have gained in status.

Although the mean age shrank by only a year over the decade—the average regional reporter in 1978 had been thirty-seven years old—the age distribution of the reporters was substantially different and a surer sign of prestige. There is an informal seniority system at play in Washington journalism: other things being equal, reporters gradually rise to assignments of higher standing. Thus, as a measure of this phenomenon, the more young people on a beat, the lower it ranks. On the diplomatic beat, of highest esteem, 5 percent of the reporters were younger than thirty in 1978, and 7 percent of the White House reporters; but 34 percent of the regional reporters were in their twenties, the highest percentage among the thirteen beats examined. So there is special significance when just 16 percent of the regional reporters in the 1988 survey are in their twenties.[41]

The regional reporters sent to Washington by their organizations—two out of three in 1988—are older and more experienced, which reflects the desirability of the assignment. Even among those who had been in Wash-

41. Although the presence of young reporters is a sign of a beat's low prestige, the presence of reporters older than fifty is not necessarily a sign of high prestige. In 1978, for example, 17 percent of the reporters on the high-prestige White House beat and 16 percent on the low-prestige regional beat were older. The decline among older regional reporters to 7 percent in 1988 is related more to the greater number of television reporters, women, and minorities in the sample.

ington a year or less, two-thirds were between 30 and 39 years old. The 1978 regional reporter had been a journalist for 6.4 years before arriving in Washington, the 1988 reporter for 8 years. And what is true of newspaper reporters is also true of those sent by television stations, whose average age and experience were about the same. It is only the freelancers who lower the age and experience levels in Washington television regional reporting.

The increased prestige of regional reporters is also suggested by their moonlighting activities. A strange measurement, perhaps, but the 1978 study showed that reporters who do the most outside work are of higher status—older, above average in terms of graduate training and the selectivity of the schools they attended, and working more important beats. In 1978 one in five regional reporters was also freelancing; ten years later it was one in three. A reporter for a western newspaper used his spare time to write articles on environmental issues, an East Coast newspaperman to write for military magazines, a journalist for a newspaper in the South to work as backup reporter for a weekly newsmagazine, a wire service reporter to write travel pieces. The boom in freelancing, however, was unconnected to the growth of regional and city magazines.[42] Only one newspaper reporter, from California, had contributed to a publication of this type.

When defining prestige in Washington journalism, the 1978 study found a strong correlation with travel. All of the high-prestige beats except law involve a great deal of time on the road. "The more exotic the travel, the more attractive the beat. As in the game of paper covers rock and scissors cut paper, Katmandu covers Peoria and Timbuktu cuts Ashtabula."[43] The 1978 regional reporter stayed home, averaging fewer than twelve days a year out of Washington on assignment; this figure jumped to twenty-one days in 1988. Much of the increase relates to the presidential election year: a *Hartford Courant* reporter who said he normally traveled ten days a year was away ten times that number covering candidates, primaries, and national conventions. But there was exotic travel as well. Various reporters claimed they did stories from Cuba, the Soviet Union, Israel, and the South Pacific.

Additionally, reporters now seem to produce more. As a rule of thumb, the reporter who writes lots of short pieces is not esteemed in Washington journalism. Reporters want time and space. The 1978 regional reporter produced nine stories a week, usually 500 words in length; ten years later,

42. See Martin Morse Wooster, "A Nation Divided: The Regional Magazine Boom," *Public Opinion*, vol. 11 (March-April 1989), pp. 12–15; and Mary A. Anderson, "City Magazines Compete for Elite," *presstime*, vol. 122 (July 1989), pp. 16–19.
43. Hess, *Washington Reporters*, p. 51.

the stories were longer than 700 words and the reporters averaged almost seven stories a week.

Also, and importantly, by the late 1980s—with a Republican president and a Democratic Congress, as well as a good scandal, Iran-contra—it was a much better time for a reporter to be "Live from Capitol Hill!"

Appendix B

Tables

THE TABLES listed in this appendix follow the sequence in which the subjects are discussed in the text. Table titles are grouped according to the chapter in which they are first mentioned, although some data appear in more than one chapter.

Live from Capitol Hill!

B-1. Washington Stories on Local Television, by Type, 1979-85
B-2. Institutions in Television Stories, and Participants Seen and Mentioned, 1979-85
B-3. National and Local Television Cameras at Senate Hearings, by Type of Committee, February 1979–June 1985
B-4. Ranking of Senate Committees by Number of National and Local Television Cameras Covering Them, February 1979–June 1985
B-5. Length of Stories on Local Television News, by Location and Washington Bureau Operation
B-6. Appearances of Public Officials on Local Television News, by Station Market Size and Washington Bureau Operation
B-7. Appearances, by type, of Public Officials on Local Television News
B-8. Government and Political Stories on Local Television News, by Focus of Story, Station Market Size, and Washington Bureau Operation

Do Press Secretaries Change Light Bulbs?

B-9. Rank of Press Secretaries in Senate Offices, by Senator Characteristic, 1989
B-10. Average Number of Media Activities in Senate Offices, by Senator Characteristic, October 1988

The Lowly Press Release

The Lordly Op-Ed Piece

The Washington Reporters Ten Years Later

B-28. Regional Print Reporters, 1978, 1988, and Regional Broadcast
Reporters, 1988, by Characteristic

B-29. Regional Reporters Working for Independent Newspapers and
Newspaper Chains, by Characteristic, 1978, 1988

B-30. Regional Reporters Working for Large and Small Newspapers,
by Characteristic, 1988

B-31. Regional Reporters, by Characteristic and Age Group, 1988

B-32. Regional Reporters Working in Broadcast and Print Journalism,
by Characteristic and Age Group, 1988

B-33. Regional Reporters' Years of Experience, by Sex and Type of News
Organization, 1988

B-34. Regional Reporters' Coverage of Executive and Legislative Branches,
by Type of News Organization, 1988

B-35. Regional Reporters' Coverage of House and Senate, by Type of
News Organization, 1988

Key to Tables B-25 through B-35

1978. The figures on regional reporters in 1978 differ from those
presented in *The Washington Reporters* (pp. 156-57 and elsewhere) because
the earlier data have been recoded to conform with the definition of regional
reporters used here. Thus there were 79 regional reporters in the first survey
and 88 regional reporters in tables B-25 through B-35.

1988. To create a stratified sample that accurately reflects the percentage
of women and minorities in this population, a few interviews were
conducted in 1989.

Regional background. This scale combines the answers to two questions:
where reporters spent their childhood years and where they went to college
as undergraduates, with twice the weighting given to the former. In 1978 the
regional breakdown of the U.S. population was Northeast 23.0 percent,
North Central 26.6 percent, South 32.3 percent, West 18.1 percent. *Statistical Abstract of the United States, 1989* (p. 20) estimates that these percentages in 1987 were Northeast 20.7, North Central 24.5, South 34.5 and West
20.4. *Northeast* includes Maine, New Hampshire, Vermont, Massachusetts,
Rhode Island, Connecticut, New York, New Jersey, and Pennsylvania.
North Central includes Ohio, Indiana, Illinois, Michigan, Wisconsin,
Minnesota, Iowa, Missouri, North Dakota, South Dakota, Nebraska, and
Kansas. *South* includes Delaware, Maryland, District of Columbia,

Virginia, West Virginia, North Carolina, South Carolina, Georgia, Florida, Kentucky, Tennessee, Alabama, Mississippi, Arkansas, Louisiana, Oklahoma, and Texas. *West* includes Montana, Idaho, Wyoming, Colorado, New Mexico, Arizona, Utah, Nevada, Washington, Oregon, California, Alaska, and Hawaii.

College selectivity. This rating system was devised by James Cass and Max Birnbaum, *Comparative Guide to American Colleges* (Harper and Row 1977). Their two top categories are here combined, and schools they do not list are rated *not selective.* The ranking is based on "the percentage of applicants accepted by the college, the average test scores of recent freshman classes, the ranking of recent freshmen in their high school classes, and other related data."

Field of study. *Humanities and liberal arts* includes English, literature, creative writing, history, political science, government, other humanities and social sciences, and general liberal arts. *Science and technology* includes mathematics, physical and biological sciences, agriculture, economics, business, education, law, medicine, and accounting. *Journalism*, the third category, includes all majors in the communication field.

Print. In addition to newspaper reporters, this category includes others who work for Associate Press, United Press International, and States News Service.

Broadcast. This category is almost synonymous with television. It includes, however, one reporter who files exclusively for radio and several who report for both radio and TV.

Chains and independent newspapers. Reporters are coded as working for independent newspapers if their Washington operation services only one outlet, regardless of whether the parent corporation owns other newspapers. For example, reporters for the *Hartford Courant* and the *Des Moines Register* are counted as working for independent newspapers even though the papers are owned by Times-Mirror and Gannett, respectively.

Large and small newspapers. The 100 largest-circulation newspapers have been put in the *large* category. The dividing line is a weekday circulation of about 115,000.

Table B-1. Washington Stories on Local Television, by Type, 1979–85[a]
Percent

Type	1979	1980	1981	1982	1983	1984	1985	Average
Legislators from station's locale								
Senate	0(0)	42.5(50)	56(60)	57(60)	41(45)	45(48)	47(50)	47(50)
House	100(100)	57.5(50)	44(40)	43(40)	59(55)	55(52)	53(50)	53(50)
Stories about Congress								
Senate	0	61	64	60	48	50	55	54
House	100	39	36	40	52	50	45	46
Stories about Congress and executive branch								
Congress	25	38	44	59	56	52	55	54
Executive	75	62	56	41	44	48	45	46
Emphasis of stories about senators								
Local	0	50	46	44	46	48	53	49
National	0	50	54	56	54	52	47	51

SOURCES: The Washington bureaus included in tables B-1 and B-2 are Belo (WFAA, Dallas); Bonneville (KIRO, Seattle; KSL, Salt Lake City); Chronicle (KAKE, Wichita; WOWT, Omaha; KRON, San Francisco); Cox (KTVU, San Francisco–Oakland; WHIO, Dayton; WKBD, Detroit; WSB, Atlanta; WSOC, Charlotte; WFTV, Orlando; WPXI, Pittsburgh); Fisher (KOMO, Seattle; KATU, Portland); Jefferson Pilot (WBTV, Charlotte; WWBT, Richmond); King (KING, Seattle; KREM, Spokane; KGW, Portland; KTVB, Boise); KUTV (Salt Lake City); Outlet (KOVR, Sacramento; WCMH, Columbus; WCPX, Orlando; KSAT, San Antonio; WJAR, Providence); Storer (KCST, San Diego; WJKW, Cleveland; WTVG, Toledo; WJBK, Detroit; WITI, Milwaukee; WAGA, Atlanta); and two independent news services, Newsfeed and Potomac, which did stories in these states: Alabama (4 stations), Alaska (1), Arizona (3), Arkansas (3), California (1), Connecticut (2), Florida (10), Georgia (4), Idaho (1), Illinois (5), Indiana (7), Iowa (5), Kansas (3), Kentucky (5), Louisiana (3), Maine (2), Maryland (2), Massachusetts (5), Michigan (4), Minnesota (2), Mississippi (2), Missouri (8), Nebraska (1), Nevada (3), New Hampshire (2), New Mexico (2), New York (6), North Carolina (5), North Dakota (2), Ohio (9), Oklahoma (5), Pennsylvania (4), South Carolina (4), South Dakota (3), Tennessee (7), Texas (12), Utah (1), Washington (3), West Virginia (1), Wisconsin (4).

a. Numbers in parentheses are percentage of time only mentioned.

Table B-2. Institutions in Television Stories, and Participants Seen and Mentioned, 1979–85[a]

Institutions and participants	1979	1980	1981	1982	1983	1984	1985	Total
Institutions								
Senate	0	17	171	268	381	378	556	1,771
House	1	11	95	177	418	376	459	1,537
Senate and House	1	16	59	100	202	242	289	909
Executive and Congress	0	31	321	357	611	537	882	2,739
Executive	6	82	464	321	707	884	1,013	3,477
Other	4	32	98	140	492	547	543	1,856
Participants								
Senator from region	0	17(13)	258(95)	337(183)	608(207)	641(207)	1,173(250)	3,034(949)
House member from region	2(0)	23(7)	202(31)	253(91)	887(120)	778(127)	1,303(132)	3,448(508)
Other members of Congress	1(2)	14(9)	93(69)	131(112)	371(147)	366(184)	460(112)	1,436(635)
Locals	6(0)	37(14)	253(35)	259(83)	693(107)	768(161)	1,527(164)	3,543(564)
Executive branch	0(4)	44(56)	329(368)	190(356)	637(535)	726(432)	1,055(651)	2,981(2,402)
White House	0(4)	8(48)	87(349)	41(303)	116(451)	133(385)	243(558)	628(2,098)

SOURCES: See table B-1.

[a] Numbers in parentheses are participants mentioned only. Senators and House members are from the area in which the story is seen; other members of Congress are legislators from outside the area where the story is seen; locals are governors, mayors, and others visiting Washington from a station's market; White House, a subtotal of executive branch, includes the president, vice president, national security adviser, director of the Office of Management and Budget, and White House staff members.

Table B-3. National and Local Television Cameras at Senate Hearings, by Type of Committee, February 1979–June 1985

Committee	National cameras[a]	Local cameras[a]
Policy		
Foreign Relations	780	313
Judiciary	491	636
Budget	302	109
Labor and Human Resources	228	363
Governmental Affairs	214	239
Joint Economic	207	146
Intelligence	39	5
Total	2,261 (61.8)	1,811 (49.4)
Policy/Constituency		
Finance	219	304
Armed Services	201	121
Banking, Housing, and Urban Affairs	132	152
Total	552 (15.1)	577 (15.7)
Constituency		
Appropriations	226	219
Energy and Natural Resources	154	257
Commerce, Science, and Technology	137	288
Environment and Public Works	87	163
Agriculture, Nutrition, and Forestry	63	96
Aging	36	59
Veterans' Affairs	10	30
Small Business	6	27
Indian Affairs	1	23
Total	720 (19.7)	1,162 (31.7)
Housekeeping		
Ethics	89	95
Rules	36	24
Total	125 (3.4)	119 (3.2)

SOURCES: Tables B-3 and B-4 are based on information provided by the Senate Radio and Television Gallery. The figures for national television consist of ABC, CBS, NBC, CNN, "MacNeil/Lehrer Newshour" (PBS), "Lawmakers" (PBS), and "Capitol Journal" (PBS). The figures for local TV do not include certain freelance cameras that we believe were covering hearings for non-news clients. The policy-constituency typology comes from Steven S. Smith and Christopher J. Deering, *Committees in Congress* (Washington: CQ Press, 1984). Modest figures for the Select Committee on Intelligence do not reflect lack of news media interest but rather that most of the committee's hearings are closed to the press.

a. Numbers in parentheses are percentages of total cameras.

Table B-4. Ranking of Senate Committees by Number of National and Local Television Cameras Covering Them, February 1979–June 1985

National cameras	Number	Local cameras	Number
Foreign Relations	780	Judiciary	636
Judiciary	491	Labor	363
Budget	302	Foreign Relations	313
Labor	228	Finance	304
Appropriations	226	Commerce	288
Finance	219	Energy	257
Governmental Affairs	214	Governmental Affairs	239
Joint Economic	207	Appropriations	219
Armed Services	201	Environment	163
Energy	154	Banking	152
Commerce	137	Joint Economic	146
Banking	132	Armed Services	121
Ethics	89	Budget	109
Environment	87	Agriculture	96
Agriculture	63	Ethics	95
Intelligence	39	Aging	59
Aging	36	Veterans' Affairs	30
Rules	36	Small Business	27
Veterans' Affairs	10	Rules	24
Small Business	6	Indian Affairs	23
Indian Affairs	1	Intelligence	5

Sources: See table B-3.

Table B-5. Length of Stories on Local Television News, by Location and Washington
Bureau Operation

Story	Number of stories	Mean (seconds)	Range (seconds)
All government and political stories	249	74.1	7–358
Location of stories			
International (out of United States)	32	59.4	12–322
Washington	104	61.1	7–251
National (out of state)	116	72.9	7–261
State (out of city)	42	70.6	18–199
Local (site of station)	59	87.2	19–358
Bureau operation			
Stations with Washington bureau	103	76.9	7–322
National focus	50	76.8	n.a.
Local focus	53	91.3	n.a.
Stations without Washington bureau	146	72.2	10–358
National focus	55	69.6	n.a.
Local focus	91	84.8	n.a.

SOURCES: Tables B-5 through B-8 include local newscasts from the following 57 stations in 35 cities: Los Angeles (KABC, KNBC, KNXT), San Francisco (KRON), Boston (WNEV, WCVB), Detroit (WDIV, WJBK), Cleveland (WEWS, WJKW, WKYC), Pittsburgh (WPXI), Minneapolis (WCCO, KARE), Atlanta (WAGA), Seattle (KIRO, KING, KSTW), Baltimore (WMAR, WJZ, WBAL), Sacramento (KCRA, KXTV, KOVR), Cincinnati (WLWT), Milwaukee (WITI), Greenville, S.C. (WYFF), Salt Lake City (KSL), Dayton (WHIO), Albany (WTEN, WNYT), Charlottesville, Va. (WVIR), Richmond, Va. (WWBT), Wichita (KAKE), Roanoke (WDBJ, WSLS), Lynchburg, Va. (WSET), Syracuse, N.Y. (WSTM, WIXT), Green Bay, Wis. (WFRV, WBAY), Omaha (WOWT), Rochester, N.Y. (WROC, WHEC, WOKR), Harrisburg, Ill. (WSIL), Paducah, Ky. (WPSD), Champaign, Ill. (WCIA, WICD, WAND), Lexington, Ky. (WLEX), South Bend, Ind. (WNDU, WSBT), Springfield, Mass. (WGGB), Washington, N.C. (WITN), Ft. Myers, Fla. (WINK), and Grand Junction, Colo. (WREY).
   n.a. Not available.

Table B-6. Appearances of Public Officials on Local Television News, by Station Market Size and Washington Bureau Operation
Percent

Market size and bureau operation	Participants			Legislature		Branch of government	
	President	Senators	House members	Senators	House members	Executive	Legislative
Number of appearances	52	67	26	67	26	90	93
Top 10 markets[a]	40.0	57.1	2.9	95.2	4.8	52.3	47.7
Top 25 markets[b]	40.2	46.1	13.7	77.0	23.0	52.0	48.0
Middle markets (26–70 ranking)[c]	25.8	58.1	16.1	75.0	25.0	43.9	56.1
Small markets (71–180 ranking)[d]	27.3	18.2	54.5	25.0	75.0	42.7	57.1
All markets[e]	35.9	46.2	17.9	72.0	28.0	49.2	50.8
Stations with Washington bureaus	38.9	47.2	13.9	77.3	22.7	51.6	48.4
Stations using Washington freelance services	47.6	28.6	23.8	54.5	45.5	63.3	36.7
No Washington bureaus	32.9	45.2	21.9	67.3	32.7	46.7	53.3

SOURCES: See table B-5.
a. 11 stations, 5 cities, 14 hours of broadcasts.
b. 24 stations, 11 cities, 31 hours of broadcasts.
c. 18 stations, 14 cities, 15.5 hours of broadcasts.
d. 15 stations, 10 cities, 13.5 hours of broadcasts.
e. 57 stations, 35 cities, 60 hours of broadcasts.

Table B-7. Appearances, by Type, of Public Officials on Local Television News
Percent

Participant and institution	Number of appearances	Seen and heard	Seen and not heard	Mentioned only
President	52	40.4	23.1	36.5
Senators	67	58.2	28.4	13.4
House members	26	46.2	34.6	19.2
Governors	35	40.0	25.7	34.3
Mayors	20	50.0	5.0	45.0
Executive branch	90	100.0	100.0	100.0
President	52	65.6	57.1	51.4
Others	38	34.4	42.8	48.6
Legislative branch	93	100.0	100.0	100.0
Senators	67	76.5	67.9	64.3
House members	26	23.5	32.1	35.7
Executive and legislative	183	100.0	100.0	100.0
Executive	90	38.6	42.9	72.5
Legislative	93	61.4	57.1	27.5
President and legislative	145	100.0	100.0	100.0
President	52	29.2	30.0	57.6
Senators	67	54.2	47.5	27.3
House members	26	16.7	22.5	15.2

SOURCES: See table B-5. Rows may not add to 100 because of rounding.

Table B-8. Government and Political Stories on Local Television News, by Focus of Story, Station Market Size, and Washington Bureau Operation
Percent

Market size and bureau operation	Number	Focus of story			
		International	National	State	Local
Market size					
Largest (1–25)	133	21.11	51.9	12.0	15.0
Middle (26–70)	76	2.6	44.7	25.0	27.6
Smallest (71 186)	40	7.5	32.5	20.0	40.0
Bureau operation					
Washington bureau	103	12.6	53.4	13.6	20.4
Washington freelance	97	14.4	41.2	17.5	26.8
No Washington bureau	146	13.7	41.8	19.9	24.7
Weighted average	. . .	13.3	46.6	17.3	22.9

SOURCES: See table B-5.

Table B-9. Rank of Press Secretaries in Senate Offices, by Senator Characteristic, 1989

Senator characteristic	Number of press secretaries	Mean rank[a]	Senator characteristic	Number of press secretaries	Mean rank[a]
Age			Party		
49 or younger	27	4.6	Democrat	54	4.7
50–59	42	5.0	Republican	43	5.3
60–69	20	5.0	Economic issues[b]		
70 or older	8	6.3	Liberal	17	4.6
Terms in office			Moderate	47	5.4
1	30	5.4	Conservative	21	4.9
2	30	4.7	Social issues[b]		
3	23	5.3	Liberal	21	5.0
4–6	14	4.0	Moderate	45	5.1
Percentage of vote in last election			Conservative	19	5.3
			Foreign policy issues[b]		
50–54	28	5.5	Liberal	23	5.5
55–59	15	4.7	Moderate	43	4.7
60–69	34	4.7	Conservative	19	5.5
70 or more	19	4.9	Region		
Year of last election			Northeast	17	5.2
1984	32	5.0	North Central	24	5.0
1986	32	5.2	South	30	4.9
1988	32	4.7	West	26	4.8
Leadership position					
Yes	39	4.4			
No	58	5.3			

SOURCE: Rank determined by staff salaries in 97 Senate offices as listed in *Report of the Secretary of the Senate*, S. Doc. 101-6 (GPO, 1989).

a. Mean rank for all press secretaries is 4.97.

b. The rating system for legislators' ideology is based on their votes on issues; it was devised by and appears annually in the *National Journal*.

Table B-10. Average Number of Media Activities in Senate Offices, by Senator
Characteristic, October 1988

Senator characteristic	Number	Mean of 5 media activities[a]	Senator characteristic	Number	Mean of 5 media activities[a]
Age			Party		
40–49	21	5.2	Democrat	46	5.9
50–59	31	6.7	Republican	33	7.2
60–69	18	6.6	Region		
70 or older	9	5.7	Northeast	11	7.7
Terms in office			North Central	22	6.5
1	27	6.7	South	27	5.4
2	32	6.3	West	19	6.4
3	10	5.7			
4 or more	10	7.2			
Next election					
1988[b]	23	7.7			
1990	25	5.8			
1992	27	6.4			

SOURCE: Survey of 79 Senate press secretaries' activities for one week, October 1988.
a. The mean number of activities was press releases, 3.7; radio actualities, 1.0; television tapes, 0.9;
newspaper submissions, 0.6; and press conferences, 0.4. The mean number of activities per office was 6.6.
b. Excludes those not running for reelection.

Table B-11. Characteristics of House Press Secretaries, 1988

Characteristic	Number	Percentage	Characteristic	Number	Percentage
Age			Years in job		
20–29	37	43.5	less than 1	27	31.4
30–39	37	43.5	1–2	29	33.7
40–49	10	11.8	3–5	16	18.6
50 or older	1	1.2	5 or more	14	16.3
Education			Previous occupation		
Not college			Journalist	49	56.3
graduate	2	2.3	Student	18	20.7
College graduate	59	67.8	Government	13	14.9
Some graduate			Public relations	7	8.0
work	5	5.7	Law	2	2.3
M.A.	17	19.5	Other	4	4.6
J.D. or Ph.D.	4	4.6	Work experience[a]		
Undergraduate major			Journalism	49	56.3 (3.5)
Government	31	36.5	Public relations	30	34.5 (1.5)
Journalism	26	30.6	Politics	62	71.3 (3.3)
English	8	9.4	Connection with district		
History	7	8.2	None	46	52.9
Other	13	15.3	Little	7	8.0
			Meaningful	34	39.1

SOURCE: Survey of 93 House press secretaries in 1988.
a. Mean years of experience are in parentheses. Percentages for previous occupation and work
experience take into account overlaps in jobs and fields.

Table B-12. Average Number of Media Activities in House Offices, by Activity and
Member Characteristic, July and October 1988

Member characteristic	Press releases	Radio actualities	Newspaper submissions	Press conferences	Television tapes
			July 1988		
Age					
39 or younger	3.0	0.3	0.6	0.3	0.1
40–49	1.6	0.6	0.5	0.3	0.1
50–59	1.4	0.6	0.5	0.1	0
60 or older	1.8	0.4	0.7	0.2	0.1
Terms in office					
1	1.3	0.3	0.4	0.1	0
2–3	1.3	0.4	0.7	0	0
4–5	1.9	0.7	0.6	0.3	0.1
6–9	1.6	0.6	0.5	0.4	0.3
10 or more	2.6	0.2	0.7	0.2	0
Percentage of vote in last election					
50–59	1.6	0.6	0.4	0.1	0.1
60–69	1.8	0.4	0.3	0.3	0.1
70–79	2.3	0.5	0.8	0.3	0.1
80–89	0.4	0.4	0.7	0.1	0
90 or more	1.6	0.8	0.8	0.1	0.1
Party					
Democrat	1.3	0.5	0.6	0.3	0.1
Republican	2.1	0.6	0.6	0.1	0.1
			October 1988		
Age					
39 or younger	2.6	0.3	1.0	0.1	0.1
40–49	1.9	0.7	0.8	0.6	0.4
50–59	2.5	0.8	0.8	0.4	0.1
60 or older	2.0	0.6	1.0	0.2	0.3
Terms in office					
1	1.4	0.7	0.3	0.1	0.1
2–3	2.7	0.6	0.6	0.3	0.1
4–5	2.0	0.6	1.0	0.2	0.2
6–9	2.4	0.7	1.3	0.5	0.9
10 or more	2.3	0.6	0.7	0.3	0
Percentage of vote in last election					
50–59	2.6	0.9	0.4	0.4	0.7
60–69	2.1	0.6	0.7	0.3	0.6
70–79	2.0	0.5	0.8	0.2	0.2
80–89	2.0	0.3	1.2	0.1	0.3
90 or more	2.4	1.1	1.5	0.3	0.1
Party					
Democrat	1.9	0.7	0.9	0.3	0.4
Republican	2.4	0.6	0.8	0.3	0.1

SOURCES: Surveys of 73 House offices, July and October 1988. Numbers have been rounded.

Table B-13. Average Number of Media Activities in House Offices, by Member
Characteristic, July and October 1988

Member characteristic	Number of offices	July week	October week	Member characteristic	Number of offices	July week	October week
Age				Party			
39 or younger	7	4.3	4.1	Democrat	38	2.6	4.1
40–49	28	3.1	4.0	Republican	35	3.8	4.2
50–59	24	3.1	4.5	Age of press secretary			
60 or older	14	3.1	3.8	20–29	20	3.4	3.9
Terms in office				30–39	13	3.8	4.3
1	7	2.1	2.7	40–49	4	1.8	6.0
2–3	16	2.3	4.3	Press secretary's years			
4–5	30	3.6	4.1	on job			
6–9	11	4.2	5.7	less than 1	13	3.9	5.3
9 or more	9	3.4	3.3	1–2	11	3.0	4.4
Percentage of vote				3–5	9	2.6	2.7
in last election				5–10	3	4.0	4.0
50–59	14	3.4	4.5	10 or more	1	5.0	5.0
60–69	18	2.9	4.3	Mean activities			
70–79	24	4.0	3.5	Press releases	. . .	1.7	2.2
80–89	9	1.7	4.0	Newspaper			
90 or more	8	3.8	5.4	submissions	. . .	0.6	0.8
				Radio actualities	. . .	0.5	0.6
				Television tapes	. . .	0.1	0.3
				Press conferences	. . .	0.2	0.3
				Total	. . .	3.1	4.2

SOURCES: Surveys of 73 House offices, one week each in July and October 1988; combined with an
additional survey of 37 press secretaries. Numbers have been rounded.

Table B-14. House Press Secretaries' Time Spent Servicing District Press, by Member Characteristic, 1989

Member characteristic	Number of press secretaries	Percent of time[a]	Member characteristic	Number of press secretaries	Percent of time[a]
Age			Leadership position		
39 or younger	9	64.9	Yes	19	52.4
40–49	38	58.2	No	88	62.3
50–59	31	59.6	Region		
60 or older	29	63.4	Northeast	25	58.2
Terms in office			North Central	26	50.9
1–3	28	67.9	South	37	68.7
4–6	44	60.0	West	19	61.0
7 or more	35	55.5			
Percentage of vote in last election					
59 or less	20	73.3			
60–69	30	64.0			
70–79	30	48.6			
80–89	27	60.6			

Source: Survey of 107 House press secretaries who were asked, "Dividing your contacts with the press between journalists in Washington and the district, what percent of your time is spent on the district press?"
a. Average percentage was 60.6.

Table B-15. Press Releases, by Type and Legislator Characteristic[a]
Percent

Legislator characteristic	Number of legislators	Advertising	Credit claiming	Position taking
Age				
House: 49 or younger	20	24.6	39.0	36.5
50–59	21	15.2	52.4	32.5
60 or older	19	23.4	52.3	24.3
Senate: 49 or younger	3	12.2	50.3	37.5
50–59	11	22.1	46.9	31.0
60 or older	9	13.2	52.7	34.1
Years in office				
House: 1–6	14	27.2	42.7	30.1
7–18	36	18.4	50.1	31.5
19 or more	10	18.6	47.4	34.0
Senate: 1–6	7	10.0	56.7	33.5
7–18	13	22.8	45.0	32.2
19 or more	3	10.7	53.4	35.9
Percentage of vote in last election				
House: 59 or less	7	22.7	39.9	37.4
60–69	18	19.5	46.9	33.6
70 or more	35	20.7	50.3	29.0
Senate: 55 or less	7	17.8	51.8	30.4
56–59	5	10.0	58.9	31.1
60–69	8	23.3	38.5	38.2
70 or more	3	12.5	58.6	28.9
Leadership position				
House: Yes	9	14.7	41.7	43.6
No	51	21.4	48.9	29.7
Senate: Yes	14	16.6	48.5	34.9
No	9	18.4	51.3	30.3
Party				
House: Democrat	31	29.6	42.1	28.3
Republican	29	12.0	53.6	34.4
Senate: Democrat	11	17.2	47.1	35.6
Republican	12	17.4	51.9	30.7
Network TV appearances				
House: None	32	14.8	54.5	30.7
1–4	20	31.5	42.9	25.6
5 or more	7	20.6	48.0	31.4
Senate: 0–10	13	11.1	54.8	34.1
11 or more	10	25.4	42.8	31.8
Economic issues[b]				
House: Liberal	7	43.1	47.2	9.7
Moderate	33	19.6	41.4	39.1
Conservative	17	16.2	61.1	22.7
Senate: Liberal	7	21.2	47.9	30.9
Moderate	10	10.5	52.4	37.1
Conservative	6	24.1	47.0	28.9

Table B-15. *(continued)*

Legislator characteristics	Number of legislators	Advertising	Credit claiming	Position taking
			Type of release	
Social issues[b]				
House: Liberal	15	37.9	38.8	23.4
Moderate	26	16.7	44.5	38.7
Conservative	16	14.5	62.5	23.0
Senate: Liberal	6	23.5	48.1	28.5
Moderate	13	14.5	48.2	37.3
Conservative	4	17.4	56.5	26.2
Foreign policy issues[b]				
House: Liberal	14	31.1	37.5	31.4
Moderate	27	21.9	49.1	29.0
Conservative	16	12.7	52.3	35.0
Senate: Liberal	5	25.8	37.5	36.7
Moderate	12	10.4	56.0	33.7
Conservative	6	24.1	47.0	28.9
Region				
House: Northeast	11	21.0	34.4	44.7
North Central	15	24.1	48.1	27.8
South	24	20.1	51.3	28.7
West	10	15.6	57.3	27.1
Senate: Northeast	3	7.4	52.2	40.3
North Central	8	16.5	45.9	37.6
South	6	24.1	43.4	32.5
West	6	16.6	59.5	24.0

SOURCES: Survey of 2,576 press releases produced by 23 Senate offices in 1984 and 321 press releases produced by 60 House offices in September and October 1989.

Senators included were Lloyd Bentsen (D-TX), Jeff Bingaman (D-NM), Dale Bumpers (D-AR), Quentin Burdick (D-ND), Lawton Chiles (D-FL), Alan J. Dixon (D-IL), Robert Dole (R-KS), Daniel Evans (R-WA), Jake Garn (R-UT), Charles E. Grassley (R-IA), John Heinz (R-PA), Ernest F. Hollings (D-SC), Daniel Inouye (D-HI), Nancy Kassebaum (R-KS), Paul Laxalt (R-NV), Richard G. Lugar (R-IN), Charles McC. Mathias (R-MD), James A. McClure (R-ID), Daniel Patrick Moynihan (D-NY), William Proxmire (D-WI), J. Danforth Quayle (R-IN), Warren B. Rudman (R-NH), and Paul S. Sarbanes (D-MD).

House members included were Joe Barton (R-TX), Doug Bereuter (R-NE), Sherwood Boehlert (R-NY), Joseph Brennan (D-ME), Sonny Callahan (R-AL), Howard Coble (R-NC), George Crockett (D-MI), Peter DeFazio (D-OR), E. (Kika) de la Garza (D-TX), William Dickinson (R-AL), Brian Donnelly (D-MA), John J. Duncan, Jr. (R-TN), Mickey Edwards (R-OK), Eliot Engel (D-NY), Mike Espy (D-MS), Hamilton Fish, Jr. (R-NY), Dean Gallo (R-NJ), Benjamin Gilman (R-NY), Tony Hall (D-OH), John Hammerschmidt (R-AR), Frank Horton (R-NY), Tim Johnson (D-SD), Walter Jones (D-NC), Dale Kildee (D-MI), Peter Kostmayer (D-PA), Jim Leach (R-IA), Marvin Leath (D-TX), William Lehman (D-FL), Tom Lewis (R-FL), Bill Lowery (R-CA), Lynn Martin (R-IL), Matthew Martinez (D-CA), Robert Matsui (D-CA), Raymond McGrath (R-NY), Thomas McMillen (D-MD), Kweisi Mfume (D-MD), Stephen Neal (D-NC), Stan Parris (R-VA), Don Pease (D-OH), Timothy Penny (D-MN), Thomas Petri (R-WI), Richard Ray (D-GA), John J. Rhodes III (R-AZ), Pat Roberts (R-KS), Martin Sabo (D-MN), Patricia Saiki (R-HI), Joe Skeen (R-MN), Denny Smith (R-OR), Stephen Solarz (D-NY), Floyd Spence (R-SC), John Spratt (D-SC), Fortney (Pete) Stark (D-CA), Charles Stenholm (D-TX), Louis Stokes (D-OH), Don Sundquist (R-TN), Harold Volkmer (D-MO), Henry Waxman (D-CA), Frank Wolf (R-VA), Chalmers Wylie (R-OH), and Sidney Yates (D-IL).

a. Rows may not total 100 because of rounding.

b. See table B-9, note b.

Table B-16. Press Releases, by Focus and Legislator Characteristic[a]

Percent

Legislator characteristic	Number of legislators	Focus of release		
		Local	National	International
Age				
House: 49 or younger	20	50.7	38.7	10.6
50–59	21	45.9	49.3	4.9
60 or older	19	39.2	48.0	12.7
Senate: 49 or younger	3	34.7	55.6	9.7
50–59	11	43.8	47.9	8.3
60 or older	9	45.4	45.5	9.2
Years in office				
House: 1–6	14	62.0	30.7	7.3
7–18	36	42.9	46.6	10.6
19 or more	10	26.7	69.2	4.2
Senate: 1–6	7	32.4	60.3	7.3
7–18	13	50.8	40.5	8.7
19 or more	3	43.3	47.9	8.8
Percentage of vote in last election				
House: 59 or less	7	47.1	47.4	5.6
60–69	18	49.5	44.1	6.4
70 or more	35	43.1	45.8	11.1
Senate: 55 or less	7	38.9	53.4	7.7
56–59	5	46.9	48.4	4.8
60–69	8	42.3	43.8	13.9
70 or more	3	50.0	45.6	4.5
Leadership position				
House: Yes	9	40.3	50.8	8.9
No	51	46.3	44.7	9.0
Senate: Yes	14	44.5	45.4	10.1
No	9	43.3	47.9	8.8
Party				
House: Democrat	31	52.1	37.5	10.4
Republican	29	39.3	53.1	7.7
Senate: Democrat	11	39.5	49.7	10.8
Republican	12	46.7	46.3	7.0
Network TV appearances				
House: None	32	43.1	52.6	4.3
1–4	20	53.1	35.5	11.4
5 or more	7	33.1	50.5	16.4
Senate: 0–10	13	39.5	52.2	8.4
11 or more	10	48.2	42.4	9.4
Economic issues[b]				
House: Liberal	7	48.6	34.7	16.7
Moderate	33	43.8	48.0	8.2
Conservative	17	50.6	42.7	6.6
Senate: Liberal	7	45.9	45.6	8.5
Moderate	10	33.4	56.1	10.5
Conservative	6	56.6	37.0	6.4

Table B-16. *(continued)*

Legislator characteristic	Number of legislators	Focus of release		
		Local	National	International
Social issues[b]				
House: Liberal	15	45.6	45.5	9.0
Moderate	26	40.2	51.3	8.5
Conservative	16	44.0	49.5	6.5
Senate: Liberal	6	47.5	43.5	9.0
Moderate	13	37.8	52.2	9.9
Conservative	4	54.4	40.7	4.9
Foreign policy issues[b]				
House: Liberal	14	48.7	35.1	16.1
Moderate	27	45.1	46.8	8.2
Conservative	16	40.5	56.0	3.5
Senate: Liberal	5	41.0	46.3	12.7
Moderate	12	37.5	54.1	8.4
Conservative	6	50.0	45.6	4.5
Region				
House: Northeast	11	43.8	43.2	13.0
North Central	15	40.6	41.5	17.9
South	24	46.3	51.3	2.5
West	10	54.2	41.7	4.2
Senate: Northeast	3	23.5	68.7	7.9
North Central	8	36.0	53.5	10.6
South	6	50.8	39.4	9.9
West	6	55.3	38.8	5.9

SOURCES: See table B-15.
a. Rows may not total 100 because of rounding.
b. See table B-9, note b.

Table B-17. House and Senate Offices Issuing Many or Few Press Releases, by Legislator Characteristic[a]
Percent

Legislator characteristic	Senators		House members	
	100 or more releases	99 or fewer releases	5 or more releases	4 or fewer releases
Number of legislators	12	11	26	34
Age				
49 or younger	66.7	33.3	40.0	60.0
50–59	36.4	63.6	47.6	52.4
60 or older	66.7	33.3	42.1	57.9
Years in office				
1–6	28.6	71.4	42.9	57.1
7–18	69.2	30.8	47.2	52.8
19 or more	33.3	66.7	30.0	70.0
Percentage of vote in last election				
59 or less	41.7	58.3	28.6	71.4
60–69	75.0	25.0	44.4	55.6
70 or more	33.3	66.7	45.7	54.3
Leadership position				
Yes	71.4	28.6	44.4	55.6
No	22.2	77.6	43.1	56.9
Party				
Democrat	36.4	63.6	32.3	67.7
Republican	66.7	33.3	55.2	44.8
Network TV appearances				
Few[b]	30.8	69.2	40.6	59.4
Many[b]	80.0	20.0	44.4	55.6
Economic issues[c]				
Liberal	42.9	57.1	14.3	85.7
Moderate	40.0	60.0	42.4	57.6
Conservative	83.3	16.7	52.9	47.1
Social issues[c]				
Liberal	33.3	66.7	26.7	73.3
Moderate	53.8	46.2	50.0	50.0
Conservative	75.0	25.0	43.8	56.3
Foreign policy issues[c]				
Liberal	20.0	80.0	35.7	64.3
Moderate	50.0	50.0	44.4	55.6
Conservative	83.3	16.7	43.8	56.3
Region				
Northeast	66.7	33.3	63.6	36.4
North Central	62.5	37.5	46.7	53.3
South	50.0	50.0	41.7	58.3
West	33.3	66.7	20.0	80.0

SOURCES: See table B-15.

a. Rows may not total 100 because of rounding.

b. For House members, few appearances mean none or one; many means two or more. For senators, few appearances means four or fewer; many means five or more.

c. See table B-9, note b.

Table B-18. House and Senate Op-Ed Pieces in Three Newspapers, by Legislator Characteristic, 1988[a]
Percent unless otherwise specified

Legislator characteristic	House[b]					Senate[b]				
	Number	Composition of House	Op-ed writers	Non-writers	Difference	Number	Composition of Senate	Op-ed writers	Non-writers	Difference
Number	429	429	48	381	⋯	100	100	33	67	⋯
Age										
49 or younger	188	43.8	56.3	42.3	14.0	27	27.0	36.4	22.4	14.0
50 or older	241	56.2	43.8	57.7	−13.9	n.a.	n.a.	n.a.	n.a.	n.a.
50–59	n.a.	n.a.	n.a.	n.a.	n.a.	38	38.0	36.4	38.8	−2.4
60–69	n.a.	n.a.	n.a.	n.a.	n.a.	24	24.0	21.2	25.4	−4.2
70 or older	n.a.	n.a.	n.a.	n.a.	n.a.	11	11.0	6.1	13.4	−7.3
Years in office										
1–6	161	37.5	20.8	39.6	−18.8	27	27.0	21.2	29.9	−8.7
7–18	196	45.7	54.2	44.6	9.6	58	58.0	63.6	55.2	8.4
19 or more	72	16.8	25.0	15.7	9.3	15	15.0	15.2	14.9	0.3
Percentage of vote in last election										
54 or less	41	9.6	0	10.8	−10.8	28	28.3	21.2	31.8	−10.6
55–59	39	9.1	4.2	9.7	−5.5	19	19.2	15.2	21.2	−6.0
60–69	122	28.4	43.8	26.5	17.3	34	34.3	39.4	31.8	7.6
70 or more	227	52.9	52.1	53.0	−0.9	18	18.2	24.2	15.2	9.0
Leader	54	12.6	27.1	10.8	16.3	45	45.0	48.5	43.3	5.2
Party										
Democrat	255	59.4	62.5	59.1	3.4	54	54.0	60.6	50.7	9.9
Republican	174	40.6	37.5	40.9	−3.4	46	46.0	39.4	49.3	−9.9
Network TV appearances										
None	188	43.8	20.8	46.7	−25.9	n.a.	n.a.	n.a.	n.a.	n.a.
One	85	19.8	18.8	19.9	−1.1	n.a.	n.a.	n.a.	n.a.	n.a.
More than one	156	36.4	60.4	33.3	27.1	n.a.	n.a.	n.a.	n.a.	n.a.
0–19	51	n.a.	n.a.	n.a.	n.a.	51	51.0	33.3	59.7	−26.4
20 or more	49	n.a.	n.a.	n.a.	n.a.	49	49.0	66.7	40.3	26.4

Rank of press secretary										
1–4	187	43.6	41.7	43.8	−2.1	45	47.4	50.0	46.0	4.0
5–7	85	19.8	16.7	20.2	−3.5	34	35.8	34.4	36.5	−2.1
8 or lower	60	14.0	18.8	13.4	5.4	16	16.8	15.6	17.5	−1.9
Not available	97	22.6	22.9	22.6	0.6					
Economic issues[c]										
Conservative	107	25.2	27.1	24.9	2.2	25	25.3	21.9	26.9	−5.0
Moderate	215	50.6	47.9	50.9	−3.0	55	55.6	43.8	61.2	−17.4
Liberal	103	24.2	25.0	24.1	0.9	19	19.2	24.4	11.9	12.5
Social issues[c]										
Conservative	108	25.6	19.1	26.4	−7.3	25	25.3	21.9	26.9	−5.0
Moderate	209	49.5	44.7	50.1	−5.4	50	50.5	40.6	55.2	−14.6
Liberal	105	24.9	36.2	23.5	12.7	24	24.2	37.5	17.9	19.6
Foreign policy issues[c]										
Conservative	109	25.7	33.3	24.7	8.6	25	25.3	18.8	28.4	−9.6
Moderate	217	51.2	35.4	53.2	−17.8	49	49.5	50.0	49.3	0.7
Liberal	98	23.1	31.3	22.1	9.2	25	25.3	31.3	22.4	8.9
Region										
Northeast	94	21.9	31.3	20.7	10.6	18	18.0	24.2	14.9	9.3
North Central	112	26.1	20.8	26.8	−6.0	24	24.0	24.2	23.9	0.3
South	138	32.2	29.2	32.5	−3.3	32	32.0	27.3	34.3	−7.0
West	85	19.8	18.8	19.9	−1.1	26	26.0	24.2	26.9	−2.7

SOURCES: Information on the *New York Times*, *Los Angeles Times*, and *Christian Science Monitor* comes from the CD-Rom indexing system created by University Microfilms International (UMI). Information on the *Washington Post* and *Wall Street Journal* comes from bound volumes of their indexes. Our survey codes only for the 429 persons who served in the House for the whole of 1988.

n.a. Not available.

a. Op-eds appeared in the *New York Times*, *Washington Post*, and *Wall Street Journal*.

b. Column entries may not total 100 because of rounding.

c. See table B-9, note b.

Table B-19. House Members' Op-Ed Pieces in Five Newspapers, by Member Characteristic, 1988[a]

Percent unless otherwise specified

Member characteristic	Number of members	Composition of House	Op-ed writers	Non-writers	Difference
Number of members	429	429	68	361	. . .
Age					
49 or younger	188	43.8	52.9	42.1	10.8
50 or older	241	56.2	47.1	57.9	−10.8
Years in office					
1–6	161	37.5	25.0	39.9	−14.9
7–18	196	45.7	50.0	44.9	5.1
19 or more	72	16.8	25.0	15.2	9.8
Percentage of vote in last election					
54 or less	41	9.6	0	11.4	−11.4
55–59	39	9.1	5.9	9.7	−3.8
60–69	122	28.4	44.1	25.5	18.6
70 or more	227	52.9	50.0	53.5	−3.5
Leadership position					
Yes	54	12.6	23.5	10.5	13.0
No	375	87.4	76.5	89.5	−13.0
Party					
Democrat	255	59.4	64.7	58.4	6.3
Republican	174	40.6	35.3	41.6	−6.3
Network TV appearances					
None	188	43.8	27.9	46.8	−18.9
One	85	19.8	16.2	20.5	−4.3
More than one	156	36.4	55.9	32.7	23.2
Rank of press secretary					
1–4	187	43.6	44.1	43.5	0.6
5–7	85	19.8	16.2	20.5	−4.3
8 or lower	60	14.0	13.2	14.1	−0.9
Not available	97	22.6	26.5	21.9	4.6
Economic issues[b]					
Conservative	107	25.2	23.5	25.5	−2.0
Moderate	215	50.6	48.5	51.0	−2.5
Liberal	103	24.2	27.9	23.5	4.4
Social issues[b]					
Conservative	108	25.6	19.4	26.8	−7.4
Moderate	209	49.5	37.3	51.8	−14.5
Liberal	105	24.9	43.3	21.4	21.9
Foreign policy issues[b]					
Conservative	109	25.7	26.5	25.6	0.9
Moderate	217	51.2	35.3	54.2	−18.9
Liberal	98	23.1	38.2	20.2	18.0
Region					
Northeast	94	21.9	26.5	21.1	5.4
North Central	112	26.1	25.0	26.3	−1.3
South	138	32.2	22.1	34.1	−12.0
West	85	19.8	26.5	18.6	7.9

SOURCES: See table B-18.

a. Op-eds appeared in the *New York Times, Washington Post, Wall Street Journal, Christian Science Monitor,* and *Los Angeles Times.* Column entries may not total 100 because of rounding.

b. See table B-9, note b.

Table B-20. Senators' Op-Ed Pieces in Seven Newspapers, by Senator Characteristic and Frequency of Appearance, January–June 1989[a]
Percent unless otherwise specified

Senator characteristic	Composition of Senate	Number of articles		
		None	One	More than One
Age				
49 or younger	28	42.9	32.1	25.0
50–59	42	47.6	23.8	28.6
60–69	22	63.6	22.7	13.6
70 or older	8	75.0	12.5	12.5
Years in office				
1–6	30	53.3	36.7	10.0
7–12	32	53.1	28.1	18.8
13–18	24	45.8	16.7	37.5
19 or more	14	57.1	7.1	35.7
Percentage of vote in last election				
54 or less	31	58.1	29.0	12.9
55–59	15	40.0	33.3	26.7
60–69	34	47.1	20.6	32.4
70 or more	19	57.9	21.1	21.1
Year of last election				
1984	33	36.4	42.4	21.2
1986	33	57.6	12.2	27.3
1988	33	60.6	18.2	21.2
Leadership position				
Yes	43	48.8	18.6	32.6
No	57	54.4	29.8	15.8
Party				
Democrat	55	47.3	29.1	23.6
Republican	45	57.8	20.0	22.2
Rank of press secretary				
1–4	49	42.9	20.4	36.7
5–7	36	58.3	33.3	8.3
8 or lower	12	66.7	16.7	16.7
Economic issues[b]				
Conservative	22	45.5	27.3	27.3
Moderate	48	45.8	25.0	29.2
Liberal	18	72.2	16.7	11.1
Social issues[b]				
Conservative	21	57.1	28.6	14.3
Moderate	45	42.2	24.4	33.3
Liberal	22	63.6	18.2	18.2
Foreign policy issues[b]				
Conservative	21	47.6	28.6	23.8
Moderate	43	44.2	23.3	32.6
Liberal	24	66.7	20.8	12.5

a. Op-eds appeared in USA Today, New York Times, Washington Post, Wall Street Journal, Christian Science Monitor, Los Angeles Times, and Washington Times. Fifty-two senators wrote no articles, twenty-five wrote one, and twenty-three wrote more than one. Rows may not total 100 because of rounding.

b. See table B-9, note b.

Table B-21. House Members' Op-Ed Pieces in Five Newspapers, by Member Characteristic and Frequency of Appearance, 1988[a]
Percent

Member characteristic	Number of members	Number of articles written		
		None	One	More than one
Age				
49 or younger	188	80.9	12.2	6.9
50 or older	241	86.7	9.1	4.1
Years in office				
1–6	161	89.4	8.1	2.5
7–18	196	82.7	10.2	7.1
19 or more	72	76.4	16.7	6.9
Percentage of vote received				
54 or less	41	100.0	0	0
55–59	39	89.7	5.1	5.1
60–69	122	75.4	13.9	10.7
70 or more	227	85.0	11.5	3.5
Leader				
Yes	54	70.4	20.4	9.3
No	375	86.1	9.1	4.8
Party				
Democrat	255	82.7	11.8	5.5
Republican	174	86.2	8.6	5.2
Network TV appearances[b]				
None	188	89.9	6.9	3.2
One	85	87.1	10.6	2.4
More than one	156	75.6	14.7	9.6
Rank of press secretary				
1–4	187	84.0	12.3	3.7
5–7	85	87.1	7.1	5.9
8 or lower	60	85.0	8.3	6.7
Not available	97	81.4	11.3	7.2
Economic issues[c]				
Conservative	107	85.0	8.4	6.5
Moderate	215	84.7	10.2	5.1
Liberal	103	81.6	13.6	4.9
Social issues[c]				
Conservative	108	88.0	7.4	4.6
Moderate	209	88.0	9.1	2.9
Liberal	105	72.4	17.1	10.5
Foreign policy issues[c]				
Conservative	109	83.5	9.2	7.3
Moderate	217	88.9	9.2	1.8
Liberal	98	73.5	15.3	11.2

SOURCES: See table B-18.

a. Op-eds appeared in the *New York Times, Washington Post, Wall Street Journal, Christian Science Monitor,* and *Los Angeles Times.* Three hundred sixty-one members wrote no articles, forty-five members wrote one, and twenty-three members wrote more than one. Rows may not add to 100 because of rounding.

b. TV appearances are for the 100th Congress (1987–88).

c. See table B-9, note b.

Table B-22. House and Senate Members' Op-Ed Pieces, by Subject and Selected Newspaper, 1988–89
Percent

Subject	Number	New York Times	Wall Street Journal	Washington Post	Christian Science Monitor	Los Angeles Times	Washington Times
House
Foreign policy	29	17.4	14.3	16.0	52.4	36.4	n.a.
Congress and politics	15	21.7	14.2	16.0	4.8	13.6	n.a.
Defense	14	17.4	14.3	12.0	23.8	0	n.a.
Social issues	12	8.7	21.4	12.0	0	18.2	n.a.
Economics	11	8.7	28.6	8.0	9.5	4.5	n.a.
Number	. . .	23	14	25	24	22	n.a.
Senate
Congress and politics	16	16.7	66.7	32.0	0	0	18.2
Foreign policy	15	12.5	33.3	16.0	0	33.3	27.3
Economics	15	16.7	0	28.0	12.5	0	27.3
Environment	9	16.7	0	0	50.0	8.3	0
Defense	5	20.8	0	0	0	0	0
Number	. . .	24	3	25	8	12	11

SOURCE: Surveys of 105 articles by House members, January–December 1988, and 88 articles by senators, January–June 1989.
n.a. Not available

Table B-23. House Members' Op-Ed Pieces, by Member Characteristic and Newspaper, 1988
Percent

Member characteristic	Composition of House	Newspaper					
		New York Times	Wall Street Journal	Washington Post	Christian Science Monitor	Los Angeles Times	Average
Number of articles	...	23	14	25	24	22	108
Age							
49 or younger	43.8	65.2	64.3	48.0	45.8	63.6	56.5
50 or older	56.2	34.8	35.7	52.0	54.2	36.4	43.8
Years in office							
1–6	37.5	13.0	28.6	20.0	33.3	27.3	24.1
7–18	45.7	60.9	64.3	52.0	37.5	50.0	51.9
19 or more	16.8	26.1	7.1	28.0	29.2	22.7	24.1
Percentage of vote received							
59 or less	18.7	4.3	7.1	8.0	4.2	4.5	5.6
60–69	28.4	26.1	64.3	56.0	62.5	36.4	48.1
70 or more	52.9	69.6	28.6	36.0	33.3	59.1	46.3
Leader	12.6	21.7	21.4	32.0	4.2	18.2	19.4
Party							
Democrat	59.4	82.6	42.9	56.0	75.0	72.7	67.6
Republican	40.6	17.4	57.1	44.0	25.0	27.3	32.4
Network TV appearances							
None	43.8	8.7	21.4	36.0	29.2	18.2	23.1
1–4	39.9	30.4	21.4	40.0	33.3	31.8	32.4
5 or more	16.3	60.9	57.1	24.0	37.5	50.0	44.4

Rank of press secretary							
1–4	43.6	17.4	50.0	56.0	41.7	9.1	34.3
5–7	19.8	26.1	21.4	8.0	33.3	9.1	19.4
8 or lower	14.0	21.7	7.1	24.0	0	27.3	16.7
Not available	22.6	34.8	21.4	12.0	25.0	54.5	29.6
Economic issues[a]							
Conservative	25.2	8.7	50.0	36.0	8.3	18.2	22.2
Moderate	50.6	52.2	42.9	48.0	70.8	59.1	55.6
Liberal	24.2	39.1	7.1	16.0	20.8	22.7	22.2
Social issues[a]							
Conservative	25.6	4.5	38.5	24.0	12.5	18.2	17.9
Moderate	49.5	31.8	30.8	48.0	45.8	9.1	34.0
Liberal	24.9	63.6	30.8	28.0	41.7	72.7	48.1
Foreign policy issues[a]							
Conservative	25.7	17.4	50.0	40.0	8.3	18.2	25.0
Moderate	51.2	26.1	21.4	36.0	54.2	9.1	30.6
Liberal	23.1	56.5	28.6	24.0	37.5	72.7	44.4
Region							
Northeast	21.9	60.9	21.4	8.0	25.0	18.2	26.9
North Central	26.1	8.7	21.4	32.0	54.2	22.7	28.7
South	32.2	13.0	21.4	44.0	8.3	0	17.6
West	19.8	17.4	35.7	16.0	12.5	59.1	26.9

SOURCE: See table B-22. Column entries may not total 100 becuase of rounding.
a. See table B-9, note b.

Table B-24. Senators' Op-Ed Pieces, by Senator Characteristic and Newspaper, 1988
Percent

Senator characteristic	Composition of Senate	Newspaper			Average
		New York Times	Washington Post	Wall Street Journal	
Number of articles	. . .	17	22	5	. . .
Age					
49 or younger	27.0	35.3	31.8	80.0	38.6
50–59	38.0	23.5	45.5	20.0	34.1
60–69	24.0	35.3	18.2	0	22.7
70 or older	11.0	5.9	4.5	0	4.5
Years in office					
1–6	27.0	17.6	18.2	0	15.9
7–18	58.0	70.6	63.6	100.0	70.4
19 or more	15.0	11.8	18.2	0	13.7
Percentage of vote received					
54 or less	28.3	11.8	27.3	0	18.2
55–59	19.2	17.6	13.6	0	13.6
60–69	34.3	58.8	27.3	80.0	45.5
70 or more	18.2	11.8	31.8	20.0	22.7
Leader	45.0	35.3	59.1	40.0	47.7
Party					
Democrat	54.0	82.4	54.5	60.0	65.9
Republican	46.0	17.6	45.5	40.0	34.1
Network TV appearances					
0–19	51.0	23.5	36.4	0	27.3
20–49	28.0	47.1	36.4	40.0	40.9
50 or more	21.0	29.4	27.3	60.0	31.8
Rank of press secretary					
1–4	42.4	68.8	40.9	40.0	51.2
5–7	35.8	18.8	50.0	40.0	37.2
8 or lower	16.8	12.5	9.1	20.0	11.6
Economic issues[a]					
Conservative	25.3	6.3	18.2	50.0	16.7
Moderate	55.6	50.0	50.0	25.0	47.6
Liberal	19.2	43.8	31.8	25.0	35.7
Social issues[a]					
Conservative	25.3	6.3	18.2	50.0	16.7
Moderate	50.5	43.8	54.5	25.0	47.6
Liberal	24.2	50.0	27.3	25.0	35.7
Foreign policy issues[a]					
Conservative	25.3	6.3	22.7	25.0	16.7
Moderate	49.5	68.8	45.5	75.0	57.1
Liberal	25.3	25.0	31.8	0	26.2
Region					
Northeast	18.0	47.1	22.7	20.0	31.8
North Central	24.0	17.6	22.7	40.0	22.7
South	32.0	23.5	27.3	40.0	27.3
West	26.0	11.8	27.3	0	18.2

SOURCE: See table B-22. Column entries may not total 100 because of rounding.
a. See table B-9, note b.

Table B-25. Regional Reporters, by Characteristic, 1978, 1988
Percent

Characteristic	1978	1988
Number of responses	88	190
Sex		
Male	81.8	73.2
Female	18.2	26.8
Race		
White	98.9	94.7
Minority	1.1	5.3
Age		
20–29	33.0	16.3
30–39	30.7	61.1
40–49	20.5	15.8
50 or older	15.9	6.8
Mean (years)	37.2	36.2
Region		
Northeast	34.9	24.9
North Central	28.7	31.6
South	24.4	26.0
West	12.0	17.5
Educational attainment		
High school only	3.4	1.1
Some college	10.2	1.1
College degree only	47.7	61.6
Some graduate work	23.9	10.5
Graduate degree	14.8	25.8
Selectivity of college attended		
Highly selective	29.1	18.0
Selective	43.0	52.4
Not selective	27.9	29.6
Type of undergraduate institution		
Public	50.0	55.3
Private	50.0	44.7
Undergraduate field of study		
Humanities and liberal arts	54.1	45.7
Journalism	36.5	48.9
Science and technology	9.5	5.3
Graduate field of study		
Humanities and liberal arts	25.0	32.4
Journalism	71.4	60.3
Science and technology	3.6	7.6
Number of responses	28	68

SOURCES: Data for 1978 are from *The Washington Reporters*. Data for 1988 are from a survey of regional journalists. Column entries may not total 100 because of rounding.

Table B-26. Regional Reporters, by Sex and Characteristic, 1978, 1988
Percent

Characteristic	1978		1988	
	Men	Women	Men	Women
Number of responses	72	16	139	51
Race				
White	100.0	93.8	95.7	92.2
Minority	0	6.3	4.3	7.8
Age				
20–29	26.4	62.5	10.1	33.3
30–39	31.9	25.0	64.0	52.9
40–49	23.6	6.3	17.3	11.8
50 or older	18.1	6.3	8.6	2.0
Mean (years)	38.3	32.1	37.6	32.5
Region				
Northeast	37.7	21.7	22.2	32.4
North Central	28.8	28.8	33.1	27.6
South	22.2	34.8	25.9	26.2
West	11.3	15.2	18.8	13.8
Educational attainment				
High school only	4.2	0	1.4	0
Some college	11.1	6.3	1.4	0
College degree only	47.2	50.0	59.0	68.6
Some graduate work	19.4	43.8	11.5	7.8
Graduate degree	18.1	0	26.6	23.5
Selectivity of college attended				
Highly selective	30.0	25.0	18.1	17.6
Selective	40.0	56.3	49.3	60.8
Not selective	30.0	18.8	32.6	21.6
Type of undergraduate school				
Public	51.4	43.8	55.5	54.9
Private	48.6	56.3	44.5	45.1
Undergraduate field of study				
Humanities and liberal arts	57.1	40.0	48.9	37.3
Journalism	32.9	53.3	46.0	56.9
Science and technology	10.0	6.7	5.1	5.9
Graduate field of study				
Humanities and liberal arts	19.0	42.9	32.1	33.3
Journalism	81.0	42.9	58.5	66.7
Science and technology	0	14.3	9.4	0
Number of responses	21	7	33	15

SOURCES: See table B-25. Column entries may not total 100 because of rounding.

Table B-27. Regional Reporters in Print or Broadcast Journalism, by Sex
and Characteristic, 1988
Percent

Characteristic	Broadcast		Print	
	Men	Women	Men	Women
Number of responses	29	19	110	32
Race				
White	93.1	89.5	96.3	93.8
Minority	6.9	10.5	3.7	6.3
Age				
20–29	10.3	47.4	10.0	25.0
30–39	62.1	36.8	64.5	62.5
40–49	20.7	15.8	16.4	9.4
50 or older	6.9	0	9.1	3.1
Mean (years)	37.5	31.4	37.6	33.1
Region				
Northeast	31.4	29.1	19.7	34.4
North Central	26.7	21.8	34.8	31.1
South	31.4	27.3	24.5	25.6
West	10.5	21.8	21.0	8.9
Educational attainment				
High school only	0	0	1.8	0
Some college	0	0	1.8	0
College degree only	65.5	68.4	57.3	68.8
Some graduate work	17.2	15.8	10.0	3.1
Graduate degree	17.2	15.8	29.1	28.1
Selectivity of college attended				
Highly selective	13.8	5.3	19.3	25.0
Selective	62.1	78.9	45.9	50.0
Not selective	24.1	15.8	34.9	25.0
Type of undergraduate school				
Public	51.7	57.9	56.5	53.1
Private	48.3	42.1	43.5	46.9
Undergraduate field of study				
Humanities and liberal arts	41.4	21.1	50.9	46.9
Journalism	51.7	73.7	44.4	46.9
Science and technology	6.9	5.3	4.6	6.3
Graduate field of study				
Humanities and liberal arts	10.0	50.0	37.2	22.2
Journalism	70.0	50.0	55.8	77.8
Science and technology	20.0	0	7.0	0
Number of responses	10	6	43	9

SOURCE: Data are from a 1988 survey of regional journalists. Column entries may not total 100 because of rounding.

Table B-28. Regional Print Reporters, 1978, 1988, and Regional Broadcast Reporters, 1988, by Characteristic
Percent

Characteristic	Print 1978	Print 1988	Broadcast 1988
Number of responses	82	142	48
Sex			
Male	82.9	77.5	60.4
Female	17.1	22.5	39.6
Race			
White	100.0	95.7	91.7
Minority	0	4.3	8.3
Age			
20–29	32.9	13.4	25.0
30–39	30.5	64.1	52.1
40–49	19.5	14.8	18.8
50 or older	17.1	7.7	4.2
Mean (years)	37.4	36.6	35.1
Region			
Northeast	34.5	23.0	30.5
North Central	28.6	34.0	24.8
South	23.9	24.7	29.8
West	13.0	18.3	14.9
Educational attainment			
High school only	3.7	1.4	0
Some college	9.8	1.4	0
College degree only	45.1	59.9	66.7
Some graduate work	25.6	8.5	16.7
Graduate degree	15.9	28.9	16.7
Selectivity of college attended			
Highly selective	27.5	20.6	10.4
Selective	46.3	46.8	68.8
Not selective	26.2	32.6	20.8
Type of undergraduate school			
Public	51.3	55.7	54.2
Private	48.8	44.3	45.8
Undergraduate field of study			
Humanities and liberal arts	53.8	50.0	33.3
Journalism	36.3	45.0	60.4
Science and technology	10.0	5.0	6.3
Graduate field of study			
Humanities and liberal arts	25.0	34.6	25.0
Journalism	71.4	59.6	62.5
Science and technology	3.6	5.8	12.5
Number of responses	28	52	16

SOURCES: See table B-25. Column entries may not total 100 because of rounding.

Table B-29. Regional Reporters Working for Independent Newspapers and Newspaper Chains, by Characteristic, 1978, 1988
Percent

	1978		1988	
Characteristic	Independent	Chain	Independent	Chain
Number of responses	34	33	28	100
Sex				
Male	85.3	84.8	82.1	80.0
Female	14.7	15.2	17.9	20.0
Race				
White	100.0	100.0	96.3	95.0
Minority	0	0	3.7	5.0
Age				
20–29	35.3	27.3	3.6	13.0
30–39	32.4	33.3	60.7	67.0
40–49	20.6	24.2	14.3	15.0
50 or older	11.8	15.2	21.4	5.0
Mean (years)	36.2	38.2	41.0	35.8
Region				
Northeast	37.0	26.5	27.2	22.1
North Central	29.0	36.7	34.6	34.8
South	23.0	19.4	24.7	22.1
West	11.0	17.3	13.6	21.0
Educational attainment				
High school only	0	6.1	0	2.0
Some college	0	12.1	3.6	1.0
College degree only	52.9	42.4	57.1	58.0
Some graduate work	32.4	18.2	7.1	9.0
Graduate degree	14.7	21.2	32.1	30.0
Selectivity of college attended				
Highly selective	26.5	21.9	14.3	20.2
Selective	52.9	37.5	46.4	48.5
Not selective	20.6	40.6	39.3	31.3
Type of undergraduate school				
Public	47.1	62.5	53.6	55.1
Private	52.9	37.5	46.4	44.9
Undergraduate field of study				
Humanities and liberal arts	52.9	50.0	50.0	53.1
Journalism	44.1	34.4	46.4	42.9
Science and technology	2.9	15.6	3.6	4.1
Graduate field of study				
Humanities and liberal arts	23.1	10.0	0	42.5
Journalism	76.9	80.0	100.0	50.0
Science and technology	0	10.0	0	7.5
Number of responses	13	10	9	40

Sources: See table B-25. Column entries may not total 100 because of rounding.

Table B-30. Regional Reporters Working for Large and Small Newspapers, by Characteristic, 1988
Percent

Characteristic	Large circulation	Small circulation
Number of responses	64	64
Sex		
Male	76.6	84.4
Female	23.4	15.6
Race		
White	93.7	96.9
Minority	6.3	3.1
Age		
20–29	6.3	15.6
30–39	64.1	67.2
40–49	17.2	12.5
50 or older	12.5	4.7
Mean (years)	38.3	35.6
Region		
Northeast	25.4	20.9
North Central	32.8	36.8
South	21.2	24.2
West	20.6	18.1
Educational attainment		
High school only	1.6	1.6
Some college	1.6	1.6
College degree only	54.7	60.9
Some graduate work	15.6	1.6
Graduate degree	26.6	34.4
Selectivity of college attended		
Highly selective	12.5	25.4
Selective	53.1	42.9
Not selective	34.4	31.7
Type of undergraduate school		
Public	49.2	60.3
Private	50.8	39.7
Undergraduate field of study		
Humanities and liberal arts	50.8	54.0
Journalism	46.0	41.3
Science and technology	3.2	4.8
Graduate field of study		
Humanities and liberal arts	42.3	26.1
Journalism	57.7	60.9
Science and technology	0	13.0
Number of responses	26	23

SOURCE: See table B-27. Column entries may not total 100 because of rounding.

Table B-31. Regional Reporters, by Characteristic and Age Group, 1988
Percent

Characteristic	Age group			
	20–29	30–39	40–49	50 or older
Number of responses	31	116	30	13
Sex				
Men	45.2	76.7	80.0	92.3
Women	54.8	23.3	20.0	7.7
Race				
White	90.3	94.0	100.0	100.0
Minority	9.7	6.0	0	0
Region				
Northeast	37.8	21.7	23.3	26.3
North Central	21.1	31.5	37.2	44.7
South	27.8	28.6	17.4	18.4
West	13.3	18.2	22.1	10.5
Educational attainment				
High school only	0	0	3.3	7.7
Some college	3.2	0	0	7.7
College degree only	74.2	65.5	36.7	53.8
Some graduate work	6.5	7.8	26.7	7.7
Graduate degree	16.1	26.7	33.3	23.1
Selectivity of college attended				
Highly selective	22.6	18.1	17.2	7.7
Selective	54.8	52.6	51.7	46.2
Not selective	22.6	29.3	31.0	46.2
Type of undergraduate school				
Public	45.2	62.1	48.3	33.3
Private	54.8	37.9	51.7	66.7
Undergraduate field of study				
Humanities and liberal arts	41.9	43.1	55.2	58.3
Journalism	48.4	52.6	41.4	33.3
Science and technology	9.7	4.3	3.4	8.3
Graduate field of study				
Humanities and liberal arts	57.1	27.5	38.9	0
Journalism	42.9	65.0	50.0	100.0
Science and technology	0	7.5	11.1	0
Number of responses	7	40	18	3

Source: See table B-27. Column entries may not total 100 because of rounding.

Table B-32. Regional Reporters Working in Broadcast and Print Journalism, by Characteristic and Age Group, 1988
Percent

| | Age group | | | | | | | |
| | 20–29 | | 30–39 | | 40–49 | | 50 or older | |
Characteristic	TV	Print	TV	Print	TV	Print	TV	Print
Number of responses	12	19	25	91	9	21	2	11
Sex								
Men	25.0	57.9	72.0	78.0	66.7	85.7	100.0	90.9
Women	75.0	42.1	28.0	22.0	33.3	14.3	0	9.1
Race								
White	91.7	89.5	88.0	95.6	100.0	100.0	100.0	100.0
Minority	8.3	10.5	12.0	4.4	0	0	0	0
Educational attainment								
High school only	0	0	0	0	0	4.8	0	9.1
Some college	0	5.3	0	0	0	0	0	9.1
College degree only	58.3	84.2	72.0	63.7	55.6	28.6	100.0	45.5
Some graduate work	16.7	0	12.0	6.6	33.3	23.8	0	9.1
Graduate degree	25.0	10.5	16.0	29.7	11.1	42.9	0	27.3
Selectivity of college attended								
Highly selective	8.3	31.6	8.0	20.9	22.2	15.0	0	9.1
Selective	66.7	47.4	76.0	46.2	66.7	45.0	0	54.5
Not selective	25.0	21.1	16.0	33.0	11.1	40.0	100.0	36.4
Type of undergraduate school								
Public	50.0	42.1	64.0	61.5	44.4	50.0	0	40.0
Private	50.0	57.9	36.0	38.5	55.6	50.0	100.0	60.0
Undergraduate field of study								
Humanities and liberal arts	33.3	47.4	28.0	47.3	44.4	60.0	50.0	60.0
Journalism	66.7	36.8	64.0	49.5	55.6	35.0	0	40.0
Science and technology	0	15.8	8.0	3.3	0	5.0	50.0	0
Graduate field of study								
Humanities and liberal arts	60.0	50.0	14.3	30.3	0	50.0	0	0
Journalism	40.0	50.0	85.7	60.6	50.0	50.0	0	100.0
Science and technology	0	0	0	9.1	50.0	0	0	0
Number of responses	5	2	7	33	4	14	0	3

SOURCE: See table B-27. Column entries may not total 100 because of rounding.

Table B-33. Regional Reporters' Years of Experience, by Sex and Type of News
Organization, 1988

Organization	Number of responses	Before Washington	In Washington	Total
Chain newspaper bureau				
Men	80	8.0	4.4	12.4
Women	20	5.8	4.5	10.3
Average	. . .	7.6	4.4	12.0
Independent newspaper bureau				
Men	23	12.1	6.5	18.6
Women	5	3.4	7.4	10.8
Average	. . .	10.5	6.7	17.2
Large-circulation newspaper				
Men	49	10.0	5.6	15.6
Women	15	7.0	3.5	10.5
Average	. . .	9.3	5.1	14.4
Small-circulation newspaper				
Men	54	8.0	4.1	12.1
Women	10	4.8	5.3	10.1
Average	. . .	7.5	4.3	11.8
Print news service				
Men	7	6.7	3.9	10.6
Women	7	3.6	2.6	6.2
Average	. . .	5.1	3.2	8.3
All print				
Men	110	8.8	4.8	13.6
Women	32	5.6	3.9	9.5
Average	. . .	8.1	4.6	12.7
Broadcast station bureau				
Men	23	10.5	4.7	15.2
Women	10	5.5	4.3	9.8
Average	. . .	9.0	4.5	13.5
Broadcast news service				
Men	6	6.8	3.0	9.8
Women	9	3.6	2.6	6.2
Average	. . .	4.9	2.7	7.6
All broadcast				
Men	29	9.8	4.3	14.1
Women	19	4.6	3.5	8.1
Average	. . .	7.7	4.0	11.7
All regional reporters				
Men	139	9.0	4.7	13.7
Women	51	5.2	3.7	8.9
Average	. . .	8.0	4.4	12.4

SOURCE: See table B-27.

Table B-34. Regional Reporters' Coverage of Executive and Legislative Branches, by Type of News Organization, 1988
Percent of time

Organization	Number of responses	Executive	Legislative
Chain newspaper bureau	99	28.7	71.2
Independent newspaper bureau	28	27.0	73.0
Large-circulation newspaper	63	29.9	70.1
Small-circulation newspaper	64	26.9	73.1
Print news service	14	27.1	72.9
All print	141	28.3	71.7
Broadcast station bureau	26	34.2	65.8
Broadcast news service	15	26.7	73.3
All broadcast	41	31.1	68.9
All regional reporters	182	28.9	71.1

SOURCE: See table B-27.

Table B-35. Regional Reporters' Coverage of House and Senate, by Type of News Organization, 1988
Percent of time

Organization	Number of responses	House	Senate
Chain newspaper bureau	94	56.8	43.2
Independent newspaper bureau	26	53.6	46.4
Large-circulation newspaper	58	54.0	46.0
Small-circulation newspaper	62	58.0	42.0
Print news service	14	54.6	45.4
All print	134	55.9	44.1
Broadcast station bureau	24	50.2	49.8
Broadcast news service	15	53.3	46.7
All broadcast	39	51.4	48.6
All regional reporters	173	54.9	45.1

SOURCE: See table B-27.

Index